THE SERIOUS ROAD TRIP

The Serious Road Trip

Simone van Kan

UNITED WRITERS
Cornwall

UNITED WRITERS PUBLICATIONS LTD
Ailsa, Castle Gate, Penzance, Cornwall.

British Library Cataloguing in Publication Data:
A catalogue record for this book is
available from the British Library.

ISBN 9781852001926

Printed in Great Britain by
United Writers Publications Ltd
Cornwall.

To my parents,
Paul and Patricia,
who opened my eyes to the world
and set me on a journey.

'I alone cannot change the world, but I can cast a stone across the waters to create many ripples...'
Mother Teresa

Contents

Acknowledgements

I would like to acknowledge the following people for their encouragement and contributions which made this book possible:

My husband Michael, for believing in me and loving me totally, as well as my daughter, family and dog who have shown love, understanding and patience during this process of writing and publishing.

Thelma Disch for editing my work before I found Malcolm from United Writers Publications, and Michael, Charles and Ted Sherrell for giving me the necessary push to contact him.

Roweena Asgarali for creating the maps.

Dallas Hall, a faithful and encouraging childhood friend.

Meni Kojaman for being a true friend since 1993, and Graeme Bint, Tony Rees and Roger Field for all your support and for endeavouring to answer tricky questions about that time.

Christophe Huette, David Rallings, Caroline (née Moore), Julie Dinneen, Meni and Roger for sharing their photos.

All the Road Trip 'skidders' such as Nev (Andrew Watt), for daring to put into action such a big vision, and all those who made their Road Trip mark from the early days to the current day, many of whom are mentioned in this book.

The many others who helped us all on our way; you know who you are, you may be mentioned and we definitely couldn't have done it without you.

My village and friends in Devon for providing me the stable space and quiet place where I could write, perform plays and journey within.

All the children and the child within the adults, who I met along the way, whether that was in Romania, Poland, Russia, Croatia, Bosnia-Herzegovina, France, New Zealand, UK or elsewhere. Somehow by just being yourselves, in whatever situation I encountered you, and sharing your enthusiasm and love, you have helped inspire me to complete this work and book.

"Now faith is the assurance of things hoped for, the conviction of things not seen." Hebrews 11:1

For more information on The Serious Road Trip:
www.theseriousroadtrip.org

Foreword
by
Bruce Dickinson

On a dark night in a British military base in Split, Croatia, four rock musicians staggered into the blackness, eyes straining after the glare of white neon blinding them, eyes streaming as the cold December air infiltrated their tear ducts.

There was a war on. A proper, brutal, shooting war. A siege longer than the siege of Stalingrad. A siege where women and children were murdered by fascist snipers and where the city of Sarajevo was reduced to three day's supply of food and fuel. In the midst of one of the harshest Balkan winters, there was an epic battle for survival.

Yet this was Europe. The much vaunted European project had signally failed to stop a brutal genocide right on its doorstep. The United Nations was often equally ineffective. Unable to choose a side, soldiers wearing blue berets had to look on helplessly as their so-called UN leaders appeased and failed to halt the aggression.

My eyes were opening in the darkness. The outline of a military, soft-top truck slowly emerged into focus. The driver stepped down and shone a torch around the tailgate. My jaw dropped. This was an old German Unimog 4x4 but it was painted bright yellow, with Felix The Cat, Roadrunner and Asterix The Gaul emblazoned on its tarpaulin roof.

The voice was from a young New Zealander; 'Get in the back, you're going.'

'Going where?'

'Sarajevo. Now.'

We loaded a crate of beer in the back.

'It'll be about eight hours. It's cold. Over the top of Mount Igman. Sleeping bags are in the back.'

Nobody moved.

'Who exactly are you guys?'

'We are The Serious Fucking Road Trip. Now get in the truck.'

Prologue

'Tell us another story, PLEASE!' the excited children begged. 'Please, please, please,' they echoed in unison. I was the class teacher for a group of seven to eight-year-olds, mainly boys, and was feeling a little flustered that I hadn't committed the latest story to memory from the Steiner school's curriculum.

'I need another day to learn that one,' I confessed, feeling a little behind with my preparation.

'Not that story!' they exclaimed, very clear about what they wanted. 'We want one of YOUR stories from the bus,' they cried relentlessly.

The children had been intrigued about my humanitarian adventures living on a double-decker bus, some 10 years prior, and working with children in orphanages and war-zones in Eastern Europe. They loved hearing about all of Johnie the clown's tricks, or any of the clowns for that matter, and what would happen when our beloved bus, van or truck broke down in some remote or forgotten corner.

'Tell us one of the red bus stories,' they pleaded. I couldn't help but smile and continue, relieved that I knew these stories off by heart.

And so I began...

'In a land, far, far away, over the seas and over the mountains, there was a deep, dark forest and on the other side of this forest there was a little village. It was on a hill, surrounded by fields. The people there travelled by horse and cart and fetched their water from the well. At the far end of the village there was a large house that looked like a fort with a huge lookout tower to one side. Inside the formidable house were 200 orphans, who had almost been forgotten; until one day a big red double-decker bus rolled in. It was The Serious Road Trip...'

The children's eyes sparkled with satisfaction as I relived one of the clown's tricks, such as the balloon trick.

'Johnie took a bright yellow balloon and blew into it. It made a few squeaks. Initially it was just a little inflated and he asked the children if he should blow it bigger, motioning with his hands. 'Mai mare, mai mare?' Those that could talk echoed back 'MAI MARE, MAI MARE!' He rubbed his hands over the skin of the balloon, making a funny screechy noise, then carried on blowing. Bit by bit the balloon grew bigger and bigger as he was egged on by the children asking for a larger balloon. That was until it was so large that – POP! The balloon popped and pushed him backwards over a chair. There he lay on the ground with his feet in the air! He was still trying to blow up the remnants of the popped balloon. Many were surprised, although some children were a little shocked by the bang at first. When they realised what had happened, many smiled and laughed.'

The class of children roared with laughter as they imagined the sight of this, and I felt liberated in some way at being able to pass on these stories.

I mostly focused on our positive actions rather than the tragic circumstance of the orphanages or refugee camps we encountered. They were too young to know about these things. The fact that it was a real-life adventure from my own experience particularly appealed to them.

I felt compelled to write it all down at some point. A friend had urged me to do so earlier, but I hadn't been ready on my return to New Zealand. I was still processing everything and had buried these experiences; almost unable to communicate all that had happened and too busy living day-to-day. After a while I gradually sensed the growing need to write. But, when would I have the time or energy amidst all these other priorities?

My sister had been chronically ill, I'd moved countries a few times, I'd met the much-awaited husband, had a mortgage and bills to pay, then a child to be mother for. I was writing and performing puppet shows locally and involved in various other community activities and theatre groups. Life can be so busy.

The loss of my sister, Ingrid, to cystic fibrosis and then my mother-in-law, Sue, to cancer, heralded a new era for us all. There was more time and some things couldn't wait any longer.

I was spurred further by the arrival of a huge parcel of articles and information about The Serious Road Trip sent from my dear friend Cynthia in Luxembourg. Cynthia had done essential fundraising for us at the time and had initiated me into this world of collecting funds for good causes. Twenty years later she had been sorting through piles of stuff. She had found this brick of paperwork that she was sending for me to either use or bin... the choice was mine.

11

Around the same time, one wise woman urged me to write now: 'Don't wait till you're retired and you have forgotten,' she warned me.

After numerous procrastinations, here I was in the attic rereading my letters to my parents from Luxembourg, London or Moscow and the old articles written about us, or by us as we lived and breathed our Serious Road Trip days. I felt determined to get the stories out and see where it led me and those that listened.

The long process of researching and recalling these precious moments began again, and once more I felt liberated to be able to communicate the many memories and stories held deep within.

After all, I had been present when key moments in The Serious Road Trip's history had been triggered, leading on to the establishment of a colourful NGO that still exists today. I wanted to give credit to some of the people who were part of this process, whether that was in shaping the happy childhood memories I could draw upon, having the ideas to do something, donating time, money and energy, with many risking their lives to help others as well. I thought it important to show what can be achieved when friends and like-minded people unite and extend love to strangers in need, some of whom ended up helping us in return. Perhaps one day we might be the ones that would find ourselves in need and as the saying goes, 'what comes around goes around'. Maybe we were some modern-day version of the Good Samaritan who didn't walk past the injured man when others did, and with limited means but huge hearts, we managed to do something. We were by no means perfect, in fact we were seriously flawed, but we showed imagination and enterprise and were determined to do what we could. We weren't going to let anyone tell us it couldn't be done, either. That just encouraged us to prove them wrong.

I hope that these stories may be of inspiration.

Simone van Kan (2019)

12

Chapter 1

New Awakenings

My stomach churned with sheer terror as I waited for the local shuttle bus into the capital. Clutching my purple daypack in front of me and my larger backpack tightly strapped over my shoulders and around my waist, it was as though I was wearing some type of armour, trying to mask my true feelings of fear from the world. And yet it was a dead giveaway that I was foreign. Concealed beneath the packs and layers of clothes was a money belt carrying a thick wad of American dollars, various traveller's cheques, my freshly stamped passport and my credit card.

It was 1991, I was 24 and I had just entered Argentina. I'd scarcely slept on the long 12-hour flight from Auckland to Buenos Aires. After a relatively relaxing holiday, back home to NZ visiting family and friends, I was now truly entering unknown territory. I was in a totally foreign country, on an unfamiliar continent, travelling on my own. I was terrified. It was true I had travelled before, mostly in Europe and on various road trips that I had embarked upon with my boyfriend and friends. But this time he wasn't coming and it felt different, as though something else was about to happen. The cautionary words of my father echoed in my ears. 'Watch out in those Banana Republics. It's not the same as in safe little NZ!' This didn't exactly instil confidence as I embarked on my South American adventure.

Admittedly I wouldn't be on my own for long, as I was on my way to meet up with good friends in Brazil. They had enticed me over to experience their colourful and dynamic country first-hand, and the excitement of a real-life carnival was fast approaching. This was just

13

the compulsory 24-hour stopover in Buenos Aires, with the connecting flight the following day. But why hadn't I thought to book a hotel for that night through the travel agent? Where would I stay? I hadn't even bought a travel guidebook to help me. The internal dialogue tormented me. 'Too late now' I muttered inwardly, boarding the bus with the sun setting in the distance. Hopefully it wouldn't be too dark on arrival and surely there would be several options near the bus terminus, I tried to reassure myself.

The doors hissed shut and the bus rumbled forwards. Still standing, I perched against some seats, unwilling to remove the protective layer of packs just yet. Besides, it was such a rigmarole to get them on and off. Most of the others had taken their seats and were travelling with suitcases, but not all. A woman with a blonde bob, also in her twenties, shouted over to me with a thick Aussie accent 'Where are you staying tonight?' Maybe she sensed my vulnerability. The timing was perfect. How reassuring to hear that other voice from Down Under even if she was Australian. I didn't want to admit that I had nowhere to go but feigned a little confidence, 'I was hoping to find somewhere in the city; how about you?'

'We've booked into a hostel. Why don't you tag along with us?' She looked to be travelling with two other women and suddenly my precarious situation evaporated when I realised that I could join their group. I crossed my fingers that there would be room at the hostel for me too.

The trip into town seemed to go on forever but at least for now my initial panic had been allayed. I just hoped that Griff, the Kiwi friend I was joining in Sao Paulo, would appreciate the extra stress that came with carrying a wad of dollars from his father. I wasn't sure what to expect but had heard of muggings happening and it would be just my luck for it to happen whilst laden with cash. But despite this risk, it seemed the least I could do as it was partly thanks to him that I was on my way to Brazil. We'd met at university, after he'd just spent a year on a Rotary exchange there and he'd been my boyfriend's room-mate and 'partner in crime'. Over the years we and other students had spent many a wild night drinking cachaça (sugar-cane alcohol) or vodka, mixed with ice, sugar and lime juice whilst dancing to bossa nova and samba tunes, along with various Brazilians who had made their way to NZ or London. I was drawn to this fun-loving bunch who knew how to live life in the moment. Now with Griff back there after many years, it had compelled me to link up with them all.

The driver signalled when we needed to get off and we approached the hostel a few hundred paces away in the dimly lit cobbled street.

The Spanish 101 course that I'd slotted into my languages degree, suddenly became very useful. It would be tight, but the four of us could squeeze into a room for three, with one of the women offering to sleep on her roll-mat. We were determined to stick together for now. It was late and we spent the night chatting amongst ourselves, despite the sheer exhaustion. The adrenalin and female camaraderie picked me up. We were all similar ages, embarking on different adventures and were just thrown together for those several hours. I must have nodded off for what seemed like a few moments but awoke famished. It was daylight and time to go and find somewhere to eat with the others. We could leave our backpacks at the hostel.

At the small front desk, we bumped into an Australian chap, who was also ready to search for something to eat and seemed to know where to go. He'd been here before and was in transit for Columbia. He must have been in his mid-twenties too but looked like a more seasoned traveller. He was quite tall, lanky and somewhat dishevelled looking. His dark curly hair was in need of a brush and his clothes were worn, but what struck me the most was his smile. His front teeth were obviously missing but he didn't seem worried about that. He exuded a certain vibrancy and I was paying more attention to what he was saying, than looking at the new environment. He was on his way to work with street kids in Bogota and had just been back to Australia to do some fundraising. He mentioned he'd repaired his local church's roof as part of this, but was now eager to get back to the children. He didn't look like a typical churchgoer.

'I lost my teeth after a fight with one of the kids' fathers. He was drunk,' he explained in a matter-of-fact manner. He proceeded to elaborate that it was quite a rough neighbourhood in the slum where he worked, with many challenges, but it was worth it for the children. You could see his excitement when talking about the children he would soon see. It sounded so far removed from my world, and as a dentist's daughter, I couldn't help wonder why he hadn't fixed his teeth whilst back in Australia. My dad would have fixed his teeth for free if he'd explained what he was doing. He had always treated various nuns and priests for free over the years.

We all meandered through cobble-stoned streets, chatting away, and eventually found a café that had a certain familiar French feel to it, with chairs and tables on the pavement outside. Coffee and croissants were available and were just what was needed.

Several hours later, I was back on the shuttle-bus headed for the airport after fare-welling my fleeting friends. I found myself alone again, but had a certain inner confidence that I had somehow managed the previous day without major mishaps and with all my luggage, money and body intact. Not long now before I would be greeted by friends at Sao Paulo airport and then I could relax.

Chapter 2

Conceived in Brazil

The first few weeks had almost sped by like an eternal fiesta. We had danced the lambada in Porto Seguro by night and sipped on coconut milk by day. The adventure had started with a 36-hour bus journey to get to the carnival; almost a party in itself. Once the carnival ended we had carried on up the coast towards Salvador, in the Northern Bahia region, visiting beaches, islands and churches. We had watched as men performed the entrancing capoeira dances in the street to the sound of an African djambe drum, and the women seemed to breathe samba moves, it came so naturally. We had dined on feijoada (rice and beans) and lashings of meat and chicken hearts on skewers in the famous Churrascarria (Barbecue restaurants).

Once we got to Salvador, children had swarmed around us outside the famous church of Nosso Senhor do Bonfim eager to sell their colourful Bonfim friendship ribbons which were said to bring good fortune or be a symbol of faith. They were almost an essential accessory in Brazil or elsewhere, and we enthusiastically procured several bundles and proceeded to tie them on our wrists and ankles right there for extra good luck. It was beautiful to see them tied to the various railings outside the church, their rainbow colours fluttering in the wind, but I was surprised to see them also dangling from inside the church along with various plastic limbs and endless photographs of loved-ones in need of healing and prayers. I had seen nothing like it before. That evening we even went to a voodoo ceremony in the favelas on the outskirts of town. Women in white dresses danced trance-like in a large circle around a solitary seated

17

male figure, to the sound of African drums. I had only read about such things when studying Haitian literature during my languages degree. Mare had asked the taxi driver to wait and we returned to the safety of the city a few hours later before anything too extraordinary happened. On our return journey south we had braved the seriously pot-holed interior roads and had even escaped a trigger-happy sheriff, who had shot a local man dead. He'd been drinking with us in the small mining town of Diamantina and a row had erupted shortly after our drunken departure. The young man was from an influential family; maybe drugs were involved, but we didn't hang around to find out or get implicated in a long drawn-out court case.

In Rio de Janeiro, we had swum at the Copacabana beach, sipped coffee at the famous 'Girl from Ipanema' café and even escaped thieves posing as tourists at the Christ the Redeemer statue, ducking into a souvenir shop to shake them off our tail during the chase. We had certainly covered lots of tourist spots and had a few close shaves. We gained a certain brave laziness, travelling in a small group and having Griff and his vivacious Brazilian girlfriend, Mare, at the helm, watching out for our safety and guiding us in the right direction. With his pale skin and red hair, Griff surprised a few unsuspecting locals as he launched into fluent Portuguese at just the right moment on our travels. I was picking up many useful words such as 'obrigada' or 'tudo bem' but hadn't been in the front seat arranging accommodation or food options.

After visiting as many far-flung parts of Brazil as possible, interspersed with true hospitality from friends in Sao Paulo, we then embarked on the last of these 'Road Trips'. Money was beginning to run out, so the return to Europe was imminent; where I would look for work again.

Then, out of the blue, my boyfriend of six years, Nev, had surprised us all by turning up unexpectedly from London. Our relationship had been at a crossroads during the last few months apart. I had even been thinking the relationship was over, but I was touched that he had come all this way to see me, after all, and I slipped back into the comfort of being together. He had a burning desire to see the Amazon. While I proudly wore a T-shirt to support an environmental group, featuring the Brazilian flag with the green disappearing (symbolising the diminishing rainforest of the Amazon), I wasn't convinced it was on our itinerary. It was so far away.

Nev was a charismatic, yet 'unconventional', son of a NZ diplomat. He was pale-skinned and a lean six foot tall. He wore motley bleached, stove-pipe jeans, his favourite Bob Marley T-shirt and pointed cowboy boots. His hair was shaved to a spiky number 1 or 2 in military style, which made his big blue eyes stand out even more. His skin was pale and he'd often been described as anti-establishment in a 'rebel without a cause' manner. He usually had a cigarette between his fingers and a bottle of beer never too far away from body or mind. We'd travelled to China and inner Mongolia, some three years earlier, invited by his father working there, and now here we were on another continent and off the beaten track. Another Kiwi friend from London, Sue, was tagging along and hell-bent on getting to Machu Picchu in Peru whatever way possible. Mare remained in Sao Paulo for this last trip, so there were just the four of us, counting Griff, answering to life's beckoning for another adventure.

We had been invited by Andrea's family (our main hostess) to stay on a real-life ranch/farm near the swampy Pantanal region. Her brother was there doing his father's monthly business of paying the wages of the farm hands, checking on various projects and planning the next month's work. We headed by bus (16 hrs) from Sao Paulo to a town in the Mato Grosso region, and then endured a very long and bumpy truck ride to the farm with no electricity or hot water. This was rough land that was still being broken in and a far cry from the lush green pastures of NZ. With a new hot and sunny day upon us we decided to visit the land by donkey and horse, much of which was still bush and scrub, checking on the construction and progress of water holes and fences. The trees were full of green parrots, the occasional toucan with its bright yellow beak, and we were pestered by what looked like giant flying crickets. In reality these were locusts as big as small birds that landed on us and generally freaked me out. Consequently it wasn't the most pleasant day out for me, so I was relieved when we ended up in a small and simple bar off the beaten track, without electricity, that had a large ice-cube for a refrigerator and horses tied up outside, just like in the cowboy westerns. The local ranch hands looked the part wearing sombreros and all the cowboy gear such as spurs and leather chaps protecting their legs. Not used to foreign clientele with US dollars burning holes in their pockets, we soon drunk them dry and ventured back to the farmhouse amidst much laughter. The following day was spent rounding up the newly arrived cattle (large white beasts with big humps on their necks) for vaccinating, which are best described as wild beasts compared to the comparatively pampered cows of NZ.

After four days on the farm we jumped on a train to get to the Brazilian/Bolivian border town of Corumbá and main hub of the Pantanal. The train journey, interestingly named the 'train of death',

19

through the Pantanal, was brimming with wildlife on both sides and was made even more exciting by the fact there was a restaurant on board with lashings of cerveza (beer) and steak a la cavalero. Griff convinced us this was horse steak, much to my disgust as I didn't like to think that horses could be eaten. I was hugely relieved when it turned out to be a steak with a fried egg on top, resembling a sombrero of the cavalero cowboys.

With the train seemingly swaying from side to side along the railway track, flanked by swampy marshlands on either side, we finally made it to the border. We were there chasing Nev's dream of an Amazon adventure, with Sue also semi-guiding the way; Rough Guide in hand and on her way to Machu Picchu. Mind you, we were a long way from Peru and the Amazon.

We ended up in a bar run by Hermann the German, definitely looking like the sort on the run after WWII, with piercing blue eyes and a much younger Bolivian wife. Already interested in stories of the Jews during WWII, this made for real wild imaginative stuff. I was convinced he was a sought-after Nazi, living in a border town so he could escape quickly if necessary by train or by boat. While there were many boats in town, parading the most gigantic fish I'd ever seen caught in fresh water, the adventure of boating up to the Amazon was laughed off by locals as being long, expensive, dangerous and not possible unless with a canoe in parts. . . hmmm. Not our budget, nor my cup of tea. I definitely wasn't prepared for that type of adventure, and nor were the others much to Nev's disappointment. Instead we were persuaded to embark on a safari of the Pantanal with the swarthy English-speaking Murillo, who seemed to be Brazil's answer to Crocodile Dundee (although much younger). He approached us in a bar on hearing our accents. He was mustering up a 'flock' of gringos for his next departure and we were promised food, lodgings and action during an overland adventure by Land Rover for three or four days. The whole novelty of a safari was something new to us and unexpected, but we were up for the challenge. We certainly thought the wildlife and area was something worth checking out after the breathtaking moments experienced on the train.

Murillo took us under his wing and persuaded us to go night-clubbing the eve of our departure. There we indulged in the local cachaça (potent alcohol made with sugar-cane) and various cocktails. In the blur of our late-night return we were stopped on the dirt road, blocked by a man lying face-down in the middle of the road with a policeman holding a gun to his head. Murillo bravely went to investigate and returned shortly afterwards. He was being arrested for drugs, we were informed, which was unfortunate for him and for us, as Murillo seemed to know the man and announced that he was meant to be the cook for our safari leaving the next day. We would need to make do without him and goodness knows what awaited him back at the police station.

Early the next morning, feeling rather worse for wear, we loaded ourselves onto the back of the Land Rover, meeting various other people on board. I was still recovering from a bad dose of hangover and ended up out of the sun in the back seat of the Rover missing much of the 'Our World' or National Geographic wildlife experience, except a massive snake that slid impressively across the road and the enormous storks flying by. Murillo explained that we had a problem with the starter motor, but no worries as he had managed to find a spare part which he would install as we waited for a ferry to cross a major river. . . and so the adventure had begun, with Murillo our tour-guide-action-man-mechanic and cook. It transpired the spare part was not the right fit, so after a lengthy and fruitless delay we carried on our way thankful that there were a few of us to push start the vehicle when leaving. Another problem that needed addressing was the radiator that kept overheating and needed frequent refilling. Subsequently the radiator cap was to disappear, further exasperating the situation. We ended up plugging it with an old T-shirt which wasn't so effective really but sort of did the trick. The terrain got wilder and wilder and there was no end of heart-stopping moments as we raced from armadillos running wild, to water pigs (Capybara), monkeys dangling from trees and hog-nosed raccoons. As if the wildlife wasn't enough to take our breath away, for us women, Murillo was there to watch with his bare torso and enviable six-pack, stopping frequently to chase after the animals on foot, bringing them back at lightning speed, held by the tail for us to photograph. We were the true gringo tourists. This would be followed by a group push start and then another encounter with an animal. At one point we stopped to replenish the radiator, only to find that moments later Murillo was holding an alligator, although a rather small one, by the lower jaw for us to examine. Griff was left bravely holding the alligator carefully by the soft spot that ensured its paralysis, while Murillo filled the radiator.

All of a sudden Murillo spotted a wild pig that he wanted to chase. The alligator was quickly abandoned, there was a big push and we were all aboard the truck ready for more action. We embarked on a massive 'cat and mouse' chase, stopping and starting, usually leaving the engine running as Murillo would spring from the vehicle, machete in hand to chase the pig, only to find that it was faster than him and we would have to catch up using the vehicle again. At one point I didn't manage to get back on the vehicle and was left stranded watching the chase happen before me and running after them. Pig chased by truck, truck chased by myself, and to my horror when I looked behind me there was a herd of those giant white cattle stampeding along behind towards me as well. Fortunately the alarm was raised, and in an almost 'bionic' jump fuelled by adrenalin and with helping outstretched hands, I was lifted to the safety of the Rover in the nick of time, as it slowed down to retrieve me before carrying on. My heart was pumping intensely after what had seemed a rather close shave of being stampeded. Meanwhile the pig met its fate in a rather noisy final battle, much to the dismay of two vegetarians on board. This beast was then placed in the passenger seat and its hoof was useful in keeping the accelerator going when stopping to open rudimentary farm gates, which Murillo also did at lightning speed, reducing the number of push starts on our way back to the sleeping area. By the following day we were enjoying the delicious meat for dinner. It was succulent and tasty and reminded us that we really were on a safari.

By night we slept in a mosquito netted outdoor room with hammocks for beds. You soon got used to lying diagonally in order to save your back from bending. In the evenings intense discussions took place around the flickering flames of the camp-fire. We chatted with two English sisters and one explained about her work with the street children of Asuncion in Paraguay, which had kept her busy for over three years. She spoke about how some of them would shine shoes whilst living on the streets, with no time for going to school, and how emotionally involved she had become in their lives. It reminded me of the toothless missionary on his way to Bogota. She was in the painful process of leaving this work with the children and her sister had caringly come to help her make the transition and spend four months trekking around South America.

'I know what you mean,' Nev empathised.

'If I wasn't here, I'd be back in Romania, building a play-room for the orphans of Ionaseni orphanage,' he sighed. 'They call them the 'irrecuperable' children. It's in Moldova, Northern Romania. Ain't never seen anything like it. Children tied to their cots and lying in their own shit. No Shit!' he chuckled at his own joke, then continued.

'I was there with volunteers helping 12 months ago and have been trying to get back there ever since.' We all listened with open ears as he described how heart-wrenching it had been.

'They just needed someone to hold them… human interaction…' he tailed off, lost in his thoughts, and the flames of the fire flickered in some sort of recognition of the pain he was feeling in that moment. I'd almost forgotten about this, there had been so much happening since then. I'd been so self-absorbed in my own worries and desires. Such a dose of this stark reality facing numerous children certainly put things in perspective and made me feel embarrassed or selfish to have worried about comparatively smaller issues in life.

The fire seemed to hypnotise me and transport me back to that time...

I had been working as a temp in the Financial Services in Luxembourg after being transferred from the London sister-office. This had suited me enormously, as travelling the world for me, meant also having the opportunity to use my French and German or other foreign languages as much as possible. Surrounded by various expatriates, who either worked in banking or the European Parliament, we frequented a bar called the White Rose. Nev and Damon, a Kiwi friend who reminded me of some big smiling teddy bear, had seized the opportunity to come over from London and visit me on the continent. We were all having a drink after work when a colleague's sister approached our group, rattling a plastic container with coins in it.

'Any donations for our trip to help the orphans of Romania? We're off on a convoy with the Red Cross tomorrow!' she explained.

'Wow! How do you get to go on such a trip?' Damon enquired. I couldn't tell whether he was attracted by the idea of a trip or spending more time with her.

'Why? Do you want to come along? There's room for more volunteers,' she announced.

'Choice!' Nev and Damon announced in unison, both excited about the prospect of another adventure.

'Let's go! Where do we need to be, and when?' Damon muttered beaming.

I was astounded by their spontaneity and a little pissed off that I wouldn't be spending time with Nev after all. The very next day, passports in hand and very little else, they were there at a warehouse, ready for action sorting out various shoes, clothing, toys, food and medical supplies. These had been donated for the children and needed sorting before they left later that day with a large 45-tonne truck carrying the goods and a transit van carrying the volunteers. They were bound for Romania, but unsure of the exact destination. The coordinator, Bob Christie, was a DJ for Radio Luxembourg but was organising the convoy in the name of the

Luxembourg Red Cross. I was at work when they set off for what was to be a 10-day trip.

It was only when they were near the border that they were asked to go to Moldova in the North and followed their noses, ending up at Ionaseni orphanage near the Ukraine border. This was one of the worst orphanages to be shown on TV at the time, where there was a handful of Scottish and Irish volunteers doing their best in dire circumstances. I hadn't really been paying attention to the situation in Romania, but had heard that their dictator, Ceausescu, and his wife had been executed on Christmas Day the year before. Since then, the situation in the orphanages had attracted attention and various people were doing what they could to help.

They had been gone over two weeks and we had had no contact with them in that time. I'd been a nervous wreck when they didn't return when expected. Nearly a week late, friends crowded round them in the pub to welcome them back, offering to buy them all drinks. They looked like they hadn't showered or shaved the whole time they had been gone. I was relieved that Nev had made it back safely, even if they all looked a little worse for wear, but was angry that we had been left without a phone-call for weeks. Now wasn't the time to voice this, of course.

'What was it like?' we asked curiously.

The tight-knit group stayed close to each other, looking at one another, wondering if any one person dared to express what they had witnessed.

'Man… it w-w-was bad,' Damon managed to stutter, biting his lip.

'The staff treated them like animals… they couldn't even speak, most of 'em. Didn't even know what a toy was… I need another drink,' Nev muttered. He seemed already quite drunk, or maybe he was stunned, and proceeded to down one pint after another.

'Every winter at least a third of the children die, due to the dire conditions and lack of resources and heating…' Another volunteer explained, and so it went on.

The appalling conditions and desperation of the children trying to survive despite all odds had made a huge impact on the hearts and minds of my friends.

The loud music of the pub seemed to drown out some of the conversations as we tried to understand what they were trying to communicate, but we were worlds apart. We were working in the banking and financial sector, frittering our money away on fine dining, wine and travel, and here they were talking about children who had been tied to their cots, with very little clothing or food, and very few staff to keep control of them using sticks, let alone care for them.

24

Nev and I stumbled out of the pub to make our way back to my hotel. He had drunk far too much and I'd managed to convince him he needed a shower and a rest. He was carrying a plastic bag with a few personal belongings.

'You just don't understand... ' he rambled as he staggered along in a zig-zag.

'Why didn't you phone, we were worried sick about you guys?' I retorted, wanting him to understand that I had found it hard too. But he was right, I really didn't understand. I felt embarrassed that I had voiced my concern as it seemed to be insignificant in light of what they had just been through.

'You don't FUCKING know what it was like!' he screamed angrily. 'Everyone is so bloody rich here! You don't fucking care... you weren't there!'

We were outside a huge window of the Pizza Hut and in his drunken rage he kicked the window. SMASH! The giant window shattered into pieces with shards of glass falling inside and outside onto the pavement. He hadn't been expecting it to break. We were both gob-smacked. Nev's instinct was to stumble down the Avenue de la Gare, as if he didn't know anything about it. I followed him screaming: 'What did you go and do that for, you wanker!' The restaurant staff came in hot pursuit and brought us back to one of the tables while they called the police. It felt surreal as we were both bundled into the police car to be taken for questioning.

A night in a tiny police cell to cool off was quite sobering to say the least. I had to sit next to him in such a small space, but we did calm down.

'I brought you a present,' he muttered.

'What, from Romania?' I enquired incredulously.

'Well, sort of...' He started to open the plastic bag he'd been clutching. 'I found these cool leather boots amongst the aid, and I thought they were too good for the mud in the village, so I saved them for you. Here, take them.' And he handed me the most beautiful pair of burgundy Italian leather boots I had seen.

I managed a 'Thank you' but I still found it hard to believe I was in a police cell and had work the next day. I felt it necessary to stay on and explain the background lest he be taken for some drunken homeless person. I think he was just lucky no one had been sitting by the window, and to have a fairly understanding police officer dealing with the case.

'How would you feel if you had experienced what we saw in Romania?' And he proceeded to explain it all, with me vouching for

25

b

him. He got off lightly with a small fine to cover the insurance excess, which I paid, and was deported to the German border, less than half an hour away, that same day. He didn't have a fixed address in Luxembourg, but managed to hitch back easily.

He and Damon tried to return to Ionaseni. They wanted to help the children engage in activities, to take them away from the continuous rocking in the cots.

Despite their huge willingness to assist, over the course of several months they met with negative responses when approaching various organisations already operating in Romania. There had been many more offers of more skilled and experienced volunteers, leaving them very frustrated, but nonetheless determined to do something positive.

There was a red hot glow in the centre of the fire and after a period of silence Nev burst out with something seemingly unrelated.

'Did ya' hear of that black London cab making it from London to Australia?'

'No,' we responded, shaking our heads.

'I read about it in the paper. Amazing eh! To think they travelled all that way!' Several minutes passed.

'Hey, why don't we do that same trip, but let's go one better, let's go all the way to NZ. Better still, let's go with a red double-decker bus! That would really capture people's imaginations!'

Nev was definitely one to think big and usually outside the square. He was always planning road trips or projects of a grand nature, many involving his friends. Just six months prior, he'd even whisked me away on a road trip with a few friends to go and celebrate the 1st Anniversary of the Velvet Revolution in Prague on November 17, 1990. The Cold War was over and Nev was always up for a celebration with beer involved. We'd been in Germany the month before that trip for Unification day.

'We can help children along the way. There are so many children in need worldwide! We need to do something!' he proudly announced.

'Sounds like a version of Cliff Richard's *Summer Holiday* to me,' Griff muttered.

This idea certainly struck a chord and seemed to be on another dimension from some of his previous ideas, mostly money-making schemes. Once he'd even tried to set up a dating agency, which involved people sending in 10 dollars in the hope of finding a partner of sorts. But this was quite a different venture. There would certainly be room for many aboard the large double-decker bus bound for New Zealand, as he dreamed and schemed into the wee hours of the night.

In the morning we attempted to go Piranha fishing. We had to wade through water, which I thought was odd if we really were in Piranha territory. Consequently I lost all my mosquito protection applied that morning and was pursued by a thousand hungry mosquitoes diving at my unprotected legs and arms. Perhaps it was the black T-shirt I wore but it was only my sweet blood they seemed to be after! With no piranhas in sight Murillo decided to head back to Corumbá on a most disastrous journey. Not only was I itching badly, covered in some 300 bites, but we had a great many breakdowns with lots of pushing and willing the motor to start again. Then a major storm hit, with heavy wind, rain, thunder and lightning, making a three-hour journey become a seven-hour test of endurance. Most of us were perched unprotected on the back of the open-air truck, clinging to each other, with a couple of people saying they would write to Rough Guide to complain about the haphazard nature of this particular safari operator. Nev laughed wildly as the rain beat upon his mad grinning face. He was happily embracing the elements on this unusual journey. It had taken coming to Brazil for him to have his epiphany of how to get back to Romania. I'm sure most Road Trippers wouldn't be surprised to hear that the idea had been born under such circumstances.

Griff returned to Sao Paulo, but we were persuaded to continue travelling with the English girls to Bolivia. We embarked on the Train of Death to Santa Cruz where we remained on high alert in fear of having drugs planted in our luggage, to then be carted off to prison unless paying a huge bribe. I needed to regularly douse my legs with alcohol to stop the itching or infection and I remember clutching my backpack for dear life and not sleeping a wink as the train rocked dangerously from side to side on the tracks. Our Spanish-speaking friends seemed to defend us adequately when approached by anyone official. After a small break in Santa Cruz, where I was fascinated to see real-life sloths in trees on the main square, we decided to head on to La Paz by bus. During this 16-hour trip we survived an encounter with angry farmers picketing and blocking the main road. The army turned up with machine-guns pointed at the crowd waving their spades and pitchforks, but this did not deter them. As the wait was long and the temperatures in the bus unbearable we went outside to get some fresh air along with the other local passengers who dispersed looking for water. The angry crowd pointed at us and jeered 'Gringos' in a nasty manner, making us feel very unsafe and almost responsible for their plight in some way. They certainly looked like they were ready to lynch someone. The bus driver could sense the volatile nature of the situation, made some investigations for alternative routes and within moments he said we were leaving immediately. Those that were able boarded the bus and we fled on a back road, leaving many local passengers behind, but safely bound for La Paz. The bus wound its way up into the Andes Mountains, until we reached the altitude of 4,000 metres where the capital city was perched.

Whilst there we had encounters with toothless miners describing their plight and poverty-stricken children pleaded for money and pulled at our hearts. Women wearing the traditional 'bowler' hats and colourful dresses were selling their wares on the streets, usually with a few children in slings or playing nearby.

Many were chewing on coca leaves to counteract the altitude sickness and numb other pain. We sipped on coca tea which had the same effect. The poverty we were to witness in Bolivia made Nev even more determined to do something about it.

I, on the other hand, was rather daunted by the prospect of facing more such heart-wrenching and emotional situations as Nev had done in Romania, where he felt it was worse. I did feel bewildered at how I might help such children in the future or even cope in the appalling conditions. Amidst all this I was celebrating my 25th birthday. Nev disappeared early that morning to return as I awoke. 'Happy birthday, Simone! I've brought you strawberries and prosecco to celebrate. You're a quarter century old!' and we feasted together, drinking from some plastic cups. He never ceased to amaze me and was always full of surprises.

My dwindling finances and a serious cholera outbreak in Peru, meant that once we reached the small fishing village of Copacabana on Lake Titicaca, we decided to let Sue venture onward to Machu Picchu on her own. There was no way I wanted to risk falling into the hands of the notorious Shining Path and with only 10 per cent of the normal tourist numbers, those that did travel were more likely to be targeted by thieves. I felt the risks outweighed the benefits. Nev agreed. Besides, he was on another mission now and was eager to get started.

By the time we returned to Sao Paulo, he was in action writing letters to many Kiwi friends, letting them know of our plans and asking them to join us back in London. He really was determined and the talk was not wishful thinking. Although the task at hand seemed overwhelmingly huge there was no stopping him, and the project started to take hold of our lives in April 1991.

Chapter 3

London Calling

With a sense of enthusiasm, various people felt drawn to the project and started meeting up in London by July 1991. The trip to New Zealand by red double-decker bus was envisaged to take one year, not including the preparation time. The objective was to help and work with underprivileged children, to highlight their plight through our positive actions and attract media attention in the various countries we would cross to get there. Nev imagined a return to Wellington, where many of us had met, helping children en route. Damon was already in London, ready to drop anything to seek his way back to Romania and quickly became the right-hand man.

Nev's brother, Christopher, gave up his short-lived career selling Kirby vacuum-cleaners and working on the foreign exchange market, to make it over to England. Another friend from Wellington days, Miles, met up with us. He'd recently met his American girlfriend Julie, whilst on the island of Eos in Greece. They were both keen to get on board. With his artistic bent, Miles set about designing the zany logo which is a mixture of Atom ant and red double-decker bus. Patrick, Myles (known as Sifty) and his young girlfriend Belinda, all from NZ, also joined up. There was Seaton and Glenda too, all eager to participate.

Tony Gaffney was an Irish accountant friend from Luxembourg; he had already run from his commitment to the nine-to-five existence over there and had joined the colourful crew in London.

Even my French friend, Christophe, had abandoned his studies at the prestigious Sorbonne in Paris, much to his parents' dismay, to join us offering his skills in translation.

Something had called us all together with a purpose.

Nev's childhood friend, Jerry (UK), was to provide financial support to buy the bus. They had lived in the same street and gone to the same Primary School in Wimbledon. Jerry's father and aunt had escaped the Jewish persecution and been sent to England as children during WWII. His father went on to become a very successful businessman dealing in hops for the beer industry, which was lucky for us. Jerry's love of reggae music and Bob Marley had influenced Nev enormously. Whereas we said 'Choice' he would say 'Wicked' and 'Aye-re man!'. Another supporter extra-ordinaire was Jerry's invaluable cousin Tessa living in Bavaria. She provided us with endless food and accommodation, moral support and guidance as a friend. She was also to become a trustee of the eventual charity. So much so a loyal supporter, a Land Rover was later named after her!

Another of their family members, working for Jebsens Shipping, offered to sponsor and provide the necessary shipping en route.

The Management team formed with four amigos: Nev, Damon, Tony and Christopher, and shortly afterward we were joined by the friendly 'grenouille' as he was known, Christophe, still based in Paris. We'd met on a bus travelling from London to Paris, some three years earlier, and had become firm friends. He was younger but very capable and forged friendships and alliances with French NGOs, in particular EquiLibre, who were to become our biggest friends, supporters and partners through our early existence. In fact, they were to give us a more concrete reason for our journey, inviting us to visit the many projects with children they ran worldwide.

The Rising Sun pub in King's Cross, London provided a perfect venue for meetings and discussions over a pint and a round of pool as the project took shape and various friends congregated in London awaiting the departure. Most of us were living cheaply in squats in the area.

In July 'Matters Limited' was formed and incorporated for the purpose of implementing and administering our project.

The project name: The Serious Road Trip was chosen, as it really was to be a serious road trip with a serious intention underneath the fun appearance.

An office space in Charlton Street, near King's Cross and Euston Road, soon became the place with a phone so people could contact us. The Rising Sun pub was still handy for regular meetings, although not quite the venue for people to take us seriously. Nev was busy contacting his father's contacts through his diplomatic ties, much to his family's initial concern, and it was all hands on deck to make it all happen. He'd not always fitted in with the conventional and privileged world he'd grown up in and yet maybe he was a product of that. By now he really was the rebel with a cause. A launch party took place and entrance to the party, held on Sunday 18th August, involved a compulsory tequila shot whilst lounging in a garden chair with your throat and eyes open and wide. The night was such a success that The Rising Sun thought it served us both if we were to organise a regular fund-raising event on Thursday nights.

Unsure of my role within all of this hype of activity, I was also attempting to pay off the huge Visa card bill that had been used to fund the latter part of our travels through Brazil and Bolivia. Nev may have got to Brazil but had arrived with no spending money and my savings had dwindled quickly. My credit card had saved the day and I was left with the responsibility of repaying that while Nev and the others focused on the actions of The Serious Road Trip. Temporary work in London was not as lucrative as I hoped, and I was not adapting to life in the squat with 15 or more of us sharing a bathroom. At least Nev and I had our own room, while the others slept with five or so to a room, but there was always a queue for the one bathroom. I didn't like my chances of getting rid of my debt fast enough either.

'Why don't you come back to Luxembourg?' remarked my wonderful Scottish friend Susan. 'My new manager says she has a project for you.' It was the perfect solution. I ended up with a job back in my old office in Luxembourg and was relieved to head off to earn some hard cash. Nev seemed happy with this idea and I went with instructions to fund-raise there too. Now for someone who had no fund-raising skills, this felt very daunting initially, but I was fortunately soon helped by an expert in this. Cynthia Albrecht was a fast-paced and well-connected English woman, aged 60 or so, married and living in Luxembourg. She had decades of experience in charity work. She was short, with dark curly hair, very vivacious and had a large dose of humour. She had been enchanted by Damon and Nev and was particularly inspired by our project. She drove me around in her lovely Jaguar to various venues, setting up fundraising events here, there and everywhere. She was not shy when it came to asking for favours and support. When I suffered from serious car sickness, we giggled about how I was going to survive on the year-long journey to New Zealand. This was without contemplating the joys of communal living again. Another great contact was Bob, the Radio DJ who had organised the original trip to Romania, and Chris, who also had been on that trip.

The White Rose and The Harp also provided venues for much

festivity and fund-raising. Everyone seemed to love supporting a good cause and fortunately these people were not short of money.

Back in London an Afro-Caribbean band, End of Culture, offered to help and even wrote a song for us. This was released on a small vinyl 45 record, which we handed out to promote ourselves, and sold for a pound. The band played endless music for the gigs on Thursday nights. They provided some much needed relaxation from the stresses of organising and projecting the work we were to embark on, in countries we knew very little about. Their concerts brought us all together, helped build bridges after disputes, getting us to refocus on what it was all about, and working as a team.

Here are the lyrics that seemed to pretty much sum it all up:

Don't flip!
But are you coming on this trip?
Haven't you heard?
The Serious Road Trip

One day this song may not be sung,
It'll happen when we're dead and gone.
They'll be singing about the brighter matters
Instead of ragged clothes and tatters.

Don't flip!
But are you coming on this Trip?
Haven't you heard?
The Serious Road Trip.

Every day is a brand new day with a journey we must make,
The kids out there need our care, you know the future is at stake.
We got ourselves a big red London bus,
We're gonna drive around the world
And do what we can to lend a hand to all the lonely boys and girls.

Don't flip!
But are you coming on this trip?
Haven't you heard?
The Serious Road Trip.

Here's a lesson we should learn
Time is short and the road is long,
The kids around don't have their say
It's up to us to change their fate.

We need volunteers worldwide to determine
This is our world.
To show that LOVE is the word,
The word.
LOVE

Don't flip!
But are you coming on this trip?
Haven't you heard?
The Serious Road Trip.

Albania, Romania, Afghanistan
It's a Serious Road-trip to many lands.
From London-town to Kathmandu
The Serious Road Trip is coming through!

Road-trip, The Serious Road Trip, Road-trip, The Serious Road Trip,
WE need volunteers worldwide to determine
This is our world.
To show that LOVE is the word,
The word,
The Serious Road Trip!

by End of Culture, 1992

A bus was sourced from adventure travel group 'Topdeck' and its previous name was PLOD. Aptly it had been a bus used on the London to Kathmandu run for years. It was a Bristol Lodekka, rather than a Routemaster as the Lodekka was less than four metres high making it easier to travel under many bridges. At huge expense, it was given a red make-over to look like a London bus and refitted with tables/seating and kitchen downstairs and collapsible seating/bunk beds upstairs. This was done by a professional company who charged a pretty fortune but did a good job. There was sleeping space for 16 people or more by night and seating for taking children and others on bus trips. The number 17 was proudly painted on as well as 'London to New Zealand.' Nev joked that this might have been to do with me as I was born on the 17th but I can't be sure what reason this number was chosen. Although our bus did not make many journeys in London, it was curiously captured by a photographer at an intersection in Camden Town and soon appeared on postcards sold locally, much to our surprise.

In February we held a historic meeting and press conference for all those interested in the project and a representative from EquiLibre, Laurent, came to speak of his organisation's support.

33

In order to capture imaginations and the attention of the various media, End Of Culture even performed on the roof of the double-decker bus when it was parked outside the Rising Sun pub. The media interest was paramount as not only were we to do the work with the children, but we were to highlight the plight of underprivileged children worldwide. There were plans to film the whole trip as well.

Another major event before leaving was to take place at Trafalgar Square, where once again End of Culture played. This was the first time a band had played in Trafalgar Square since the Beatles, so it was a big deal. There were all sorts of activities as part of the fund-raising effort, and I remember the joy of dancing around wearing a mini-red-bus-decorated-cardboard-box in front of our real bus. The TVNZ crew was filming, the music blaring, jugglers and entertainment doing their thing and collections being made. The big departure was imminent but more details were being finalised and more funds were needed to pay for the bus and other project costs.

As I was operating 'solo' from Luxembourg, I valued these regular short returns to London to reconnect with Nev and the gang and to help with London fund-raising. I boosted my energy through the music and finding out the latest developments for the trip. The novelty of operating as a 'Lone Ranger' in Luxembourg was starting to take its toll on me. I had managed to pay off my debt relatively quickly and save some funds, but now with weeks to go till our planned departure date, I had been keen to spend some preparation time in London. There had been virtually no time to connect with Nev one-on-one. We were theoretically still romantically involved, although indications to the contrary were beginning to show. Was I just imagining that there were other women hovering rather closely? If I questioned this he would reassure me that while we were still together, there wasn't really room for 'couples' on the bus. Obviously, under the circumstances, there was never a moment for quality time, but there never really had been. We had usually been surrounded by friends, mostly male, with Nev a main ringleader and me his faithful side-kick. I consoled myself with the hope that once we were on the road, we might finally find some time together. I really was tired of waiting for this moment, but there was no point in giving up at this stage.

The disheartening reality was that I was not so useful in London, and was asked to return to Luxembourg where I could be more help organising a fund-raising weekend extravaganza. The bus would pass through a few weeks later, as part of a Western European tour, and I would be instrumental in organising the gigs there. The band End of Culture was to provide music for concerts in various indoor and outdoor venues through Luxembourg, France and Germany before the more 'serious' work was to begin in Eastern Europe.

Funds weren't the only major worry. There was rising concern that we had no bus driver for the Trip and our one and only mechanic (my cousin Grant from NZ) had decided to put his relationship first. At the time this seemed a rather unusual choice and we couldn't see why he would let his relationship get in the way of such an important journey. Losing our mechanic was one blow, but the one critical person needed for such a road trip was a driver! This person was yet to be found and it needed to be someone who felt confident driving a Bristol Lodekka full of well-meaning volunteers.

One week before departure, 35-year-old Liverpudlian Paul Kirwan walked into the Rising Sun pub with all his driving, mechanical and travelling experiences. He was meeting his stilt-walking friend Justin there. They saw our project proposal on a table in The Rising Sun and decided to act spontaneously. After a couple of beers, Paul made his way to our office down the road.

'Can I be of any help? Do you need another driver by chance?'

He was greeted with smiles of relief all round. Our prayers had been answered.

Little did he realise that he would be the one and only experienced driver! Justin would also join us as our one and only experienced performer for the Western leg, aside from the band, although we would all go on to play our parts in our own unique ways.

Chapter 4

Fundraising through Europe

First Stop – Luxembourg! (May 1992)

Once the bus was ready and paid for, the bus did actually leave London in a huge furore including a big send-off on ITV's Gimme 5. The first stop was Luxembourg where Cynthia and I waited with anticipation. There was a mix of familiar and unknown faces. We had prepared the ground for an outdoor concert, sponsored haircut and general fundraising activities. Many of these were centred around The Harp and the White Rose. What a thrill to see all the hard work come to fruition. There was also an amazing last-minute sponsorship from Luxair, who would proudly place their logo on our bus. It was quite affirming for me to have organised such an intense and profitable weekend and a huge relief finally to be on the bus. I put on a brave smiling face as I climbed aboard the bus and waved goodbye to my financial services buddies (especially Susan, Jacqui and Noel). Cynthia was nervous for us on such a long journey, but at least the shaky bus didn't seem to affect me as much as her sporty Jaguar.

'Will you come back and visit us?' Cynthia asked.

'I don't think so,' I remarked, slightly insensitively. As far as I was concerned I was on my way back to NZ.

'Do let us know how you get on... Bon voyage.'

'Thank you. I couldn't have done it without you. Goodbye,' I cried.

Farewells were hard at the best of times. It was the end of an era, in some ways a more stable and predictable Kiwi overseas experience, and the beginning of another very unpredictable adventure into more volatile and unexplored waters.

I waved until there was no one left to wave at and climbed upstairs. There were people everywhere and the smell of sweaty bodies was already evident. I avoided the bucket that doubled as an emergency toilet, as I stowed my purple backpack in a spot under one of the benches. I wasn't sure there was space for me to sleep as most of the bunks were spoken for. My stomach was in knots.

'Welcome aboard!' Nev grinned.

After Luxembourg came Brussels, where two women hosts had arranged for us to perform and collect money on the Place de la Monnaie, not far from that Manneken Pis statue.

A Revolutionary Idea in France

Then we travelled to Normandy where Christophe's artist uncle had organised an art auction and concert in Bayeux. I was beginning to realise how vital my language skills were becoming, as Grenouille (Christophe) and I were the only two that had French and English.

Although I would naturally choose a back-seat and prefer to be led and fit in with the crowd, I was now at the centre of things. This was especially important when it came to sorting out everyday matters such as sourcing food for everyone and electricity for the band, while Christophe handled most of the press attention. It was exhausting and exhilarating at the same time. I thrived on speaking French and with such a large group there was always something to keep me busy.

There really wasn't space or privacy on the bus for everyone and many chose to sleep outside in various Botanical Gardens.

Then it was on to Paris for a press conference with Alain Michel, President of EquiLibre, offering his support to this collaborative project. We were also invited to join him later in Lyon at their headquarters.

A couple of women who had joined the fundraising team, Andrea and Jane, met up with the bus in Paris and I was becoming more aware that my intuition had been right. One of them was definitely paying Nev a lot of attention. I was in a tricky situation, as Nev explained that she was one of the people responsible for finding necessary funds for our journey, as I had been too. My emotions had to be suppressed, as under the circumstances it felt impossible for me to voice anything without jeopardising the project.

Then it was Orleans beckoning, where Christophe's family and support network had arranged various concerts, indoors and outdoors. The Road Trip and supporters slept in their garden and the Huette family (Josette and Pierre) provided meals for over 20 people. This amazing family had provided a home away from home for me during my first year after NZ (whilst teaching English in France) and now they were being so hospitable to a crowd of people that they had just met. It was almost like some giant Christmas gathering as they were all there to farewell Christophe and the rest of us on our year-long journey.

The big bombshell came when we arrived in Lyon to spend a night at the EquiLibre warehouse and headquarters. Their president, Alain Michel, needed to speak with us urgently.

'Will you join us in a Peace Convoy to Sarajevo in Bosnia? A war has broken out in Bosnia and no Western Leaders 'ave chosen to acknowledge its existence. We are leaving in a couple of weeks with an Italian group. Zey are inviting all sorts of people to join them with trucks and vehicles laden with supplies for the people under siege in Sarajevo. Per'aps your red bus could lead the convoy in?' He asked with his persuasive French accent.

'Let's go!' Nev exclaimed with a resounding yes.

'Of course!' announced Damon and Christophe with no hesitation.

'What? Hang on a minute. You're talking about a war zone. It's not even on our itinerary,' remarked Australian Matt. 'This is a political act as well!'

'Sara... what?' I asked.

'Sara-yay-vo,' Christophe enunciated clearly as if the 'yay' in the middle of the word begged us to say yes.

The name was vaguely familiar, having watched the Winter Olympics several years earlier.

'Is this what we set out to do? I mean... that means we will be going into a war zone.' I questioned.

It's true that in one ambitious itinerary plotted by Christophe, there had been 'plans' for an accompanying Land Rover (which we did not actually have) to go off into Croatia to explore the situation there as there had been trouble between the Serbs and Croats, but Bosnia was definitely not on the itinerary of the one-year journey to NZ. Although we were ready or blindly accepting the unexpected twists and turns of travelling, this was a huge detour besides targeting a country at war.

'Are you serious, man? Are we really ready to risk our lives crossing front lines to get there?' Miles asked incredulously.

What's more, it was suggested that the red bus be the lead vehicle waving the white flag. Would this be like waving a red flag to a gun-trigger-happy bull?

'I just wanted to help children... ' remarked Julie incredulously. 'I didn't think we'd be crossing front lines to do so,' she continued.

38

'Same,' echoed Belinda, Amanda and myself. 'Yeah, we just wanted to help the kids,' we wailed in unison.

'Well, if you're not prepared to go into Sarajevo, then you're not ready to be a true Road Tripper!' announced Nev quite boldly.

Belinda started to sob and her boyfriend Myles tried to comfort her. Similarly Miles stood next to Julie for moral support.

'You can't make us go into a war zone mate.' Miles defended us as he addressed Nev.

'Yeah, I agree,' muttered Myles.

'Me too!' a number of us repeated.

'So you haven't got what it takes to be a Road Tripper then...' Nev persisted.

'WHAT! Fuck You! Who do you think you are? A dictator or something!' voiced Miles boldly.

'What about all the street children and orphanages in Romania expecting us at that time?' Matt pointed out. 'We don't want to let anyone down.'

'You don't 'ave to decide tonight!' exclaimed Alain Michel. 'We are leaving in two weeks. You can join us at the Austrian Border or not. This is a big decision, so you need to sink about it. We would love you to be zere and our actions could r-really make a differ-ence, but it's up to you, of cour-se. I'll leave you to discuss amongst yourselves. I will let you know where we will meet on the border, if you agree. Good night dear friends.'

The discussions were heated and fraught with extreme reactions. What a hoo-haa erupted, with many tears and emotions unleashed as we contemplated crossing into the war-stricken lands. It was obvious that we were not going to come to some mutual agreement that night.

One of the true ironies was that Murillo, the brave Crocodile Dundee of the Pantanal in Brazil, who we had persuaded to join us, almost as though he would 'protect' us in such situations, was one of the first to say that there was no way he was heading into a war zone.

'Do you really know how it feels to have someone chasing your arse and out to kill you? No fucking way!' he confirmed.

Eventually, we managed to come up with a wise solution. Those who wished to go on the Peace Convoy could do so and those that chose to travel to Bucharest to work with the street children could do so by train, where we would wait for the bus to join us afterwards. There was time to work out which group you fell into, and with fewer people on board the bus, more provisions could be transported to the hungry Bosnians.

It was quickly apparent who would be on board the bus or not. Nev,

Damon, Paul (the driver), and Christophe were definite, although later Myles also joined the hardy group.

This Peace Convoy now became a newsworthy point in our concerts through Europe as we ventured over towards Bavaria and Southern Germany. Once there, Murillo announced he was off, quite spontaneously, and disappeared with a German friend before we had a chance to think. I'm not sure whether he had befriended her on one of his safaris or at one of the concerts.

Outbursts in Germany

I was relieved when we reached the familiar terrain of Übersee am Chiemsee, where Tessa and Wolfie welcomed us into their spacious home and gardens. I'd stayed here a few times before when Nev, Damon and Tony G were helping to restore their ancient mill. We'd all headed off to the famous Oktoberfest to indulge in the ritual beer-drinking there or over the border to Austria and to Prague. This time was different, although we still managed to sample the local beer alongside our other actions. As an English teacher, Tessa had arranged for us to entertain local school children and the general public whilst fundraising at the same time. 'We're off to Sarajevo to try and stop the war, then heading to NZ working with underprivileged kids en route!' we announced. Our band performing on top of the bus roof certainly amazed a few in nearby Bad Reichenhall and brought in a few Deutschmarks for our journey.

We were in the vicinity of the Kehlsteinhaus, otherwise known as Hitler's Eagle's Nest retreat, aptly perched on a mountain peak. It was now operating as a restaurant with panoramic views of the Alps.

'Let's check it out!' announced Nev.

So we ventured on up.

'To think, this is where Hitler and his friends used to hang out!' Tony announced as he took a seat at a table and sipped on his beer.

'Prost!' we all clinked our glasses.

Was this one of the tables where he and his Nazi friends had plotted their evil? I wondered. It was a breathtaking view from there.

'Yeah, it feels strange to be here really...' I trailed off thinking about what a contrast it all was. Where they had dreamed of being a superior Aryan race and the annihilation of Jews and other groups of people, we were dreaming of helping children and plotting our journey to New Zealand. And yet some of our group were now heading into a war.

As I had sensed earlier, Nev was not only showing more interest in

40

the future of The Serious Road Trip and its journey to Sarajevo, but also in the advances of fellow fundraiser Andrea who came with big connections to charitable causes in London. How could my Visa card and relatively smaller fundraising actions compare if that was what it took to gain the attentions of Nev? I wasn't sure what was going on. I sensed there was something happening but maybe it was just a short-lived crush? Or was it just the location and what it represented that made me feel uncomfortable.

We didn't linger as it had been a long day and we needed to get back.

I decided to pile into Andrea's car with him and a few others, which made a change from the spacious bus. He was in the passenger seat with Andrea at the wheel, while I managed to squish in the seat behind him.

Nev looked stressed. I decided to give him a wee massage on his shoulders since I was jammed up against the back of his seat and he was so close. It didn't last long before he gently moved his shoulder away. We travelled in silence for a few minutes before I tried again.

This time it was clear he didn't want this attention and definitely not in front of Andrea. Perhaps it was an act of provocation but I had needed to find out some way or other. He had clearly chosen this newcomer while I had been conveniently working away in Luxembourg; or did he not want any display of affection in public? The emotions started to well up and I was grateful that night had descended and I could hide my face. Andrea didn't seem to have noticed and kept her cool.

We definitely needed to talk when we got back. Nev continued to drink one bottle of beer after the other and toked heavily on cigarettes as we drove in almost silence.

Finally we arrived after what seemed an interminable time. We piled out of the back seat, but Nev and Andrea didn't move. I waited for him to get out but just when I thought I would have my moment, the car suddenly reignited and sped backwards in reverse and then stalled.

'Where are you off to?' I screamed with a jolt.

'I'm giving him a driving lesson,' Andrea announced with a Cheshire-cat smirk on her face.

'What! In the middle of the night?' I didn't want to believe it and looked at Nev to confirm.

Nev was quite drunk and nodded with a silly grin on his face.

The car engaged first gear and sped off, leaving me behind. Initially I was too choked up to talk. I made my way back to a small group outside.

'I'm leaving the Road Trip! Enough is enough!' I announced my decision in the heat of the moment. This heralded the end of a very long relationship. Perhaps it was partly fuelled by my fear of the future plans in war-stricken and impoverished lands, but everything had come to a head. I was left heart-broken, jealous and sobbing into the small hours outside on a garden bench. I tried to contemplate my options of where I should go and did I dare to return so soon to Luxembourg? Most of the others had gone to bed, except gentle Ben from the band. His kind look conveyed he understood my pain and he placed a comforting blanket around me. My outpouring of grief was followed by a welcome deep sleep. I awoke with a sense of calm.

'You can't leave, Simone. You're just as important to this trip as Nev!' exclaimed Belinda, Julie and Miles.

'We won't let you leave,' they reaffirmed.

'Anyway, Andrea's going back to London today and Nev is off to Sarajevo soon.'

'There's no point in leaving over this, you're coming to Bucharest with us,' they begged me to reconsider.

Finally, Nev found time to speak with me one-on-one; the situation was so dramatic. He too wanted me to reconsider, especially as our friendship went back years. There was no apology mind you.

Partly to stand my ground and also not wanting to leave the security and moral support of my friends at such a time, I decided to face the challenges ahead and venture on.

Andrea and her friend left that day. Their summer break was over and they needed to return to London. I was glad she was gone but something had been broken.

Next stop was Berlin where a concert was planned at Humboldt University. Far from Tessa and her organising nature, I stood out of the group once again as the only German speaker. There was much that fell again on my shoulders as I sourced electricity for the band and pointed people in the direction of shops for food supplies. With the departure for Bosnia imminent we wanted to do all that we could to protect our brave friends. It was decided that we needed placards on the sides of the bus 'DON'T SHOOT' and so various people set about making that happen. We worried that the Bosnians may not speak English and so the decision was made to paint 'NE PUCAJ' on the other side, for the snipers to think twice before shooting. This emphasised further that our bus and our friends really were heading into a war zone.

For publicity purposes, as well as the novelty, we arranged for the bus to travel under the Brandenburg Gate and managed to have Justin juggling on the roof of the bus whilst doing so!

I organised a permit for us to 'busk' in the central spot, the Kurfürstendamm, next to the church that remains with its bombed roof as a statement about war.

This proved to be the most successful concert of them all, with hundreds gathering for the appealing tunes of End of Culture and a sound-system that surpassed your usual busker. Even the TV reporters were alerted to our presence and projects and came to film and interview. The red London bus was heading into war-stricken Sarajevo on a Peace Convoy. The public reached into their pockets. Not only was the music and entertainment fantastic, but we were off to help the starving people of Bosnia. Within the hour though, the police sirens were blaring and I was carted off in a paddy wagon along with Nev to explain the situation all in German. We had a permit, that was true, but the decibels were well beyond the acceptable limit. The music had to stop! Fortunately with a few language delaying tactics, by the time we unplugged the electricity a good collection of funds had been made and it was time to call it a day anyway. Phew! At least we hadn't ended up in some police cell.

The band and the sound technician were next to leave us, after five weeks on the road. They too were heading back to London. The Western European leg was at an end and it was time for us to head to Prague. The focus was changing from fun-loving fundraising to serious humanitarian work.

Chapter 5

Prague and Peace Convoy to Bosnia or Bucharest

The bus rattled over the potholed roads of Eastern Germany and shook our nerves as well as the pots and pans as we rumbled on to Prague. There was a silent sombre mood on board, apart from one excited East German woman catching a ride to Dresden. She was full of conversation and questions during her brief encounter with The Serious Road Trip.

From Prague, one group would board a train for Bucharest, Romania and the others would stay with the bus and head to the border to meet up with the Peace Convoy.

We were filled with dread at what might happen to our loved ones as they headed to more dangerous territory. It somewhat tainted the mood of visiting Prague again.

The last time I had been there, I'd jumped in a car with Nev and Tony bound for Czechoslovakia to celebrate the first anniversary of the Velvet Revolution of 1989. It had been aptly named 'Velvet' as there had been virtually no violence. It was just weeks after the Berlin Wall had been torn down and had started with a small group of students protesting and marking the 50th Anniversary of a violently suppressed demonstration against the Nazi storming of Prague University. Eventually there had been hundreds of thousands protesting in the streets against the communist government. The communist party eventually handed power over to the influential playwright Havel. I wasn't sure what to expect for the anniversary celebration, but the main square decorated with American flags had really caught me by surprise. President George Bush was arriving shortly as the first American President to visit in the country's 70-year history.

He spoke clearly to the crowd:

'Thank you my Czech and Slovak friends! It is a tremendous honour to me to visit this proud and beautiful country and to be able to join you on the first anniversary of the extraordinary Velvet Revolution. What a powerfully moving sight it is... Your declaration of independence proclaims: "The forces of darkness have served the victory of light. The longed-for age of humanity is dawning." Today, the freedom-loving people of the world can bear witness that this age of humanity has now finally and truly dawned on this splendid nation. . . God bless Czechoslovakia. Thank you very much.'

The hundreds of thousands waved their flags alongside American flags and I was just metres from the black limousine as the American President and First Lady waved from their window and made their way from the square. The Revolutions of 1989 had swept across many of the Warsaw Pact countries with much hope and optimism and yet here we were faced with another result of such freedom. The disintegration of Yugoslavia had brought with it a scramble for land and a complex war. Would our friends be successful in their bid for peace?

We were equally filled with anxiety as to what might happen to us without the security the bus provided, both for shelter and a focus to unify us. Emotions ran high as we bade farewell to our friends Nev, Damon, Christophe, Myles (aka Sifty) and Paul. Would it be a matter of weeks or would this be the last time we saw each other? Belinda was particularly in pieces over saying goodbye to Myles, although he tried to reassure her that he would only accompany the bus to Zagreb or Belgrade. There was even a chance that the convoy might not even travel further than that, in which case they would all be in Romania much sooner. Nothing was certain and I just remember Belinda sobbing more than I allowed myself to. She was only 21 and this was her first big trip away from her family in NZ.

I'd cried myself out just days before.

Bucharest or Sarajevo!

The overnight train for Bucharest set off and once again we headed into the unknown, clutching our back-packs for dear life, like snails holding onto their shells. My nerves would not have endured a Peace Convoy. How brave our friends seemed, or were we just all plain ignorant and naive?

45

The rattling train and slamming doors of compartments did not encourage much sleep. Our passports and tickets were checked at the borders. Those travelling on NZ passports had to pay $20 US for a visa into Hungary, where we didn't even leave the train. The friendly Hungarian controller left us when we entered Romania and so we were finally in Romanian territory where seemingly it had all begun. Well, at least the motivation for The Serious Road Trip had been sparked some two years prior, just after the fall of dictator, Ceausescu. The seed had been sown in that Institute for the Irrecuperable Children of the Botosani region, in the small village of Ionaseni.

Mind you, our train was heading to Bucharest and that was quite some distance from the Northern Moldovan region. It would be several weeks before we made it up to Ionaseni.

Our train rolled in to Bucharest train station and we piled into a taxi in the direction of EquiLibre's Headquarters. There we were fortunately greeted with open arms by EquiLibre's French chief of Mission for Romania. We were feeling dirty, tired and hungry but were shown into a dining room with fabulous Romanian cooking. It was delicious and gave us the safe haven that we needed. From there we piled into an EquiLibre mini-bus and headed off to a huge house where there were at least seven bedrooms, each with no fewer than four beds. They were far comfier than the hard beds of the bus. Were we really in the down-trodden Romania I had expected? There were all sorts of clean-cut young men coming and going from the building. Were they really humanitarians? I had no idea what to expect and had vaguely been expecting the types that would enter a monastery. Once again my French came in use as we tried to explain who we were and what we were doing in Romania. Hang on a minute... I thought they were expecting us to work with the street children... and weren't we participating in a huge EquiLibre driven convoy to Sarajevo? Weren't they the same organisation?

Now we were starting to discover the difficulties in communication between head-office and local head-office. On top of that, the prior planning had been made between Christophe and a former member of staff, neither of whom were there now. And, of course, with the focus in our group being the red double-decker bus travelling from London to New Zealand, we felt somewhat vulnerable in our identity and maybe came across as a lost group of volunteers, as opposed to a dynamic group of individuals with a mission.

'Are you doctors or nurses?' they asked.

'Are you child psychologists or special needs workers? Have you worked with street children before?' We shook our heads, understandably surprised and perhaps wishing we were such people.

46

'No, we're here to help clean, paint and redecorate the orphanages and do what we can,' enthusiastically remembering some of what Nev and Damon had thought might be needed based on their experiences two years prior.

'But most of that has been done already and our two year plumbing project is almost at an end...' they said.

'Oh...' I remember saying, followed by a lengthy silence.

'Don't you have a music concert? How big a stadium do you need?'

'No, we're not the band! That was for the fundraising in Western Europe,' we explained, internally horrified at how much they had been misinformed or at how much Christophe had been dreaming and scheming to bring the band that far. I think we tried to explain about the bus but they didn't seem to understand the significance of our bus being on the peace convoy to Bosnia.

'But aren't you clowns? Don't you have a show?' They probed further. I was lost in thought remembering all the clowns who had supported our fund-raising events and all the juggling balls on the bus and wishing they were there, but fortunately before I could respond negatively, Miles Dinneen, with his 'she'll-be-right-Kiwis-can-do-anything' attitude said, 'Yes! Yes, we have a show!'

I did an internal gulp as did a few others. I didn't dare contradict him and this idea had featured in some early proposals.

'Magnifique! We're having a big get-together tonight, maybe you can perform at that!'

Big gulp.

'And it would be great if you could do your show for the children at Orphanage Number One tomorrow,' he continued.

'Of course, of course,' as we latched on to the one thing that we could theoretically offer.

Needless to say the 'concert' for the adults that evening was held together by Matt on the guitar and Miles Dinneen doing brilliant Elvis impersonations, backed up by us gathering some Dutch courage after a few drinks and finishing on a Kiwi haka (the Maori war-dance that the All Blacks rugby team perform famously before international matches), a la Serious Road Trip. Although it was not quite what they expected, there was a small applause from those that could see the situation for what it was, and we excused ourselves saying it was better for children as they would see the following day.

So rather than retiring to bed as we felt like doing after such an exhausting day, we stayed up late rehearsing what was the skeleton of a show with the main song being 'Old MacDonald had a Farm'. We all gravitated to one animal or another for our show identities with just a

47

few mock face-paints (really palettes of water colours rather than genuine face-paints) and colourful clothing for costumes. Matt, the dog, played guitar and howled away brilliantly, while Miles continued with his Elvis songs and huge face-painted sideburns. It was such a hoot getting ready for it and our spontaneity was starting to work its charm, even on ourselves.

The following day we were taken to a spot outdoors under a tree in the gardens of Orphanage Number One, which is the best known Orphanage of Bucharest, right in the middle of the city. The children were organised in a semi-circle with various staff attending too, and off we went with much enthusiasm despite a bit of stage fright.

We launched into song and were able to find confidence through knowing that we had animal identities and besides, no one knew us in this foreign land. The children were delighted to recognise the various animals including a cat, dog, mouse, chicken and cow to name a few... and we naturally went towards the children to pick them up and dance interactively much to their delight. In fact, there were some surprised staff watching us as we picked up various children from one group to the side that looked to be suffering from missing limbs... it was leprosy, but that didn't stop us. Our motto, 'Every child deserves a chance' was ringing in our heads. Miles' rendition of 'You Ain't Nothing but a Hound Dog' with Matt on guitar howling away, was hilarious and was to become much of a theme song for the show. Another scene included myself, as a bull charging at the red cape of the matador.

Importantly, the show had a positive response with huge smiles all round and lots of clapping and squeals of enjoyment. Most of all we were relieved to have responded so aptly to a need, thus justifying our arrival in Romania.

EquiLibre were pleased and were keen for us to visit all sorts of orphanages with whom they had contact nationwide (40 to choose from), when and if the red bus made it safely to Bucharest after Sarajevo.

There was the occasional phone call to the London office, which also tried to follow the progress of the bus in Bosnia.

There was such a mixture of emotions from the highs of the show to the lows as we waited for news of our friends. Would we see them again? Belinda was a nervous wreck wondering where the heck Myles was if he wasn't on the bus. She had been told he would be with us shortly, but he never arrived.

Then, much to our surprise, as we sat watching the news in the lounge area of the canteen, there it was... The big red bus with 'Don't

48

Shoot' capturing the attention of the TV crews amidst all the other vehicles waving their 'Mir Sada' (Peace Now) flags. We brimmed with pride and relief that they looked to be okay, although we didn't see any faces, just the bus amidst many other vehicles. This also confirmed to the others present, that the bus really did exist and was not a figment of our imagination. It also showed that the Peace Convoy seemed to be gaining the attention of the world leaders as it had hoped, as well as delivering the much needed provisions of aid.

While we waited for two weeks in Bucharest we met such an assortment of people, all intrigued to meet Kiwis and Australians quite a way off course from their usual European pathways.

There was the young Frenchman, who told me I was like a 'flower that needs watering'. While this didn't make sense at the time I can see he was quite perceptive beyond his years. He explained how he had come to do humanitarian work. As a 16-year-old he had invited a homeless man back to his house for food and shelter. How brave this all sounded. He was so positive and encouraging about us too.

There was another Frenchman who was a doctor and was very busy with sick children, particularly those in an Aids hospital. There were others driving four-wheel-drive vehicles and popping in to Bucharest to collect materials for their irrigation projects up-country. These were the ones that reminded me of the men in Levi jeans advertisements at the time. Very cool.

There was a monk from the Order of Don Bosco who explained that some of his fellow monks were also on the convoy for Sarajevo and that their founding father had worked using theatre as well.

There was the jolly Romanian cook and his wife who just provided hearty meal after hearty meal. And of course the French Chief of Mission and his wife who endeavoured to make us useful with activities such as sorting out clothing for distribution in the villages.

We were introduced to the staff and children of the Gavroche Children's Street Centre and performed our mad show for them too, aided by percussion on pots and pans from the kitchen and shakers we had made using plastic bottles filled with stones. Their ages ranged from 5-11 years. Each of these children had been 'rescued' from the street and had a story to tell. The eldest boy, Alexander, was a real scallywag, but looked after the others almost as if he were the father figure. Alina, also 11, had run away from home because her mother was beating her up and her father was a drunk. Her dark brown eyes were really badly crossed and Belinda really identified with her as she had also suffered from a similar thing. She let her try her glasses on and it was as if she could finally see properly. It was good to take our

49

minds off waiting for the others as we would see these children regularly over the next couple of weeks. We were delighted when they performed a rendition of *Little Red Riding Hood* for us and were impressed with their recitations of poems by heart as well.

These children had found shelter in this centre, unlike the many children we found in the streets sniffing glue from dirty plastic bags. They were as high as kites; it was heart-breaking to see. Yet they introduced themselves politely to us and asked us for food. Our guide Vali, wanted to know how we dealt with such issues in NZ, but I hadn't encountered this back home.

By now we had registered ourselves as a Non-Governmental Organisation (NGO) working in Romania with the Ministry of Health. We had established a few links with other organisations such as Caritas and also with 'Studio 24' who were a semi-professional theatre group who performed in the street and on stage.

We sent faxes off to London and our supporters in Luxembourg and still we waited for news of the bus.

One Sunday we visited parts of Bucharest which seemed dirty and grey in general. We heard how Bucharest had been a mini-Paris but what we saw was a depressing city littered with bleak Communist blocks of apartments, lots of roadworks and lots of dirty, dusty roads.

We were overwhelmed at the colossal size of the People's House, which was in fact the largest administrative building in the world. In order to build this, Ceausescu had demolished seven square kilometres of the old city centre in the Uranus area. This included the site of a Monastery, a hospital, numerous factories and thousands of homes with 40,000 people relocated from the area. The works were carried out by forced labour of soldiers and some say 3,000 people died building it. It was the brainchild of a delusional dictator and was still not completed with only 400 of the 1,100 rooms actually finished and used, including a huge bunker in the event of nuclear war. I remember Miles juggling in front of the many grand fountains, spurting water before this huge monster Palace. It was sickening to think of the pain Ceausescu had inflicted on his people. It was anything but a House of the People!

The following week brought our first invitation to an orphanage outside of Bucharest. However, with the bus's imminent arrival, Belinda, Amanda and I decided to wait in Bucharest and let the rest of the team head off to Horia in the Black Sea region.

And still we waited for what felt like an eternity for the bus to appear, but in reality was a mere couple of weeks.

It was Saturday 27th June 1992 and we had been in Romania since the 12th of June. Suddenly, there it was, a little later than expected, but who was on board? Our hearts soared when we realised that they were alive and well and we were reunited amidst hugs and much chatter of all that had happened.

Our driver Paul Kirwan was no longer with them, as he had been asked to join one of the other groups. His mechanical and driving skills had proved invaluable on the road to Sarajevo as apparently he had heroically fixed a truck which had broken down and which threatened to stop the whole convoy at a critical and dangerous moment. How amazing to hear this news, but where did that leave us now he had been commandeered elsewhere?

Damon and Myles (who did accompany them to Sarajevo after all) had been driving the bus now. Mind you, they were beginners and they were certainly not mechanics. Nev and Christophe seemed rather detached from the crowd and deeply affected by all that had happened on the convoy. They certainly didn't appear interested in what had been happening in Bucharest, with such extreme needs prevailing in Sarajevo. They hid themselves in the offices of Bucharest, taking over phones and fax-machines, such was the urgency.

We couldn't help but think that this Project Romania was just a huge inconvenience to them and to the people of Sarajevo who needed them more urgently. They were out on a limb in Bucharest and London was calling in many ways. Our head-office in Charlton Street was receiving all sorts of calls from the media in Britain as we had been the first British NGO to enter war-torn Bosnia and had been easily identified by our bus. ABC news wanted to interview someone from the convoy, and TVNZ (Paul Holmes Show) too, as we had been in the first convoy to break the siege of Sarajevo.

We listened with open eyes and hearts to all that had happened on the convoy. The bus had not led the group as previously anticipated, but had been placed in the middle of the thirty-vehicle convoy. It had provided much needed light relief during a very tense time when crossing front lines and entering the besieged city of Sarajevo. One by one, various people took their turns to board the bus for some much needed respite from the relatively cramped travelling conditions of the other vehicles and very necessary conversations over cups of tea. It sounded like a travelling café where a genuine sharing of the human fears and common bonds that connected them all took place.

We learnt that the true destination of the convoy had been Medjugorje, where many pilgrims journey since the Virgin Mary made her appearance in Bosnia. Nev described with delight how a small group of monks had blessed the bus in a water-sprinkling and chanting

51

ritual one night as they encircled the bus. How mysterious and magical! They must have been friends of the monk we had already met.

Nev proudly told us how the Croatian word for God was Bog and how that had given him a new meaning for going to the Bog! Or even looking for a Bog.

He and Christophe went on to describe the mood that prevailed when they finally arrived in Sarajevo amidst the bombing and sniper fire. They had entered the city along the airport's runway and had downed a bottle of vodka between them in the time it took to drive from one end to the other. Whilst doing this they had aptly listened to Bob Marley's 'Coming in from the Cold'. Typical, I thought as Nev was an avid Marley fan. I wondered whether this had helped to numb the fear. Myles later confided to me that at this point he was beyond fear and was just completely in the moment. After delivering the supplies they were told to seek refuge in the famous Holiday Inn. There, amidst all the shelling and gunfire Damon, the barefooted gentle giant, had seized the moment when he sat himself down at the Grand Piano and proceeded to give a concert with the Richard Clayderman repertoire his mother had taught him. Everyone was speechless as he looked an unlikely sort to play piano as they wondered if these were to be their last moments. They had been approached by people from the Children's Embassy, asking if they could transport 50 or so orphans in the bus from the besieged city. Unfortunately the paperwork did not arrive in time and the bus had to leave three days later, without the children. Nev and Christophe tried to organise an airlift to see these children to safety, but Bucharest was too far removed. Their efforts were also focused on securing peace as they pleaded with politicians to intervene and 'Stop the War!' before it took hold further. They were shaken and understandably emotionally involved with the plight of Bosnia.

The rest of the team returned from the Black Sea. Here they had exceeded all expectations and delivered an amazing performance in conjunction with two French volunteers from our host organisation EquiLibre. They returned elated and excited to see the bus as well. We were ready for more action.

News about our presence spread amongst the NGO staff working in Romania and the orphanages were beckoning us left, right and centre to come and do a show for their children. After all, many of the basic needs were being met in the form of repaired shelter, plumbing and heating, medical and food supplies. Now was the time to also endeavour to meet the psychological needs of the children. Although we were not child psychologists or social workers there was room for some much-needed laughter and love. Both would go a long way in these still desperate situations, where the children were severely deprived and under-stimulated.

But the happy reunions on the arrival of the bus soon turned to frustration for Nev and Christophe. Nev was determined to return to London at the earliest possible date rather than continue on with the bus. I found this rather hard to process, particularly as Nev had previously seemed hell-bent on returning to Ionaseni orphanage, where his dramatic transformation had taken place two years earlier. What about the orphans that he had met and had desperately sought to see and help again? I also had my selfish reasons of wanting to see if our relationship could continue again, away from the intervention of the 'other woman' in London. But in the end the sequence of events took their course and we were to be separated again, once and for all. Nev returned to London and Christophe went back to Lyon on a mission to join EquiLibre's second convoy to Sarajevo.

However, there were still things to be done in Romania. We selected a few places to visit on our way North to Ionaseni. We were down to nine volunteers (Damon and Amanda, Patrick, Matt, Julie and Miles, Belinda and Myles and myself) as we farewelled Bucharest, the much-loved children of Gavroche, and our hosts. We navigated some busy streets in Bucharest and then in typical style our bus broke down on a major roundabout, blocking traffic in all directions. What were we to do now? As if by magic, a swarthy-faced man appeared and leapt under the bonnet of our bus's engine. It didn't take long for him to sort it out... I asked if he was a mechanic or bus driver, but he was neither. He was a sailor and said that he knew the sound of a Gardner engine anywhere as these were also used in boats. How handy I thought, but before I could say a word more, he disappeared as quickly as he had arrived.

We headed to our first stop, Pitesti, venturing over pot-holed roads to the city centre in search of the venue. This was a mining town and it was lunch-time. The square was swarming with workers all dressed in blue. The buildings were grey and there we were in a bright red bus with our colourful costumes searching for the next lot of children to delight. It was an outdoor venue for a small crowd of children on holiday.

Damon had easily slotted into the show as a bare-footed Red-Indian with his long hair and a head-band complete with feather. I watched with wonder and worry though as he proceeded to swing the slender Belinda around in Merry-Go-Round fashion, much to the children's amazement. Afterwards they all wanted to be swung around, which he happily obliged to do until he himself was dizzy and on the ground.

Chapter 6

The Road Back to
Ionaseni Orphanage

The bus stopped in Hirlau, which had an institute housing hundreds of children and adults. It was like an orphanage, nursing home and psychiatric ward all rolled into one. Absolute bedlam! There we discovered children in their beds, shockingly under-stimulated and in need of love. Many of their hygiene and care issues had been addressed, but the lasting effects on the children created by this environment hit us in the face. We'd heard about these places and seen images on television but the reality was truly appalling. In one room there was a teenager who had been left so much in his child-sized bed that he was the size of a young child, but with lengthy arms and legs that seemed to curve around the edges of the cot-bed. How could this be?

In another room the children begged to be picked up, craving the smallest ounce of attention. We put smiles on our brave faces and tried to meet this need in that small moment. The children clung for dear-life to that human warmth they so craved. It was frightening. It was all too much for one child who gave a huge bite to Patrick and drew blood. We were worried for him. He brushed it off, humorously saying that he had just survived being bitten by a 'radioactive' kid. He was referring to our close proximity to the Chernobyl nuclear disaster some six years prior and a mere 500 kilometres away. Honestly, we did start to wonder if he might have contracted some more serious illness such as Hepatitis, or dare I say HIV?

Aside from the emotional stress, there was also an incredible stench of urine and faeces in these rooms. It was hard to stop ourselves dry retching and yet we had to put on a smile and reach out for them, just to keep sacred that small moment of joy and human touch. These children had already faced so much rejection, we dared not do that to them again. And so for those brief moments we held the children on our hips and swung around as if dancing with them, while Matt strummed tunes on the guitar. There was something about being in our close-knit group that made it more bearable, and the fact that we were doing something, rather than just looking, that helped us along.

We were invited to stay a little longer, however, we were on a Road Trip, and our destination of Ionaseni was beckoning. Off we went in the big Red Bus, direction Botosani and from there, right out into the very rural Ionaseni. I was lost in all sorts of thoughts, reflecting on our experiences that day with the children, when suddenly we passed an entire field of what looked like marijuana growing. That stopped us in our tracks. How odd! Was it not illegal over here? Damon pulled over and there were hundreds if not thousands of these eight-foot plants towering over us. Of course the surprise didn't last for long when we realised that it must be hemp, which resembles 'weed'. Someone mentioned it was used for making rope, clothes and other things.

Some seemed disappointed by this but grabbed a few buds to test out later, just in case. After stretching our legs, we piled back onto the bus. It shouldn't be too far now. At least Damon had been there before and we felt safe having him as our driver and experienced aid-worker.

What were we doing in this unknown world, completely out of our comfort zone? What would we find in that Orphanage for the Irrecuperable that Nev and Damon had chanced upon some two years before and had given us all the impetus for the whole Serious Road Trip project. It felt quite surreal as we headed to meet those very children that had motivated Nev and Damon to help. At least the Scottish folk who'd first started working there had been making progress. But Nev had chosen to return to London, to respond to the Bosnian crisis. How meaningful then, was our return to Ionaseni for him? He was seemingly rallying to another cause. I allowed myself to focus too much on his not being there. For all his saying that there was no room on the bus for couples, there were three couples after all; making me the only female on her own.

Yet I was living this adventure thanks to him. It was also true that I had invested much time and energy in this project and had my own journey to make.

It was here at Ionaseni that my humanitarian self was stirred, and that something else inside me was born... not straight away, but it started to grow slowly. It was July 1992, and I was 26.

The orphanage building stood like a 'concentration camp' with a formidable tower on a hill surrounded by fields of hay. We later found out it had been a former hunting lodge, but its notoriety had preceded our first view; we didn't quite see the grandeur at this moment. It was above the main road and our huge bus slowly pulled itself up the dirt road to the main entrance. The bus only just squeezed under the metal archway announcing 'Camin Spital pentru Copii'. We passed the gatekeeper, who was half asleep, and made our way into the courtyard and over to the building. It did seem grander than it had on my first impression.

From outside it was a sleepy place, with just a handful of children at the front door who squealed with delight when they saw our huge red bus roll in. They were sitting on the wall of the porch entrance rocking backwards and forwards in unison, one child in a wheelchair. I remember hearing an Irish accent from one of the volunteers, and soon there was Rupert Wolfe-Murray coming to welcome us. He was the Scottish journalist who had 'discovered' Ionaseni. He had broadcast the plight of these children, whilst covering the story of the Romanian Revolution in December 1989. He had been motivated to set up a charity in Edinburgh to 'rescue' the children, help them clean up the place and rebuild and renovate. Through his work, experienced nurses, therapists, teachers and many well-wishers had come to see what they could do to help these forgotten and abandoned children.

I remember being ushered into an attic room that had become the volunteers' room and 'off limits' to children and orphanage staff. It was purely for the expatriates and it felt like a safe-haven in an establishment that held many dark secrets. There were always the unpredictable and needy children, roaming if they could, and a language with which I was still unfamiliar. Now I was one who did not understand the local language. My fellow Trippers had probably felt that way since we left England and were already used to it. This room provided some sanctuary from that 'unknown' world outside and had various supplies such as PG Tips tea-bags, Nescafé coffee and tins of baked beans, as well as other familiar treats from the UK, including books and newspapers. There, after all these months, was a link with the UK and the outside world.

However, the food store-room had other invaders. There was the familiar smell of mouse droppings and the cupboard definitely needed cleaning out.

We were quickly shown around the rest of the orphanage and the difference from what Nev and Damon had described was enormous. Romanian Project UK had made major progress and renovations.

There was even a huge supply of hot water in the boiler room beneath the orphanage-come-hospital. For those of us desperate for a shower, there was a pipe gushing water, with a wooden pallet to stand on, but this was better than imagined, and a huge improvement on our bus. Things were far from perfect, but one could sense that the place was brimming with developments and potential.

The children at this stage were much of a blur amidst the smell of urine and the occasional cry that echoed through the halls. Many of these children could not talk. They had not learnt to talk in such dire conditions, and for many the possibility of learning to talk had gone. The situation was similar with walking: many had not learnt to walk, confined to their beds and rooms. I was shocked. They were starved of love, stimulation and interaction and most seemed to be lost in their own little world. The building and conditions may have improved, but the long-lasting effects on the children lived on. Such a leap from my sterile office work in the financial services to this other world: I wondered how on earth I would cope?

Amanda and I quickly busied ourselves tidying the volunteers' room and cleaning out their larder; as we clung to being useful, without having to risk it with the children, just yet.

Having the fairly tall, dark-haired and dashing Rupert Wolfe-Murray on site, as a link between the two worlds, was helpful. He kept us all on track. They needed help transporting clothing and food to various villages further away as well.

We were also embraced by the almost mad but fun-loving Scottish Henry who spoke like Billy Connelly and was much loved by the local village folk and children. He was a talented water-colour artist and had painted pictures of the orphanage as souvenirs for the volunteers or visitors. Other volunteers included a speech therapist and physiotherapist.

The novelties of the next few days included attending a local wedding and visiting one of the several painted monasteries, for which this region was famous. I remember seeing the ornate hand-painted frescos on the inside and outside of the building and feeling so surprised to see that Christianity had somehow survived the communist era. It was the last thing I expected. These monasteries of Bucovina (Voronet, Moldovita, Sucevita, Humor and Arbore) were declared World Cultural Heritage sites by UNESCO in the 1990s. The buildings dated back to the 16th Century and the unique frescoes were decorated to teach soldiers and farmers the history of the country as well as the Bible.

However, our focus at that time was helping the orphanage, so this

57

seemed a bit of a side-track whilst making a delivery of provisions to a neighbouring village.

Those that needed cigarettes quickly discovered that the filterless Carpati were by far the cheapest and we laughed about the name sounding like 'cowpats'. In fact, the guys thought they almost tasted like them too.

The hemp cigarettes had definitely not had the effect that some had been hoping for.

Within days we managed to perform our Old MacDonald's Farm show for the children of Ionaseni orphanage. They watched from blankets under the shade of a tree in front of the building. What a relief to be outside, away from the confines of the orphanage walls. What amazed me was that children who could barely utter sounds, who looked lost in their own worlds, seemed to respond to the music, colour and movement of our show. Even if it didn't make much sense to them, some of them still managed to smile. Others looked more caught up in watching the tiny ant walking past their picnic blanket, rather than the colourful performer several metres away. One particular child caught my attention. Adriana looked the size of a three-year-old and yet I was told she was seven or even older. She had huge brown questioning eyes and stood rocking from one leg to the other whilst watching the animation.

The carers and volunteer staff had to watch out that one of the older and more violent children, Mihaiella (who reminded me of a cheeky monkey), didn't pick on the smaller ones. A few years prior, I was told, some of the staff had used sticks and violence to keep the children under control. Now some of the children were copying behaviour that, to them, was 'normal'. I guess it was a situation where victim had become aggressor.

Back then, there had been too few staff, none with adequate training to cope with such situations, and with limited resources. With sub-zero conditions, broken windows, lack of clothing, heating, food and medical care, a third of the children died every year during the harsh winters. Under those circumstances, and with children behaving like animals, how would one act? It was hard to believe that this had all happened here such a short time ago. Now, to us, the staff didn't look capable of beating the children.

The majority, however, were untrained women from the village, who had to balance work with family responsibilities. Their summer work in the fields included bringing in the harvest and preparing for the bitterly cold winters. For them it was non-stop work.

Our elation from the show soon turned to drama in the team that night. One of our group, Matt, an Australian physio and our guitarist, told us his mother was suffering from cancer in Australia. I asked him if he felt he should return to see her and I'm not sure if I voiced my opinion too loudly, or that I said what he wanted to hear, but in the dark of night and probably after a few too many drinks, Matt took off for Australia. It could also have been that he was used to travelling alone in a more independent one-man band style, than with our chaotic bunch of friends. Whatever the reasons, he would still be missed along with his guitar renditions of 'You 'Aint Nothing but a Hound Dog' along with Miles 'just-call-me-Elvis' Dinneen.

In the following days, various team-members such as Belinda, Myles, Julie, Miles, Patrick, and Damon were busy interacting with some of the children and accompanying them on walks. Amanda had even given a few of them a much needed haircut, which looked better than some of the usual shaved heads we saw.

I was concerned that we needed visas for our onward leg to Poland via the Ukraine. This need for essential paperwork provided a perfect excuse, once again, to escape from the emotions of dealing with the children in the orphanage. I didn't want to admit it, but I was frightened of them.

Another distraction had also emerged. Moona, the much-loved younger brother of Rupert, had arrived from a holiday or a training trip elsewhere. His real name was Magnus, which was a name I'd never heard before, and Moona was his equally different nickname: it encouraged my mind to wander off into another realm. He bounced into the volunteer room to introduce himself and his energetic youthful approach to life contrasted enormously with the more conservative, gentle and serious Rupert.

Here was a guy, high on life, who completely charmed us with his dreamy, piercing blue eyes. Barely containing his excitement, he asked constant questions as to why we were there, what we had done and what we had planned? The arrival of The Serious Road Trip bus had shaken things up for him and he wanted to find out more: 'What was this about Bosnia?'

Here was the sort of guy who could have jumped on top of the bus and pretended it was a giant skateboard or surfboard, such was his enthusiasm and readiness to embrace something new. He was also a keen surfer, skateboarder and climber of trees. The positive energy he oozed was infectious.

We decided that a day trip for the older children in the bus was possible. With Moona's help we managed to load up many of the older children onto the upper deck of the bus. We all escaped from their reality for a day and embarked on a trip to a nearby lake. Our beautiful magic bus, the 'Masina Mare', which had been admired from the outside by the children, now became a means of transport that whisked them on a magical trip away from the orphanage. It reminded me of the concept of a magic carpet, except much bigger.

The view from the top floor was quite unique, as the local vehicles and horses and carts did not afford such amazing views. The excitement was highly visible and nervousness too, as leaving the orphanage was something they didn't do often. The bus lurched past carutas (horses and carts) and many surprised faces on our journey. All of a sudden our fairly slow bus, nicknamed PLOD by the previous owners, felt rather fast alongside these local slow-coaches.

Later that day, in the volunteer room, I managed to grab hold of a weekly International Herald Tribune and to my astonishment read news of our friends in London: a world away from our very remote corner in rural Romania. Here, making an international phone-call required a journey by car to a PTT building (post-office and telecom-munications) some 30 minutes drive away. The orphanage did have a director's office with a phone where local calls could be placed and received; you were lucky if an international call ever got through.

Anyway, here was news of The Serious Road Trip in a story covering the situation in Bosnia; on the front page too! It seemed that the Peace Convoy had succeeded in shaking up a few governments who were embarking on talks, but for now the British Government had not responded and the only British organisation seemingly doing anything was the rather obscure group, 'The Serious Road Trip', who were agitating for intervention or peace, or something along those lines. How proud I felt... we really were achieving our goal of 'generating the maximum amount of media attention and public interest in every country we pass through' as per our original proposal. Nev's dream was coming true! Could they really stop the war? I mused naively.

Moona said he would help me obtain the necessary visas for the Ukraine from the neighbouring city of Suceava, but we would need a few days to process the paperwork. It was decided that, in the meantime, the bus and Trippers would venture over to Podriga, another institution for adults, linked with Ionaseni. Volunteers from the UK were working there and they would benefit from the much-needed relief The Serious Road Trip could provide. We were starting to realise that while we thought it was the children of the orphanages who would most benefit from our visits, it was also the volunteers working in these dire situations, who needed new energy and some contact with the outside world.

By all accounts the situation in Podriga sounded worse than at Ionaseni. Adults with severe psychiatric needs and physical disabilities were harder to face for the team. On top of that there was no plumbing in the institution. I truly was spared that horror for now, as I was swept up in spending time with Moona and fulfilling my administrative role.

We applied for the visas, made necessary phone-calls from the telecommunications centre in town and I was introduced to Moona's daily life. This meant driving around more swiftly than the bus, in a silver Nissan Hi-Lux, running errands, spending lots of time with locals in the village speaking Romanian, sorting out various situations or things that needed mending and hanging out with the children on our return from the activities. We bought bread and provisions from the local market and Moona even surprised me with a huge bouquet of flowers. Wow! This interest in me was welcome.

He introduced me to Mama Puiu and family, who would later help me learn Romanian with Moona's help too.

The ease with which Moona communicated with everyone was inspiring and opened my eyes and heart to a whole new world of 'love'. He was in love with life and it showed. It was also contagious as I started to shed some of my fears and embraced the children he knew so well after over two years of being in Ionaseni. All of a sudden he was putting names to the faces for me and the children loved him so. He hugged them and they hugged back. From being a stranger, I was now a friend of Moona's to them. From being a bunch of wild children, some were now starting to become little individuals with their own quirky personalities.

Moona was also explaining the intricacies of humanitarian work. We were so naive. We had no idea how it all worked, or needed to work for long-term success. It really wasn't a matter of just giving what we thought were the much-needed clothes, toys or money. For the long-term, the orphanage would need to budget for these requirements, and the staff would need training. For now however, the situation was still relatively urgent and the supplies and volunteers would come from Scotland and other parts of Britain. In fact, there was even a Royal Mail truck parked near the main entrance that had arrived on convoy in some of the early days of their involvement. I think Moona had driven it overland, and subsequently it had been donated to the orphanage. I loved hearing him speak in that mesmerising Scottish accent and he seemed to know so much about it all. As a linguist, I also admired the way Romanian rolled off his tongue. He was most certainly catching my attention, especially now that I was a 'free' woman after the seven-year relationship with Nev had come to a grinding halt.

As they say, where one door closes another opens.

It was liberating to be 'off' the bus and away from the group too.

And so when the departure date loomed, after some two weeks in that northern Moldovan region of Romania, and I voiced my feelings of not wanting to leave, Moona responded with a 'why don't you stay on then? Let's enjoy the summer together!'

Throwing caution to the wind and swept up in the moment, I decided to leave the bus and stay in Romania. Of course, I had no idea what that would mean and maybe nor did Moona, but we were living in the moment and were prepared to take a risk. I could also spend more time getting to know the children.

'You're doing what?' Nev's voice asked down the phone at the PTT building.

'I'm staying on in Romania.'

'Really? This isn't a tit for tat situation is it?' he enquired, which suggested he knew about Moona.

'Well if you reckon this is a tit, then there must have been a bit of tat!' I retorted, relieved that he had somehow communicated what he was up to, when he actually sought to hide it from me.

The numbers on the bus were dwindling, but there were more recruits due to join the team in Poland. Before they left, we organised a big feast with a whole sheep bought from local farmer Costica. We chatted around a large bonfire that night. I was tearful even if I was excited to be staying. I wasn't certain when I would see them all again when the bus drove off into the Ukraine, bound for Poland, on 29th July 1992. I would join them before they left Poland, or so the plan was, but it felt like anything was possible.

The reality was both daunting and exhilarating. My role within the group of Trippers had become more defined. Plus I had known some of these friends for nine years. How trusting I was, but this Romanian situation, complete with a budding romance had become more familiar and enticing than the unknown territory towards which the bus adventured.

Chapter 7

Off the Bus

With the bus gone, where was I to base myself? Soon a couch in a village apartment, occupied by other volunteers, became 'home'. There was no regular plumbing, so I learnt to bathe in a hand-basin with a flannel and jug of water. From this apartment a lot of the admin for the charity took place. When various people returned from their summer trip back to the UK, I moved down the road to Mama Puiu's, where a room had become available. Her grandchildren, Daniella and Mihaita (little Mihai) came to my aid and were intent on helping me learn Romanian.

Mihaita carefully drew a table in my new vocab book that Moona had initiated, then wrote the word 'Masa' next to it.

'Masa,' he and his sister pronounced carefully.

'Masa,' I repeated, making way for this new word and image. They continued with drawings of 'lingura' for spoon, 'furculita' for fork, 'cutit' for knife and 'farfurie' for a plate. They both giggled as I pronounced the words after them.

So it all started to make more sense. This foreign language was starting to become more familiar, and having the vocab book to refer to was invaluable for learning and remembering.

It was no surprise by now that there was no running water and one of the daily chores was fetching water in a bucket from their own 'funtana' (well) rather than the communal village one. Early in the morning, the cock would crow and one could hear all the cows being led down the road in one massive herd, off to the fields and pastures. Once again it was a splash bath system and a trip to the 'long John' at the end of the garden. This was similar to some of the beach houses in NZ, where these toilets were a holiday feature, except this was their daily reality. Fortunately, due to Mama Puiu's steady flow of volunteers, she was well stocked with toilet paper, which was a relief.

The smell of frying eggs would greet me in the morning as these were plentiful at this time of year. There was also cheese made from sheep's milk, some large red tomatoes and a strong cup of coffee with the grains still floating in it. However, she also had 'Ness' available, which was a version of Nescafé, a real luxury for them, and some fresh milk to go with it. It was here that I even tried my hand at milking the cow with mild success. Most food was served with the traditional Mamaliga, boiled cornflour bread, which I somehow grew to enjoy. Mind you, I still preferred eggs with a slice of wheat bread, no matter how hard it was, if available.

'Buna Dimineata,' Mama Puiu would say with a serious look in her face as she placed food in front of me.

Whilst I ate at a table on the wooden deck in front of one of the bedrooms, she could be seen fussing around outside, sweeping the earthen courtyard area clean ready for the day. Her little granddaughter imitated her with her own little homemade broom. These were just like witch's brooms made from sticks and soft twigs. As her name indicated, Mama Puiu, really was like a mother hen taking care of all her family and household responsibilities, as well as taking on the various straini/foreigners that were sent her way. How lucky I was to have been taken under her wing.

Where I slept was quickly tidied away and became the lounge once more, decorated very brightly with handmade cloths and embroidered wall hangings. These were interspersed with some old fashioned family photos, made to look like coloured photos with some water-colour paint technique I had never seen before.

What was fascinating too, was that the house wasn't one big house, but a series of separate rooms that stood alone with the courtyard in between. Whilst there was electricity to power a few lights, the summer kitchen really consisted of an old fashioned wood-fired oven and a small wooden table where she prepared food. The walls were hand-painted sky blue, and roller stencils had been used to decorate them with little flowers. There wasn't even a floor made with floor-boards. We were literally standing on the same earth as the courtyard. How handy for sweeping any crumbs outside, for the wandering chickens to greedily peck at.

It was a fair hike up to the orphanage so I was grateful when Moona would turn up to transport me there, to see what that day would bring.

Having been the driving force behind some nearly completed extension or renovation, Moona was looking for the next project with which to busy himself.

One of the experienced physiotherapists working there for some time, Di Hiscock, introduced me to another volunteer and the local staff. We made sure that the children from Copii Mici wing (Little Children), aged 3-7 years were fed, watered and clean for the morning. There were so many of them, I don't know how the local staff had been managing alone. This was where little Adriana lived and she was fascinated by my coconut necklace which she loved to handle and play with. Then we needed to make sure that these little ones had a chance to stretch their legs; as they were used to sitting for prolonged periods on little white plastic chairs. I found this so unusual, when children back home were usually wandering around and playing at this age. Not all of them could manage alone and needed a caring pair of outstretched hands to hold while they clumsily tried to walk. To think they weren't even capable of what some one-year-olds or toddlers were usually doing and they were much older. They scarcely spoke and seemed locked away in their own little worlds, unable to communicate with one another. One of the little girls, Luminita, did smile however, and was fascinated by threads. She would spend her time pulling knitted clothing to pieces. At least she was able to walk, unlike Bogdan who was recovering from dysentery, and Batir or Felitia, whose legs were bent. Nicolae was left in a cot and when he did try to walk, he shook a lot in spasms.

Once this routine was over, I would be swept up by Moona into organising something that would require a journey: to make phone calls, send telegrams, or find provisions.

Having a thrill-seeking nature, Moona had befriended the instructor and head of the local parachuting club in Suceava, where he had learnt to sky-dive. He often called in to see what the weekend had planned parachuting-wise. The lessons he had been attending, prior to my arrival, included a few folk from Russian Moldova; some of the equipment dated back to WWII.

One weekend I went to watch the action at the airport. The group disappeared into the plane, and then the instructor, Mr Soare, motioned for me to join them. Being caught up in a summer romance gave me the courage needed to jump aboard, and I took my seat by the jump door. I watched as they prepared for their dives (without speaking, or maybe unable to speak, such was the noise) from the plane, which also seemed to date back to WWII. I managed to take a few photos as one by one they literally disappeared out the door just centimetres from where I sat, belted in and watching their chutes open. I definitely didn't feel brave enough to do such a thing, but felt that I had overcome some other fear by just being up there in the air with them all.

Some weeks later it was Moona's birthday. Some of his friends at the Suceava airport had organised for both of us to go up in a glider. How amazing to look down on the fields of haystacks and ant-sized people below, flying high in the sky with the sun shining and smiling down on us all. It was uncannily quiet and smooth in comparison to the noisy jump plane. Once again it was also a relief to be on solid ground afterwards. It was only then that my travel sickness hit me in a delayed fashion for a few hours.

Mama Puiu took Moona's orders seriously about teaching me Romanian customs. One day I remember sitting on a stool in the kitchen for a good few hours. She draped a traditional scarf over my hair and tied it back to keep my hair out of the way, and showed me how to make Sermale. These are little packages of mince-meat and rice, wrapped in cabbage leaves, then boiled and baked; they soon became a favourite dish for me. I'm not entirely sure, but we may have prepared them for St Mary's Day which was quite a celebration around here, especially as Mama Puiu's first name was Maria. At various times of the day I would also be offered little drinks of Tsuica, which was a local firewater/moonshine made from sugar beet. It was potent and I soon became accustomed to drinking little shots of it, when offered, as is customary when visiting local folk.

At night the grandchildren would come to say 'Noapte buna' (Good night) and then later they elaborated with 'Noapte Buna, somn usor, sapte purici, pe-un picior'. We laughed about this image of seven fleas biting on one leg, and I couldn't help but draw the parallel with our own saying 'good night, sleep tight, don't let the bed bugs bite'. We may have seemed to come from worlds apart, but some things were the same.

In the morning I would be back at the orphanage where some children there were learning another useful language. Those who had not learnt to talk were being taught Makaton, a simplified version of sign language with some 200 gestures. The extremely dedicated Di Hiscock had set up a prefab, dubbed the Casuta (little house) where they would go to learn and make things, almost like a mock school. It gave the children a much-needed routine and was a space away from the bigger crowd of the orphanage.

I was remembering names now, which pleased me. Silviu, Emil, Borobita, Andreus, Tomita, Cesar, Florin. I remember Di saying that for these children, who lived in a communal setting where nothing belonged to them, their names were the only thing they owned. So it was important to use them. I tried as best I could.

My accommodation was changing as the valuable space at Mama Puiu's was needed for new visitors. Moona invited me to stay where he lived, with another family. It started off well and they even built a new room to make it possible, using a mixture of mud and hay. How handy to just be able to build a new room in little more than a day, with the whole family pitching in, plus a few days drying out.

However, this arrangement did not go so well. It's hard to remember exactly the reasons, but I realised that each day some item of clothing would disappear from my bag. I finally knew I had to do something about it when we returned one evening to find that someone had been rifling through my bags again, and emptied some of my treasured pots of Body Shop creams. It was probably just a little curiosity with the temptations of Western products within reach, but to me it felt like an affront and I took it personally and overreacted with a few tears.

There was an argument of sorts involving Moona, the father and his daughters. I think my arrival had upset the family balance and it was mutually decided that we needed to find somewhere else. On top of this we were an unmarried couple and that was probably another factor. Moona couldn't really understand the fuss caused by a few creams and clothes, when as Westerners we had so much. After all, they were just a few material possessions, but he was sympathetic too. I am sure all the stresses of the previous months hadn't helped, and with all the changes and situations we had faced, I was probably starting to feel somewhat vulnerable and out of my depth. It may have easily been like the straw that broke the camel's back.

Thank goodness Moona knew many people; so another house to stay in was soon found, with the elderly mother of a friend. Here we found space in the quiet household along with the crowing of cockerels once again. I did miss the company of Mama Puiu's grandchildren nonetheless.

Meanwhile a war had broken out closer to home than Bosnia. The Republic of Moldova (also known as Bessarabia) had just gained its independence and had become involved in a conflict against local insurgents in Transnistria, who were aided by locally stationed Russian armed forces. This former Moldovan SSR had been separated from the region of Moldova in Romania since WWII. They still spoke the Romanian language and the rural setting looked similar to ours. It felt like their Moldovan brothers needed their help. Moona could see that there was surplus aid in the orphanage and more where it had come from. Possibly inspired by The Serious Road Trip's recent actions in

Bosnia and his own convoys to Romania, he decided to organise a humanitarian aid convoy to the Republic of Moldova. It would be Romanians helping Romanians.

To obtain the necessary paperwork and for other projects afoot, we made a journey to the beautiful capital of Moldova, Iasi (pronounced Yash) over two hours drive South East of Ionaseni. What a stunning city, with a statue of Stephan the Great in front of the Palace of Culture on the central square. This had been the capital of Romania 1916-1918 and traditionally one of the leading centres of Romanian social, cultural, academic and artistic life. It certainly showed. We connected with some students Moona was establishing links with, made some more phone calls from the PTT building and organised some paperwork on the proposed convoy. I'm not sure at what point it was done, but Moona also made sure that I had an extended visa for Romania with multiple entries possible.

As the day was drawing to a close we made our way back to Ionaseni with a perfect sunset. En route, we passed by a garden centre in the middle of nowhere, where roses were cultivated. There were all sorts of roses in varying colours and perfumes. How beautiful it was to see them all. Moona rushed inside for a few moments before reappearing beaming.

'Here, some roses for you!' said Moona, presenting me with a colourful bunch.

They seemed to wash away all the previous stresses. Wasn't life simple and beautiful here in Romania?

Moona had some contacts in the capital, Chisinau (formerly known as Kishinev), from his parachuting lessons and so the convoy started to take shape. Once the paperwork was in order, the Royal Mail truck was packed full of clothing, medical supplies and tins of food. At the crack of dawn the team of volunteers (local and international) piled into the white transit van. We were all interested to see how things were on the other side, so to speak, as well as to help.

The sun was starting to rise as we set off on our long 250km trek towards Chisinau to the East of Iasi. I don't remember the border control being tricky. I do remember the border official laughing at my story of how my sister's puppy had gnawed away at the corner of my British Passport, which explained the nibbled corner and tooth marks. The border guard laughed, thinking how hungry the dog must have been to try and eat a passport.

When we arrived in the capital city I remember very wide boulevards lined with trees and very tall towers or blocks of flats, characteristic of most communist countries, although reminiscent of the HLMs in France too.

I later found out that 70% of Chisinau needed to be rebuilt after WWII, following the effects of Soviet occupation in 1940, a devastating earthquake the same year, and subsequent bombardment from Nazi air-raids of the newly formed Moldovan SSR.

Here we were in the recently internationally recognised Moldova (founded in Aug. 1991 but only recognised in March 1992) where the Russian alphabet was still very prominent. There was no evidence of the conflict here which was going on further East in the Transnistrian breakaway republic. In July 1992 a ceasefire was negotiated for this area, which was good timing for us.

We headed to the mayor's office where we were welcomed and interviewed by local radio. What a story this made... a group of volunteers from a Romanian orphanage, both Romanian and International, here to help! They were able to put us up in a giant hotel in one of those communist-looking buildings, where we would rest our weary heads that night.

From there we visited an orphanage to deliver the medical supplies. I remember being shown around the orphanage with all the accompanying Ionaseni staff, including the director; the feeling was that they were far better off than the Ionaseni orphanage, but nonetheless we were there to give them aid. What struck me most was that there wasn't that familiar smell of urine, to which I had grown accustomed in Romania. The children were even able to speak.

Then we headed East to the Transnistrian area, where the rural houses were very similar to those on the Romanian side of Moldova. Many of them had windows missing, and were obviously abandoned and empty. The people had been evacuated or had fled. The roads were also dotted with the familiar potholes we knew from Romania.

I do remember going through checkpoints with Russian soldiers tightly holding their Kalashnikovs, while the lead vehicle negotiated our passage. We carried on towards a village on the river Dniester, where another orphanage needed our donations of food and clothing.

We delivered our supplies and were then treated to a huge party with someone playing the accordion into the night, while we ate copious amounts of watermelon and drank local wine. How unexpected it was to have a party. I remember dancing into the wee hours.

The following day we made the long trek back to Ionaseni with our fuzzy heads.

There were all sorts of conversations as Moona and others wondered whether it would be more practical to send the Ionaseni staff just over the border for training rather than to the West. They had similar cultures and languages and it was far less expensive. We were grateful to crawl into our beds in familiar territory later that night.

I couldn't wait to tell my friends how it was all going and especially about our recent convoy to the Republic of Moldova. So a trip to a PTT building was in order to call London.

My own convoy to an area in conflict seemed rather insignificant as I was given news of the convoys being organised for Bosnia and for the besieged people of Sarajevo. These convoys sounded like they were on a much larger and more urgent scale.

And the bus was happily trouping through Poland and making its way to Warsaw.

Now was the chance to link back up with the bus if I wanted, since the plan was to drive across Belorussia to Moscow and then South to Georgia.

'Are you on the bus or not?' The London crew enquired. I questioned my long-term future in Romania, and reminded myself that I had initially intended the stay to be short-term. In any case, it looked like Moona had a few projects to tie up, then he was in need of a well-earned break from all that he had contributed for over two years. He was also keen to join The Serious Road Trip in some way at a later date. His intention was to set off elsewhere, destination uncertain, so staying on in Romania, even if I felt like it, did not seem viable or appropriate.

Having packed up my huge purple Macpac, I reluctantly bade farewell to the many children and adults in Ionaseni who had touched my heart. I felt quite emotional about it all. Moona accompanied me on an overnight train down to Bucharest, where, amidst many tears, I caught a flight to Warsaw. From the plane, I remember seeing the land below and a river snaking beneath the plane, which reminded me of the shape of a crocodile and the poetry of many adventures with Moona, including those in the air. I was missing him already and wondered when I would see him again. My time in this lost corner of the world seemed to have awakened something within me on many levels.

Chapter 8

Back on the Bus!
Poland to Red Square

I arrived in Warsaw before the bus, and was nervous about how I would feel linking up again. It had been such a wrench leaving Romania. What happy reunions we had when the bus rolled in the next day. Oh, the stories they told of entertaining so many children all through an area near Krakow, where many workers' children were spending their holidays on summer camp. On top of this, the show had developed into a much more professional affair with the arrival of a new group of volunteers.

There was Brett, a very accomplished 'devil stick' performer from London, but with African origins; and Sly, a youth worker from London, who made a very unlikely but hilarious fairy with a magic wand. His friends Jason, Lennox and Darrel were also youth workers from London and Felicity from NZ. Various other members had spruced up their acts. Julie from the USA now appeared to the music of Johnnie Cash and she really looked the part in her cowgirl outfit throwing a lasso, whilst shouting 'Howdy' in her friendly American manner. Damon had dyed his long hair black; wearing short cut-off jeans with a bare torso and feet, he looked like a cross between the Hulk and Hiawatha.

Instead of the raw acoustic guitar, there was now a relatively sophisticated beat-box with speakers and taped music.

My charismatic friend, Tony Gaffney, an Irish accountant we'd originally met in Luxembourg, had also joined the red double-decker bus from our London office; he would travel to Moscow with us. He was far too fun-loving to be pigeon-holed as your normal accountant type, so it was no wonder that he had chosen to put his skills to good use as our financial director in London. Now he was the one responsible for sorting out our Russian visas while we visited a few centres for disadvantaged children in Warsaw. My administrative duties were now replaced with a part in the show as a clown. The patchwork blanket was donned, a pillow was belted beneath to create a round belly, and I had a wig for disguise. I remember the slender Belinda also dressed up as a clown and we bounced bellies together, danced and wobbled around in front of delighted children. What a change from Old Macdonald's Farm. Meanwhile the audiences and venues also seemed far more sophisticated and modernised, compared to the hidden institutes of Romania. This was unfamiliar territory once again and a language that bore no resemblance to the Romance languages and German I knew, understood and found comfort in. There were more challenges in store for us now though, as we prepared for the next change of country.

A Red Bus on Red Square

Within days we had left Warsaw on the long haul to Russia, via Minsk. The bus rattled over long motorways and once again the tower blocks of apartments dotted the landscape. Everything seemed so grey and colourless and it was cloudy or raining as well.

Our bright red bus seemed to light it all up as we rattled along, all 15 of us now. The numbers had doubled since leaving Romania, although we had been at least this many, if not more, during our Western European Tour. My regular sleeping spot was the upper bunk, just next to the stairs going down to the rear of the bus and the main entrance. During the day these bunks were dismantled to form bench seats. By night I was glad to have my Kermit green sleeping bag as my little private space in these communal quarters. I crawled inside my little haven and imagined I was back in Romania where it felt my heart had remained. I clung to a poetry book, entitled *Weathering*, by Scottish poet Alistair Reid, whom Moona had met. He'd given me the book, and the poem 'Curiosity' seemed to hold deep significance. This dealt with the woes and joys of being itinerant; likened to the unpredictable, independent nine-lived cat with many tales to tell. I definitely identified with the cat rather than the predictable dog, in these relatively uncharted territories.

I needed to readjust to all the changes in team, language, country

Safari in Brazil
with Murillo,
Nev and
Simone.

London office
with Tony G,
Christophe, Nev
and Chris.

Fundraising at Trafalgar
Square, 1992.
Simone and Belinda.

Band on bus concert – outside the Rising Sun pub.

Fundraising during Western European Tour. Simone and Julie.

Getting ready to go to Sarajevo.

Bus in Bucharest with street children from the Gavroche Centre.

Julie and Miles – face-painting.

Bus in Bucharest.

Show in Pitesti with Miles and Matt.

Ionaseni Orphanage.

Belinda helping at Ionaseni.

Florin on the bus at
Ionaseni.

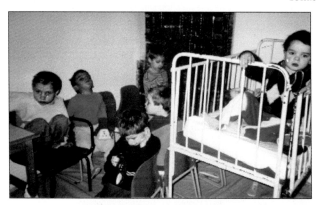

Orphans
at Ionaseni.

Damon,
Miles, Julie,
Simone and
Belinda – in
Moldova,
Romania.

Moona parachuting in Romania.

On Red Square, Moscow:
Damon, Felicity, Patrick, Brett,
Tony, Simone, Myles
and Belinda.

Mural by Miles and
Julie in Moscow
orphanage, 1992.

Johnie at Ionaseni with
unicycle volunteer.

Caroline during the carnival
at Ionaseni.

'Long john' at Mama Puiu's.

Getting ready to tow the combi:
Johnie, Simone, Andy McG. and Bob.

After show at
Ionaseni Village.
Mania 4 Romania
team with Alex and
Henry King, 1993.

Simone face
painting at an
orphanage during
Mania 4 Romania
tour.

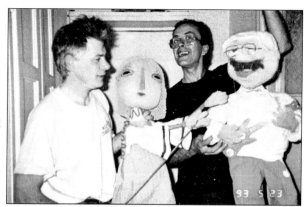

After the show at Bacau Puppet Theatre. Johnie and Puiu.

Piatra Neamt High School, 1993. Our largest show during Mania 4 Romania.

Balloon fun during show at a centre for children with HIV+.

Bananas 4 Split van with Johnie and refugee children in Croatia.

Outside Magda's pension, Podstrana, Croatia.
On 'Ragga' – Paul Kirwan, Isabelle, Caroline, Johnie, Yoyo and Simone.

'Ragga', with refugee children in Croatia.

and situations and found comfort in my own company, thoughts and reading the poems. Would it really be like this all the way to New Zealand and would it really take a year or maybe more?

Most of the other vehicles on the roads were trucks, mostly army style with the odd Lada or Moskvich car. Sometimes trucks were parked on the side of the road with loads of people queuing up for produce such as potatoes and onions. Or we could see queues of people outside what looked like a derelict warehouse but was in fact a bakery of sorts.

On our approach to Moscow I remember a scene vividly. We were driving through the dreary outskirts of the city, and along the streets there were various people going about their normal business, walking into town or coming home from the shops. There was a small child with his mother, who had stopped to chat with a friend, but it was the observant child that spotted us and tugged at his mother's hand, pointing with such a look of surprise on his face. What is that, Mama, he seemed to ask, although he remained speechless with a look of awe and wonder. Our bright red bus could have been a UFO for all he knew.

And onwards the bus rolled, unable to stop until reaching its next destination. After all, the day was ending and we wanted to get to Moscow before nightfall.

I don't know how Damon did it, but he managed to find his way to Red Square where our Red double-decker found a space to park just as the sun was setting.

It was late but Tony still managed to phone the Moscow office of EquiLibre to let them know where we were. Dear EquiLibre provided some sort of anchor in the midst of these unknown countries. Someone would join us in the morning, but for now we camped out preparing some dinner on our gas-stove in the kitchen, and slurping on some vodka that street hawkers wearing Russian hats had sold to us. Well, we had to celebrate as the locals would do! Unsure of the terrain, we stayed close to the bus, but we were metres from the immense Kremlin and the brightly coloured domes of St Basil's church.

This was still only 1992 so it felt quite a feat to be on the other side of the Iron Curtain so soon after the Cold War had ended.

We crept into our sleeping bags in the wee hours, so it was a shock to the system when someone arrived early the next morning and almost banged the door down to get our attention. I'm not so sure we looked as ready for action as they anticipated and many of us were hungover. But they were nonetheless very enthusiastic to see a Red Bus on Red Square and eager to welcome us.

We cranked up the bus and made our way to EquiLibre's offices,

d

guided by their representative. It was here that we met the lovely Martine from NZ. She was also a linguist, speaking Russian and French, and would become our main point of contact for the next few weeks. She had been helping with a soup kitchen programme, feeding mainly elderly folk, but welcomed this new change in focus. She would help us with the itinerary of orphanages we were due to visit and being a New Zealander, she enjoyed meeting a few Kiwis from home too.

We had huge difficulty in deciphering the Russian alphabet. This posed more than the usual difficulty of being in a country whose language I didn't speak. At least with Romanian being a Romance language I had managed to understand certain words with my studies in French, Spanish, German and some Portuguese. Russian, on the other hand, completely floored me for now.

Before we knew it, the EquiLibre crew gave us a list of plenty of orphanages and institutes to visit with our show, and Martine was able to meet us early in the morning, map in hand, to guide us through the streets of Moscow.

We would arrive at an orphanage to be greeted by very welcoming staff. The children looked extremely well cared for by comparison with Romania and extremely receptive to the humour, colour and action of the show. From the sound of it, the children of Russia seemed to be well catered for; it was the old people and refugees who were not managing, hence the soup kitchens that EquiLibre had set up. There were 40 of these kitchens feeding 10,000 homeless and old age pensioners one meal a day. Our bus came in handy on occasions for transporting some of the supplies to these kitchens.

Meanwhile, whereas in Bucharest we had managed to base ourselves at a house for EquiLibre staff, this was not the case in Moscow. Fortunately, they were able to set something up for us and we were directed to an area in the Fili district, not far from Stalin's Dacha. Here we were to stay in what appeared to be barracks at the entrance to an enclosed wooded area with rather grand houses within. We imagined that this large building must have housed the former KGB staff who guarded the area. How amazing to think we were now being welcomed there, although there was just one elderly man in charge of the whole building. Even with our large crowd, we did not take up much space as the rooms were huge having previously catered for hundreds. After the close quarters of living on the bus, it was a welcome change to use the kitchen and dining rooms.

I remember the excitement one day at having the caretaker approach the group asking for me as there was a telephone call. Wow, it seemed amazing that someone had tracked me down to this spot, had managed to get a telephone line, and that we were even there and not on the road to a show. He led me to a distant room and the telephone.

My heart beat wildly, as of course 'he' had not been far from my thoughts. While many others wrote diaries I had been composing letters to Moona, and now here he was on the phone. Unbelievable! He echoed my feelings of missing each other, which was such a relief to hear, but where to from there? How were we to meet up? Should he come to Moscow? He would have to liaise with London, although that could be tricky. We decided that he would call back a week later.

In the meantime a heart-felt letter from Moona even arrived, sent through our London office in a bundle of many letters from all our loved ones. What a joy to have this contact. Everyone was in need of this as we floated around in our red bubble in distant lands. This was the time before e-mails or mobile phones and so letters were our way of staying in touch. Unfortunately post was also rare whilst on the road, so we were all caught up in our small ounce of contact with the outside world, and were able to read and reread the letters over and over.

My joy and anticipation of the next phone call turned to exasperation as the call never came the following week. I waited and waited but there was still no call. I tried to go over it in my head again and again. Maybe I had sounded a little sceptical about him dealing with my ex, to arrange for him to join us? Or had something else or somebody else come up for him? Maybe the phone lines were down? Whatever the reasons, Moona seemed unlikely to join us in Moscow for now and my romantic dream of being reunited was presently thwarted.

Not far from the building we occupied, surrounded by trees, and within one of these mansions, there had been a hospital set up for victims of the Chernobyl disaster. They did not want us to visit the children, they were so ill; but we did have contact with the children of a diabetic centre nearby. We were asked if we could clear some trees and rustle up a play-park area in the woods for the visiting children. While we did manage to set up some nature trails and play areas such as camp-fire sites and bivouacs, the fancy play area seemed an unlikely task without tools or skills in designing play equipment. Moreover it would need to be sturdy, safe and able to endure the harsh wintry conditions for which Russia was well-known. I remember wandering through the woods with everyone searching for solid bits of wood to use, only to find that the branches we found on the ground were already rotten. What may have sounded like an exciting request was out of our capabilities or budget.

At least we were able to feel useful elsewhere, with our bus to transport children and our show to excite the children.

What a surprise for these children to see our bright red double-decker bus turn up, Damon driving it almost permanently in his Hiawatha Indian costume. As already mentioned, his cut-off jeans, bare torso and feet and long hair dyed black with a band around his crown and a feather poking out, looked like something from a movie. Then there was Brett Smith with his shiny black skin and dark leather outfit covering him top to toe. He had all sorts of things dangling from his attire which shook as he walked, making him sound like a mobile rain stick. During the show his devil stick antics were awe-inspiring. He remained a rather lonely figure in our group though, and as far as I remember, never removed those clothes in the couple of months we were together. This was incredible as we sometimes endured hot and sticky conditions, living on board a bus with no insulation or air-conditioning.

There was a distinct lack of dark-skinned folk in Moscow, so Brett and a few other members of our team were a huge hit and novelty. While Brett may have been very short, the others were tall and looked more like basket-ballers with their baggy sweatshirts and caps worn backwards. How very cool the children thought they were.

We had the New Zealand 'haka', or at least a version of it, as a signature to our performance. Although the Maori war dance was out of context, this definitely brought smiles to the surprised onlookers. And, of course, there was our male sugar plum fairy, female cowgirl with lasso and colourful clowns. We really were a motley crew from many corners of the world.

Day trips with children on the bus included an outing to the Moscow Zoo, where I must admit the conditions were less than desirable for the animals at this time. Obviously the children were excited to see monkeys, and a polar bear pacing up and down his concrete enclosure. We might have hoped for better conditions for the animals, but the children appreciated time away from their usual routine and a chance to escape on the top deck of our red bus. It really did give them a different perspective on life as we chugged around the capital. I definitely think the bus was overloaded with children and accompanying adults on occasions, but health and safety issues didn't seem to matter and fortunately we didn't have any accidents. We didn't want to turn anyone away.

Frighteningly there was a scary moment with the brakes not working at the traffic lights once, but guardian angels must have been watching over us. The bus mounted the pavement, swerving almost out of control to avoid whatever was in front and we just kept going up and over, back onto the road. Fortunately no one on the pavement, road or in the bus was injured and we managed to get everyone home in one piece, although rather shaken by the experience. I think it heightened our realisation that we were on this massive overland trip to New Zealand without a mechanic on board. I'm not sure what had caused the brakes to fail on this occasion but they seemed to work again later. Another issue was also emerging: the starter motor did not always work, or was it the battery starting to fail? We managed to get around this with everyone push-starting the bus to get going. This proved quite hilarious for the children after the show and they enjoyed helping us push. We weren't the only ones wondering how we would get all the way to New Zealand.

It was just impossible to get to one orphanage, no matter how hard we tried. Martine knew the way, but our bus was 3.8 metres tall and couldn't go the way she knew. We had to reschedule another two times and make sure she had a good map to follow. On the third attempt we felt sure we would get there, and still a low bridge blocked our way. I hated to think of the children's disappointment, but we had tried our best.

I remember an outing along the river and seeing the Kremlin and other important buildings. Memories of these monuments were overshadowed by something else: sadly we also saw the body of a woman who had been pulled from the river and was lying abandoned on a wharf for all boat-onlookers to see. We tried to turn the gaze of the children in another direction, but I for one was shocked. This was the first dead body I had seen, and under most peculiar circumstances. It certainly made an impression on me, more than the impressive sightseeing we were doing in a country that was just starting to open up to the West. Meanwhile, those seated on the other side of the boat remained oblivious to the scene.

On another trip to Red Square, several members of our group visited the embalmed body of Lenin in the specially dedicated museum and a few of us remained outdoors. Someone needed to stay with the bus at all times. Later, I remember seeing a woman wearing a Body Shop T-shirt being filmed by a BBC camera on the square. How I loved the Body Shop creams, so I eagerly wandered over to say hello. Spotting my accent from New Zealand, the woman, who looked like Anita Roddick, founder of the Body Shop herself, remarked that she had lots of Kiwi staff in the shops. She was in the middle of a report with a television camera filming, so the encounter was brief. She must have been surprised to have come all that way to meet more English-speaking folk. I remember kicking myself for not asking for some type of sponsorship on the spot.

Other members of the group had been fascinated by the huge queue to McDonald's that we had passed en route to an orphanage one day, and had gone off to indulge in a hamburger. We only received a meagre allowance, but they had been saving up for a treat. By the sound of it, it was worth the several hours' wait.

We were told by EquiLibre that we needed to be very vigilant and stay in small groups on outings. They were particularly worried about Brett disappearing, as he did enjoy wandering off away from the group. They kept on emphasising that Russians were not used to Africans and there was a risk he might be abducted. We found it hard to believe that it could be that dangerous in the street, but nonetheless Brett needed to stay close to the bus. I'm sure he didn't like this restriction and still wandered on occasions, once keeping us waiting for at least half an hour, wondering if we would need to contact the police. If a ransom needed to be paid, they had targeted the wrong people.

Such were the frustrations of being in a large group. If one person was late, the rest would wait.

I breathed a sigh of relief, thinking about an instant where I had been trying to change money in a market. The man offered me a certain rate for the dollars, but said if I wanted an even better rate I could follow him to some secluded area... 'No thank you,' was my instinct at the time. Now, on hearing this news of abductions, I wondered if this had been a ruse for something more sinister and if I had had a close shave.

Meanwhile, back at the forest area where we resided, we were starting to wonder more about the number of fast black cars with dark tinted windows that would pull into the enclosed area and speed over to the mansion where the Chernobyl children resided.

One Sunday we were even allowed into the sauna and swimming pool area of one of the mansions, where we really enjoyed a dip in the pool. It did look like a little maintenance was needed, but that didn't curb our enjoyment of the fresh water. We were a long way from New Zealand and I missed the regular swimming there during hot weather.

Further afield in the woods, we stumbled across a number of wooden cabins in a row, surrounded by lovely gardens with flowers. One of the women there for the weekend, approached us and conversed in English. She was a professor from Moscow University in the English department. How wonderful to be able to tell her all about our adventures. She invited us back the next weekend for tea.

78

Others in the group came across other activities in the park. Patrick told me of stories of playing chess with men in the park and slurping vodka together.

The location did feel rather surreal and the Chernobyl victims remained elusive, although I thought I may have seen a sickly child sitting on a bed by the window with tubes and drips hanging nearby.

One day, we did manage to stop a nurse who was leaving the building to ask more about the set-up. She looked rather stressed. She said she didn't know who she was working for really and that she and the others hadn't been paid in months. She commented that whoever was in charge didn't have the interests of the children at heart as she and the staff did, working for nothing. I could well believe this as she looked like a real babushka type, who loved the children.

On top of this we had stumbled across a whole collection of large white rabbits near the centre. What were they using these rabbits for? Drug testing maybe, or fancy warm hats?

We did start to worry that we were living near some humanitarian racket of sorts, but our Russian language skills were lacking and our imaginations were wild, so who knows what was really going on. It could have been a front for siphoning foreign funds or maybe just huge mismanagement.

We mentioned our concerns to Martine about the suspicious black cars and unpaid workers and she enlisted the help of the director of a centre for children of alcoholics, who we had visited in the local Fili area. We were welcome to base ourselves in their centre. At very short notice we left the park and set off back where we had already had a particularly warm welcome.

We were invited to eat with the children in their dining hall, much to everyone's excitement. It was lovely to sit and eat and attempt to communicate with the children. Some of them looked like they were out of a Russian version of Oliver Twist, with most of them smoking cigarettes already, aged 12, yet small enough to be 10. The walls were mostly bare. I could hear fellow Kiwi, Miles Dinneen, thinking out loud. Being an avid artist amongst other things, he could soon rectify this. Within days, he, with the help of his girlfriend Julie, had painted the most amazing mural on the walls, called the Children's Crusade. It was a beautiful image of our red bus entering the city of Moscow, with a procession of animals and children led by a young boy carrying a white dove. They had left the darkness of the forest and were arriving in the city where the streets were brimming with abundance, full of mountains of watermelons and other tasty fruit and vegetables. To the side, there was a frightened Gorbachev figure running away. A crowing cockerel announced the arrival of this crusade from the high perches of the bus rooftop. What a feeling of hope and light for everyone it gave, not to mention an amazing collection of vibrant colours and energy.

They also decorated the serving hatch leading to the kitchen with a giant fire-breathing dragon.

We were excited to hear that there was an unused dormitory in a side wing of the centre and we soon claimed a bed each. What a luxury after the close quarters of the bus, even though they were old-fashioned hospital beds with sagging mattresses. The children were keen to learn basic English, and we some basic Russian. They were mostly children of alcoholics, as excessive vodka drinking was a huge problem in Russia. However, one child explained that his parents had both been killed in the Afghanistan war. How awful that both parents had been taken. The Director was very happy to have us stay and set about organising various outings for us and the children.

At this point, Damon, our lead driver, and one of the co-founders of the project, decided that he needed to return to head office in London with his girlfriend Amanda too. He was concerned about our next leg to Georgia, dwindling funds and the need for a mechanic, and could sense that the head office needed assistance. Our phone calls to London were proving fruitless in this area and difficult to make. Myles Stratton would take over as sole driver of the bus.

I remember taking a group of children to a theatre in the area, where dogs and fluffy cats performed the most amazing tricks, alongside a clown. We had never seen such amusing things where dogs walked on their hind legs, pushing cats dressed as babies in miniature prams, and cats swung like acrobats from trapezes. It was so unbelievable and hilarious at the same time.

The weather was starting to cool and we were grateful for the warmth of the centre at night. It was time to start worrying about getting some antifreeze for the bus and it seemed to be the eternal mission to find some, no matter how hard we tried.

We would need to find some before we left on our onward leg to Georgia. Then the plan was to travel over to Kurdistan.

One night, on our way back to the orphanage, we decided to stop at one of the few restaurants. We were too late for the kitchen in the children's home and were excited by the prospect of some different food for a change. It was Georgian, as chance would have it, and we proceeded to talk with some friendly Georgians, who were also dining there. We told them of our impending departure for Georgia in our red bus. They chuckled and asked us if we were looking forward to the sound of machine-guns? There was conflict in the area so we needed to be prepared. Most of us didn't quite see the funny side to this, especially as many of us had chosen not to go into besieged Sarajevo when given the opportunity. At least our driver, Myles, had this experience behind him. The others who had undertaken this journey were all back in London or in Bosnia itself.

How had we missed hearing about this conflict? No doubt the lack of newspapers in English hadn't helped... or maybe the conflict wasn't publicised. We started to think about other routes, even contemplating going back through the Ukraine and Romania. I was totally up for that, excited by the thought of seeing the familiar children's faces again.

Before we could think too much about this, we were asked to take the children on a trip to a mansion on the outskirts of Moscow, where artists once gathered. What a lovely day out it was, visiting the rooms full of paintings. I managed to buy a carved wooden egg with a huge cross on it for my father. The pain of the Russian folk seemed etched into this cross on the egg, for they had suffered bitterly. What a long day it seemed as the bus shook and rattled over the pot-holed roads that evening. Darkness was fast approaching, the temperature had dropped sharply and our un-insulated bus felt like a fridge on wheels. We had not been prepared for this, and frozen to the bone, we were grateful to arrive back safely, piling into the warmth of the centre for a hot meal inside. We did wonder about the bus without antifreeze? How cold was it going to get? Someone muttered about building a fire under the engine overnight, but that would mean someone would have to stand watch all night. After such a long and tiring day and maybe hoping for the best, we weren't thinking straight and fell asleep in the safety of our warm dormitory. We were utterly exhausted from the events of the day and our precarious future. Meanwhile an early freak blizzard enveloped Moscow, taking us all by surprise as we slept more soundly than we had in months.

We awoke the next day to discover snow everywhere. How beautiful the layer of white looked and how exciting to be able to make snowmen and snowballs. The first snow of the season and much earlier than expected in the first week of October!

However magical the snow appeared, especially for us New Zealanders unaccustomed to snow in the city, this did spell disaster for the bus. Our fears had been realised. The engine had cracked with the cold. What a hopeless situation. Now we not only needed a mechanic, but we also needed another engine! How had we let this happen? I thought of the countless hours we had spent looking for antifreeze with no success, in a country that undergoes freezing temperatures regularly. How had we failed to find a most basic essential?

Likewise refilling our gas bottle for the cooker had been totally impossible for the length of our stay in Russia, so we couldn't even make a cup of tea to console ourselves.

We managed to phone and fax London the following day in a panic. This was the last thing they needed to hear. We had already reached the moment when it was time to go, but moving forward was an impossible task. Our whole group's mission depended on the bus or so it seemed to us. And yet our future projects had seemed very unclear, even with a functioning bus, especially as we heard more of the conflict brewing in Georgia. Our head office in London didn't seem to be very focused on this major hurdle we faced. They were now organising more convoys of humanitarian aid to war-torn Bosnia and its refugees. Even Damon had been commandeered to this effort. Winter was imminent and the food was crucial in the besieged Sarajevo. The people there were starving, not to mention everything else they were dealing with. Sadly and understandably, the back-up we needed from London was not a priority. However, there was a blessing in this crisis, which was that we would not need to worry about some trigger-happy Georgians for now.

Our lives hung in the balance as we wondered what action to take next, and all the while our visas for Russia were about to expire. Tony Gaffney was in charge of organising this aspect, while we tried to find things to do. Some of us accompanied some children to a concert at the Kremlin. The director of the children's centre seemed to know the right people to facilitate this and the concert was even televised.

Other days we were busy doing our washing at the laundrette with Martine, our translator and life-line in Russia, who took us under her wing. We met her boyfriend from Algeria, Farid, who was studying in Moscow. Funnily enough, years later I crossed paths with him while touring the South Island of New Zealand with a French band. I hadn't even realised that he and Martine had moved from Russia to Dunedin and were now the proud parents of a little boy. He and his friends were a great help to us at this time of relative purposeless and uncertainty.

We now travelled by Metro, and that was so impressive with some stations reminding me of museums, they were so ornate. I remember some kind passer-by offering us their bread on the metro; maybe we looked so hungry. What an amazing taste. Warm fresh bread with a delicious cabbage mixture within. There was only enough for a few mouthfuls each. We never managed to find that type of bread again, most probably someone's home-made bread as it had been wrapped in a tea-towel.

Outside on the square, people were queuing for an ice-cream. It seemed the thing people did at this time of year as I hadn't noticed these kiosks in the relative warmth of September. The ice-creams were reasonably priced and very yummy.

It was time for us to think about buying warmer hats and I proudly managed to find one of those grey Russian soldiers' hats with the badge on the front and warm ear-muffs that could be worn down over the ears or tied upwards over the hat.

The endless wait for visas seemed to go on and on, but it was increasingly looking unlikely that we would ever manage to leave Moscow by bus. We were in a stalemate, completely blocked by lack of a functioning vehicle, the snow, finances and visas.

There was no way we could stay on indefinitely at the home and so we started looking at the possibility of returning to London by train. We would have to wait for some money from London to enable this. What an anti-climax to what was meant to be our year-long trip to New Zealand.

I, for one, was not happy at this prospect and was not ready to give up what we had started. The children of Romania were on my mind and in my heart. After all that I had seen and experienced, they were the most in need.

Chapter 9

From Russia to Romania - alone

My Romanian visa, that Moona had organised, allowed me multiple entries into the country for another few months. I looked into the possibility of getting a train down to Moldova and over to Romania. I sent a telegram to Ionaseni Orphanage. I received a prompt response saying that Moona was no longer there, but in my mind, the children beckoned and I was convinced I needed to return there.

With Martine's help I set about buying a ticket. Did I want the international price of $50 US to take me to Iasi, in Romania, or the local rate of an equivalent to $4 US which would get me to the border where I could buy an onward ticket for the remaining 30kms? On a budget I aimed for the lower one, of course, and felt quite chuffed with myself being able to embark on a 24 hour journey for a mere $4.

I sent a telegram to Ionaseni to let them know my expected arrival time and heard back that one of the volunteers, Jon, would meet me at the station. How simple was that?

I bade my farewells, once again, and headed off into the unknown but towards familiar territory. What a lovely feeling to be on the way back to Romania. Would Moona hear of my plans and join me there where we had shared so many happy moments? After all, the last time we had spoken, he was missing me and wanted to join us. Unlikely, of course, as he was ready for new adventures, but it was not entirely impossible in the mind of an optimist.

On the train I sat next to a student from Peru who I managed to converse with although I'm not sure if that was in English or basic Spanish. It certainly wasn't Russian as this language had not come easily to me beyond a few basic words. It amazed me that Moscow seemed to attract so many foreign students from exotic lands.

I kept a tight grip on my small backpack, had my money belt well concealed and felt certain that no one would make off with my other very heavy MacPac. I chatted and dozed quite comfortably in the train compartment.

The time passed quickly and we neared the border area. The reality of not having a ticket all the way to Iasi was setting in and I did start to worry a little. The train conductor arrived and explained that I would need to disembark at the border town station and purchase a ticket for the final leg, then climb back on. They would be stopping for a few hours, I thought he said, but I may have misunderstood.

With my luggage weighing me down, I left the safety of that small world on the train and joined a queue. I was definitely sticking out in this environment with my purple backpack and bright-coloured clothing. I finally got to the counter and discovered I had been in the wrong queue. So I then started queuing in another line of locals. I glanced over to where the train had stood and suddenly realised that it was no longer there. How could that have happened? Had it gone early? Surely no more than 40 minutes had passed. It was only several months later that I learnt that the train hadn't left the station; it had been changing tracks in another part of the station. The railway lines were a different size in the former Soviet Union.

At that moment, as far as I was concerned, the train had gone without me! What a feeling of panic, especially as Jon was waiting patiently on the other side to greet me and take me back to where I wanted to be. Here I was stranded at the station!

Someone in the queue reassured me that there were other trains to Iasi. Phew! But only the following day! I most definitely had missed my ride to Ionaseni with Jon and there was no way of letting him know. I would have to sit out for the night in a waiting room at the station, with two armed Russian soldiers with those big furry hats for company.

Well, that's what I thought, until later as darkness fell, it turned out that a few other folk were in the same boat. I felt grateful for the company of some Romanians who had been turned away at the border for having too much produce and sparkling wine. They were buying goods more cheaply in the former USSR to sell at a higher price over the border. There was only one thing for it and that was to consume the surplus produce that prevented them from entering Romania. What could have been a dreadfully lonely night turned into an unexpected feast with much festivity, as we ate amazing hams, cheeses and bread washed down with some fine Moldovan wine. I entertained them with stories about the big red bus and working with the orphans and felt safe in their company through the night.

The soldiers looked on as we popped yet another bottle open, and talked and sang into the wee hours. We were waiting for the first train to leave early the next morning and for a number of reasons chose not to fall asleep.

Feeling rather stiff from the hard wooden benches and a night staying awake, we amassed our possessions and queued for the onward train together at daybreak. By now there were hundreds of us, all queuing to board the train. We needed to show tickets and identity documents. I remained the only foreigner and stuck out like a sore thumb with my bright purple backpack. It came to my turn and the border guard looked through my passport. He pulled me to one side. There was a problem. I was an international citizen, trying to cross the border on a local train. He was not used to dealing with foreign passports and despite my pleas to describe my predicament in simple Romanian, I was told I was not able to travel on this train. I remember bursting into tears when I lost the companionship of my new-found friends, and once again ended up in the train station waiting room. I felt miserable and needed to wait for a consul who would look into my situation.

Hours later he arrived and I proceeded to try and explain in Romanian the story of the bus breaking down, working with orphans and needing to get back to Romania. It must have sounded rather far-fetched. We discovered he spoke fluent French and it was a huge relief to be able to converse more freely. The fact that my Russian visa had expired was the biggest issue and to further complicate the situation, it was the weekend. I could be blocked for days. However, for a fee of $120 US, he could sort it out today and then I could be on the next international train passing through that evening. It seemed rather a lot of money, but sounded like my best way forward.

Relieved to be able to leave, I paid the fee (or was it a bribe?), and waited for the onward journey. The cheap ticket from Russia to Romania had ended up rather expensive after all and my impatience to leave before the visa extension came through hadn't really paid off, although it had added some adventure to the trip. Finally, my train rolled into Iasi in the darkness of early evening, a whole day later. Of course, there was no one to meet me at the station and I did feel vulnerable in the swarm of unfamiliar people on the platform, with darkness falling. Luckily, in my notebook, I found the name of one of the students we had met some months earlier with Moona. In my money belt I even found the correct coin, and phoned him. He was home, and would come and get me from the station. What a relief! I waited and waited but he didn't appear. What was I to do? I phoned again and we realised neither of us remembered what each other looked like and he hadn't found me in the crowds. I gave a description of myself and where I would be. By this stage it was a relief that he spoke English when we finally linked up. Once again I managed to rely on the Romanian hospitality that I had experienced thus far and was welcomed into his home with his father. The following day we would ring the orphanage and arrange my onward travel by train.

I was collected from the Suceava train station and ended up on the couch again at Jon and Mary's apartment in Ionaseni. By now the weather was much cooler and I was appreciating the heating from the 'soba'. This was an intricate heating system made from bricks that was fuel efficient and kept us toasty warm. I was starting to hear how cold it actually gets during winter, but for now the snow and sub-zero conditions were a month or so away.

Obviously the children were excited to see I had returned and some looked perplexed to see me without the big red bus and without Moona. Where was he? Was he returning, some asked?

I got involved once again with helping the little children with breakfast in the morning and the occasional walk. Adriana connected once again with me and my circular coconut necklace around my neck. It was familiar and she showed some recognition of this. She scrutinised it and held it tightly.

I went for walks into the forest with some of the older children and got involved in role-playing at the casuta, school-room. They were running a make-believe restaurant and I was their first customer. What fun to see them cooking and serving food. Cesar proudly showed me his chef's white hat. I'm not sure I managed to eat anything as the waiter ate my portion en route from the kitchen. One of the boys I helped with eating, Murgurel, quickly stuffed his mouth full of food, then tried to eat the plate and had a go at my arm too.

Meanwhile, back at Mama Puiu's I managed to stay a few nights and curled up on the bed in the lounge, which was conveniently located on top of the Soba. The courtyard was a muddy mess with the arrival of rain and I dined in the outdoor kitchen huddled around the stove. The familiar chicken eggs were no longer on the menu as the chickens had stopped laying or were laying fewer eggs due to the cold. The family was preparing their stores for the winter and I could feel that my purpose here was still rather unclear.

I phoned London to let them know I was safely in Romania and heard news of how the rest of the group were faring. They had travelled by train from Moscow to Warsaw and had picked up a Eurolines bus for London. Ironically this bus also had broken down on its way and they had had a long journey back. Belinda was missing NZ and planning to return home. The group was disbanding for now, or getting involved in helping in the office co-ordinating convoys and aid donations for Bosnia. For now I felt happy to be in Romania as I tried to work out my next steps.

Then a couple of weeks later, I got a message from Moona. He was back in Scotland and could be reached on the office number or his mum's.

My heart was in my mouth as I rang to speak to him from the PTT building in Suceava.

He was missing me and wouldn't I join him in Scotland? I explained that I had just travelled such a long distance, but he persuaded me that for a variety of reasons he would not be travelling to Romania and that it would be best if I headed for Scotland. He would do the same for me if the situation arose.

Chapter 10

Soul-searching in Scotland and Ireland

It all made sense as I also needed to access more funds from England. Nev had been repaying some money he owed into my account there. Feeling eager to get on with the next part of my journey and see Moona, not to mention avoiding the impending winter, I set off to Bucharest. I stayed one night with a translator, and then took my flight for Heathrow. I was also to carry lots of post for the volunteers, including several letters that I had sent to Moona from Moscow. He hadn't received a single one.

The plan was to phone from Heathrow on arrival, but as fate would have it, there was a bus leaving for Edinburgh, just moments after leaving the arrivals hall. Rather than miss this bus to announce my arrival, it felt meant-to-be that I was getting to Scotland faster than anticipated. I couldn't wait.

It was dark when I arrived in a wet Edinburgh, but there was a taxi rank nearby. It felt easier to climb into the black cab with my various bags and head straight to Moona's mum's. What a surprise it was when the cab pulled up outside. Moona was outside for some reason and couldn't believe his eyes to see me roll in. The bags were brought inside and we sat talking about our adventures over a warm cup of tea.

Although welcoming, it did feel rather odd to be face to face in a completely different world and staying at his mother's.

By now Moona's mind was set on exploring the needs in Bosnia. But before taking the next step, he was planning a surfing trip to

Ireland in a VW combi and would I join him? In fact, before leaving for Ireland I was also shown numerous beaches where Moona would proudly demonstrate to me how he rode the waves. I was not only impressed by this, but also the freezing temperatures. Of course, there are wet-suits, but after the sunny weather of New Zealand, surfing in sub-zero conditions in late November seemed madness.

He had a few things to sort out to do with his trip to Bosnia and I enjoyed wandering the streets of Edinburgh and also chatting with his mum. Then off we set in the combi.

In Glasgow we danced at a Ceilidh with some of his friends, before taking the ferry over to Northern Ireland. There we caught up with some volunteers from Romania, Paddy and Colette, and then headed to the Giant's Causeway. All the while, Moona would surf by day with me watching, and then he'd collapse with exhaustion after expending so much energy. I'm not so sure I was cut out to be a 'surfie chick' but I enjoyed some quiet moments thinking, soaking up the atmosphere of the windswept Irish coastline and listening to music by Enya.

Moona touched base with his office in Edinburgh and it seemed there was something pressing happening there and he needed to return a week sooner than expected. He seemed obsessed with making his way to Bosnia and maybe I was expected to tag along. We had just arrived in Ireland and this was a country I had heard so much about. I felt at home here and I couldn't leave without trying to see some of my friends. Besides, I had no desire to head into a war zone and felt I was more of a hindrance. Moreover, I was not ready to return to London and face Nev and his girlfriend.

We were in Sligo. Moona found a local bed and breakfast and dropped me off, asking the woman running the house to look after me for now. We parted ways in what seemed a huge anti-climax, not knowing where and when our paths would cross again. Perhaps our romantic reunion had not lived up to our expectations.

There I was all alone again, but this time in the backwaters of Ireland. It felt like a second boyfriend had been lured away towards Bosnia. I'm sure I cried very hard that first night, but certainly the emotions were cleared by the following day and the hostess made me feel so welcome. I made a few phone calls and heard that Frank, a friend from Luxembourg days, was back in Ireland for the week, not far from where I was. I headed to Roscommon and was made to feel very welcome staying with his family. We spent the week going from pub to pub for various music sessions. He played the bodhrán drum; other musicians joined in with their fiddles, tin whistles and voices. It was such a treat; the music touched my heart and soul. It seemed that

90

everyone in Ireland could play music or sing spontaneously with no written notes in sight. It was in their blood and veins. How inspiring to see such music live. I wished I could join in, but I had learnt music in a more classical fashion and was not familiar with ad-libbing in this way. Still, I managed to move to the rhythm, almost dancing whilst sitting, and soaked up every note and beat I heard. The music was in my blood too.

My next port of call was Galway, where Tony Gaffney had grown up. He was back in London at The Serious Road Trip office, but his parents and sister Pat, welcomed me like family. I was able to relate some of our Russian bus adventures to them and they hoped to see him soon. For now I was a link for them with the life he was now leading. After the relatively quiet backwaters of Roscommon, I remember Galway being a lively city and I discovered that the Aran islands were not far away. As a youngster in New Zealand I had grown up wearing Aran sweaters, hand-knitted by my mother, so this felt like the next place to see.

It was early December by now and I took the ferry to the largest of the islands, Inishmore. I spent the day wandering around the island, where the Irish language was very alive. There were hundreds of stone walls containing small plots of land for grazing animals or growing vegetables. The locals had used seaweed and sand on top of the rocks to create fertile soil for their crops and grass for the animals. Of course, the wool from the sheep would be used to create those lovely knitted sweaters, shawls and hand-woven garments. We passed cemeteries with huge Celtic crosses on our way to a prehistoric fort on the clifftops, Dún Aonghasa. This is a Bronze Age and Iron Age fort with triple wall defences, on a cliff some 330ft (100 metres) high, overlooking the Atlantic Ocean. The views were spectacular and this was the closest we could get to America from Europe. I wanted to get as near to the edge as possible, but only managed to do this lying down for fear of being blown off the edge. It was a sheer drop and the noise of the waves crashing against the cliffs below was intimidating. Coming from the relatively new country of New Zealand, I felt transported back in time just being there. It was quite mystical being in such a place that bore the name of the mythical King Aonghus mac Umhor.

After an amazing day sightseeing we headed to a local pub in the harbour to enjoy a pint of Guinness whilst waiting for a lunar eclipse. It was almost eerie with the moon blackened out like that. It felt like I was teetering on the edge of something both ancient and new in my life.

My next port of call was Dublin! I boarded a bus for the city, where I was welcomed by Linda Moore, whose sister Caroline I had befriended whilst teaching English in France for a year. Caroline was finishing off a teaching stint in Italy for now, but I was welcome to join her sister and flatmates in their house on the quays, just opposite the Guinness factory. It was a mad time with the added bonus of having a local pub right next to the factory where it all came from. Caroline arrived a few weeks later and so began a new adventure.

Christmas was upon us and we all headed down to her parents' home in Black Rock, Cork. Her parents were both retired doctors with Caroline's dad being a well-respected orthopaedic surgeon. A good amount of time was spent visiting the people in hospital as they lay in their beds on the wards on Christmas Day. Dr Moore was also a Sean Connery look-alike so that added to the excitement for some. My family finally had a fixed address to send post to me and I was excited to receive useful gifts and warm messages at Christmas time. Caroline and I both went and kissed the Blarney stone, which felt quite a feat as you had to do it while dangling from a pole, upside down in jungle-gym fashion. I was most amused to see it covered in what looked like lipstick. I wondered if people caught nasty diseases just kissing that stone. But the risk seemed worth it, even if I aimed for the side. Her brother Donald also combed the coast with us and showed me the tourist sights that Ireland had to offer.

All the while Caroline listened with open ears and heart to all that I had experienced in Brazil, Bolivia, Romania, Poland and Russia. She was fascinated by the receptivity of the show in the orphanages and my missing the children in Romania. How she would love to do something like that too. With the bus out of action for now, we could maybe do a smaller scale project to Romania in a VW combi campervan! And so the idea for a follow-up project began. We wrote down our ideas and how we would fund-raise. We would need some performing volunteers as neither of us felt confident in this area, although seriously willing to take part. We would also need a vehicle and driver.

Once back in Dublin we visited the premises of an organisation working in Romania and told them of our rough intentions, hoping they might have contacts, funds or ideas as well.

Then it really was time for me to return to London to set the plan in motion as best I could from there, whilst Caroline would join me later.

Off I set by ferry and coach to London, with my eyes set on this new goal. What would I find going on back there? My mind boggled with the possibilities.

Chapter 11

Yellow Trucks and London

My first point of contact was Nev, who was happy to see me return. The romance was no longer on of course, but we were still friends. He was excited to tell me of the new offices in Greenland Street, just off the High Street in Camden town. There had been a few convoys to Bosnia, but for him that wasn't the focus or the intention of The Serious Road Trip. He wanted to set up a football match between Red Star Belgrade and Sarajevo 11, in an attempt to unite people through sport. There was talk of arriving in a helicopter. Nev was full of big ideas, and whilst we had been with him on the idea of setting up The Serious Road Trip double-decker bus to New Zealand, many could not see the point in these outlandish ideas.

His brother, Christopher, did embark on a hair-raising fact-finding mission to Belgrade, travelling by a Eurolines Coach to attempt to make this football vision happen. He quickly returned after a brief attempt to meet with the notorious Arkan, who was a paramilitary commander but also a leader within the Redstar Belgrade football team. I think Christopher was worried they thought he was some sort of spy and might deal with him accordingly so was relieved to return a few days later.

Nonetheless, the fact remained that there were starving people in Sarajevo and convoys of food were a priority. Nev's football ideas would resurface some years later in another form, but he was alone on this project for now, and had distanced himself from the group because of it. He really was on another planet at times, but I could see how he thought that convoys were steering the Road Trip in another direction and had taken on a life of their own.

By now a few convoys had taken place and some of the stories were a little hair-raising. All sorts of risks had been taken, including some of the trucks not having the correct insurance, although this seemed to be a rather minor one. Various people had rallied to embark on these convoys from all walks of life. Some had heard of the plans on the radio, others in local papers and even the BBC.

Some had military backgrounds, some had huge hearts. Some needed absolute organisation and some had a more happy-go-lucky approach. Some had their feet on the ground and others had a screw loose. There were all sorts of ages involved. Despite everyone leaving for Sarajevo with what seemed like a united vision, the cracks started to appear on the road and under the pressure of entering a war zone. No one had been vetted for suitability, apart from the ability to drive a truck. Bringing together such a team from all sorts of backgrounds and age-groups had been difficult. If I remember correctly from what I heard, certain volunteers wanted to take charge and others didn't want to listen to their command. One driver had even taken an extreme risk by having a large knife on board for self-protection. There were certain rules that needed to be followed and one person could easily jeopardise the lives of others. Something needed to be done to prevent these issues arising on future convoys.

Another issue had arisen. Our original bus-driver, Paul Kirwan, who had changed track after the Peace Convoy to Sarajevo, to focus on driving aid into Bosnia, had been shot at, even though he was driving a humanitarian aid vehicle. He and his Kiwi navigator, Greg Bond, had been entering what was meant to be a peaceful area when they came under fire from a sniper's bullet. By chance, Greg had bent down when the bullet entered the cab, maybe to reach for a map that had fallen on the floor. The bullet narrowly missed him and proceeded to ricochet around the cab and off the steering wheel, before landing in Paul's side. Their guardian angels were certainly looking after them, as Paul's pocket knife was located near his jeans side pocket and took the impact of the bullet. What could have been a serious injury in a war zone turned into a very close shave, with a nick on one finger and a bruise the size of a dinner plate down Paul's hip. How lucky was that? But this highlighted the risks that the drivers were taking. His truck had been a Bedford painted white with a red cross on the side. Had they been mistaken for the UN or the Red Cross, and why should someone shoot at peacekeepers or an aid vehicle? The same truck was later stolen by irregular Croatian soldiers during an ambush, but that is a whole other story…

Another issue was the fact that some of the larger trucks, while being able to carry large amounts of aid from Britain, were unable to navigate the treacherous mountain roads to Sarajevo. These roads were also damaged further by shelling during the ongoing conflict.

Experienced SRT convoy drivers, Graeme Bint (UK) and Doug Meacham (NZ) were here to recount the challenges faced. A round trip from the UK to Sarajevo could take roughly three weeks, with a large portion of the costs being spent on the travel across Europe. Meanwhile aid was arriving in Croatia with no one able to take it further.

We decided to tackle these problems by buying a fleet of Bedford trucks and an accompanying Land Rover, and to set up a base in Croatia. These ex-army trucks were needed for their ability to navigate the treacherous roads.

A set of volunteers had to be recruited. Application forms were filled out, providing us with background information, details of next of kin and the like. There would be a convoy leader, and to avoid any confusion that we were somehow connected with the UN or governmental agencies, Damon felt that we should paint the trucks canary yellow, rather than white. Midge, a local artist who had decorated the first articulated truck, was enthusiastic to paint the truck canvases with cartoon figures such as Smurfs and a wolf. These characters had been part of the logo for the winter Olympics in Sarajevo in 1984 and would certainly bring a few smiles. We wanted to meet the needs of the fun-starved children the drivers would meet on the road or at various checkpoints, but we also wanted to eradicate any possible loss of life due to a perceived army connection.

TSRT began the process to buy three Bedfords and a Land Rover through the British Army. The Serious Road Trip was registered as a potential buyer and when they investigated to see that we were a legitimate humanitarian agency needing equipment, the purchase was approved. Promptly, work began on the fleet down at Charlie and Linda Robson's yard near Windmill Lane in Tower Bridge, South London. They were in the transport business and provided the perfect base for preparing and painting the trucks. It was January-February 1993.

Meanwhile I had my own project to work on and based myself in the huge Greenland Street offices. We shared the space with another organisation that had sprung up, called War Child, but there were four or five large offices, a kitchen area, and toilet facilities.

One of the rooms had been converted into a large dormitory for returning drivers and volunteers. Some were working in the office or in between projects like myself. I camped out there for the next three months alongside some of the original team from the bus. Once again there was no personal space, but this meant we could be working on the project day and night, such was the enthusiasm and need. When we needed a shower, we would head down to Euston Station or across the road to a flat occupied by Christopher Watt and Chris Fleury, alias Goblin, who were part of the main office team. Given the nature of their heights, they were our own version of Laurel and Hardy with a semi-serious focus. Humour and a laid-back approach were essential to our way of operating.

When we needed to call a meeting and our office was too busy with all sorts of people dropping in and out, we would head down to one of the local Camden pubs, with Liberties becoming a regular. How apt the name seemed at the time. The local pubs and Camden market would also provide a good source of fundraising venues over the next few years. Sometimes this was as simple as shaking a donation tin during the hustle and bustle of Camden Market.

Caroline and I had drafted the project proposal to spend three months in Romania, touring all sorts of orphanages and hospitals. We still needed to find two talented volunteers.

Shortly after Caroline had touched base with an Irish organisation stating our need for a performer, a clown had walked through the door announcing his desire to do something for the children of Romania. How lucky was that! A real-life professional clown called Johnie Kavanagh, willing to join our team. He had even been trained at the Blackpool Tower circus! The only downside was that he didn't have a driving licence. So that left me as the only driver, and I definitely didn't feel confident at the thought of driving all the way to Romania on the other side of the road, then touring for a few months.

Caroline and Johnie would stay in Ireland fundraising, organising pub quizzes, raffles and charity dinners. Meanwhile I set about sourcing a Volkswagen combi-van and driver, while carrying out general administrative tasks to prepare for the journey. It was hard to stay focused on this project with so much happening in the office related to the urgent convoy preparation to Bosnia-H and Croatia. We heard tales of how Christophe, alias Grenouille, had ventured into the Bosnian capital and, together with another chap, had dodged bullets to climb to the top of the Unis Tower to set up a radio antenna. As a result of this brave act, the outside world could contact the besieged capital.

It all sounded far too dangerous for me and so I was relieved to be able to work towards the safer Romanian return.

Mind you, even on the home front there were dangers. One weekend, we heard a loud explosion and then numerous sirens outside.

When we tried to venture out of the Greenland Street offices, we realised that our street and a few others had been cordoned off with police tape. The streets were empty except for scores of policemen patrolling the area. There had been a bomb explosion in the litter-bin on the curb outside McDonald's on the High Street just metres from our office. We had been parked with one of our vehicles right next to that bin, just 30 minutes earlier, and we could have taken the brunt of the explosion. My imagination raced wildly, wondering if it was somehow connected and had we been targeted? Or was it someone who didn't like the hamburgers? It turned out that the IRA had claimed responsibility for this act of terrorism which resulted in 18 people being injured, including two seriously (27 Feb 1993). What a close shave. We toasted our luck, and sympathy for those injured, in the pub later that day with the recently returned Christophe, wondering if the dangers of Sarajevo were somehow following him.

Meanwhile, on the Romanian front, I was relieved when we were contacted by a guitar-playing chap from Manchester, who could also double-up as driver. Bob Butcher answered our prayers and became the fourth member of our Romanian team. With the help of my cousin Grant, a Kiwi Volkswagen mechanic, I managed to find the right campervan for the project. There were plenty of Kiwis doing the overseas adventure thing in VW Combis and so there were a number to choose from. If we needed a Romanian translator, we could also engage the services of a local who was used to working at Ionaseni orphanage. All aspects of the trip seemed to fall into place, including a series of Dracula Party fundraising events planned for our departure from London and en route in Luxembourg.

Caroline finally joined me in London for the final preparations amidst the various convoys. Not only was our office busy organising aid for Bosnia, there was even a smaller convoy to Kiev in the Ukraine, driven by Henk and Seaton, friends from our Wellington University days. This was funded by a Jewish organisation we had met through our Bosnian actions. How amazing to think that the original idea of driving the bus to New Zealand had transformed into a multi-national venture covering a number of countries.

Meanwhile, fundraising in New Zealand was taking place with Damon's mother and Belinda from the bus at the helm. On top of this, Belinda was expecting a baby that had been conceived in Moscow; her boyfriend Myles had returned home to help. There was news of another child (Jason and Felicity's) on the way, after our delay in Moscow. Thank goodness we hadn't carried on to Georgia.

We awaited Johnie's arrival with eager anticipation. I remember

e

finalising the ferry details one morning, trying to get as much done as possible, when I was interrupted by someone who stumbled into the offices volunteering for Romania. He didn't seem to be all there, a few sandwiches short of a picnic, but he was dead-set on going to Romania to help the orphans. He wore shorts pulled up above his waist and a green hat with flaps over the ears and had seriously thick circular glasses. He'd been listening to a story on the radio about the plight of the orphans and felt called to help them. He stuttered as he talked about being ready for anything, like painting the walls, and he could do murals of little duckies for the children if needed. I wished someone else would deal with this guy, as he was certainly not the type of person we wanted to take with us and I had other things to prepare.

But there I was, alone in the office, having to deal with this confused chap, who was like a fox-terrier hanging onto this idea that he wanted to go on our trip to Romania. He explained he was a 'weally' good musician too and went on to tell me he could 'play the spoons'. I'd never heard anything so wacky. I explained we were full up and had no space for extras. In an attempt to get the guy off my back, I got him to fill out a volunteer form on a clipboard for future trips. He could scarcely write, so he did so slowly, which at least gave me some brief respite. That was short-lived as he needed a better pen and then help with spelling. I admit I was seriously wound up and he was testing my patience when suddenly the pace changed.

He handed me the form, shook my hand and slipped into an Irish accent.

'Delighted to meet you!'

The penny dropped! This was Johnie himself, fooling me completely into believing he was some idiot wanting to get to Romania. The funny thing is, these sorts of characters do exist.

We were definitely in for some fun with Johnie on board. He wasn't like any other clown I had previously imagined a clown to be and certainly wasn't the stereotypical one with stripey trousers and a curly red wig.

He certainly entertained our supporters with his dim-witted 'Brian Melley' renditions as we fundraised before leaving. Meanwhile Caroline and myself were dressed as wenches from the grave, posing either as Dracula's victims or accomplices, I'm not sure which. Using face-paints plastered on by Johnie the professional, we had nasty looking faces stitched onto our necks and we drank red-coloured punch posing as blood from wine glasses. Bob had a black cape and was dressed as Dracula himself.

The send-off party in London was enjoyed by all, including those heading imminently on convoy to Bosnia and the Ukraine. That initial, exclusively Road Trip convoy was made up of Tony Gaffney and Damon Hinton from the bus days, joined by an American newcomer Josh, in 'Ragga' the leading Land Rover. Charlie and Linda Robson were in their own Bedford, Richard and Allan Cooper (Aus) in Richard's own van, Roger Field (UK) and Peter Gulliver (NZ) were in a Volvo from previous convoys and Liam and Meni Kojaman were in the Ford cargo Fridge. Doug (NZ) and Graeme had already headed off earlier in another of the Bedfords. On top of this Henk, Seaton and another Pete (NZ) were also setting off for Odessa in the Ukraine in a single truck, although I later heard they only needed to go as far as Kiev and then to Poland to leave the truck there with EquiLibre. That also sounded like quite another adventure.

We didn't know when we would all next meet and the anticipation of our own adventure certainly made the adrenalin flow.

Chapter 12

Mania 4 Romania Tour
(1993)

Amid last-minute chaos we set off from London for Dover at 5.30pm on 31 March 1993, with our arrival in Calais almost dead on April 1st. How appropriate for a clowning tour to begin on April Fool's Day.

The first port of call was my old stomping ground of Luxembourg. With almost no sleep, after a journey through the night, we managed a comedy crawl of various old haunts such as the Harp Bar, Pygmalion, Black Stuff and White Rose, not to mention my old workplace, Corporate Funds Management Services. Once again the people generously dipped their hands into their pockets for the project. After all, the initial trip to Romania undertaken by Nev and Damon had also started from here, so the expat community remembered us well. The next day we even managed to hook up with a local bus transport manager and double-decker bus enthusiast who also supported our cause, and long-time fundraiser and friend Cynthia Albrecht. Another Dracula party was called for at the White Rose, but the next day, with no time to waste, we left for Germany, stopping in a car park beside the Autobahn to sleep a few hours.

The mustard-coloured Brazilian combi van needed some livening up. In true spontaneous fashion, Johnie had us spray-painting bright squiggles all over the van with the words 'Mania 4 Romania' on one side, a red nose on the front in between the headlights for eyes, and the words 'Clowntown Express' above the bumper. On the other side of the van we had already placed a giant sticker of a red cross and The Serious Road Trip bus logo in the middle.

Being on the road with Johnie and Caroline was hilarious and there was always some bicycle hooter or duck caller going off to brighten the hundreds of kilometres we covered. Meanwhile, Bob drove slowly while I navigated. With our in-built kitchen, we could stop for endless cups of tea and food cooked in one pot. At night we would park up, pull the curtains and could sleep four with a squish in our sleeping bags. It really was like being on the bus again, but in miniature this time.

It was a time for getting to know each other. At the time, Johnie seemed much older at 35 years of age and came from a comparatively rough background. His arms bore various tattoos and it sounded like he had got up to serious mischief before embarking on his vocation as a clown. With drug addiction and time in prison behind him, we were thankful to have someone so street savvy on the trip, not to mention his natural talent as a clown. We crossed Germany, Austria and Hungary on fairly good motorways and after sleeping in the van in Budapest, close to a red double-decker bus transformed into a café, we awoke to Romanian gypsies surrounding the van. We sped off, amidst their pleas to donate our van to their worthwhile cause, on a mission to find gas for our stove and coffee to wake us up.

Finally we arrived at the Romanian border to find another British group there, who had been held up for 18 hours. Our passports were checked and the van inspected near the border town of Bors, not far from Oradea. Then we were waved on after a mere 30 minutes. The clowning magic seemed to be working and we had made it into Romania! This was where the serious adventure would begin. Bob proudly announced that he had never driven more than 25 miles in a row and he was chuffed to bits to have driven so far over these last few days! I'm sure we would have preferred to remain in our ignorance of thinking he was an experienced driver, but at least we could celebrate this achievement. We crawled across the north of Transylvania on pot-holed roads, overtaking many horses and carts in the dark and finally arriving in Cluj-Napoca with no petrol left in the van, and no local money in our pockets. There we found a parking spot in the city centre for the night. Once we managed to change some money, we 'launched' the project with a cheap bottle of sparkling wine and a basic pizza for dinner.

By the morning we had a number of street kids gathering around our brightly-coloured van with its steamed-up windows. Johnie didn't disappoint them and even actions such as his cleaning his teeth in the morning were full of gurgles and gargles that would make the most serious of us giggle. He also had his unicycle on board and numerous balloons, juggling balls, clubs and costumes.

101

He was an early riser and had the kettle on to awaken us from our slumber and hangovers. He was fairly hyperactive and seemed to have endless energy.

We waved farewell to the gypsy-looking fan club and set off in search of a Peco petrol station. They were few and far between, so this was something we would need to watch as one could easily be caught short. From there we headed towards Vatra Dornei in the Carpathian mountains, as we crossed Romania towards the Moldovan region in the north east. It was the beginning of April and the fields in the mountains were still covered in snow. It would be another 220 miles before we would reach our destination of Ionaseni.

There were not many motor vehicles and, of those that there were, they were almost entirely the Romanian-made Dacias. We sped past many horses and carts carrying giant piles of hay, so big you could scarcely see the cart beneath. Much to our excitement, we even discovered a hotel on the main road called the Hotel Castel Dracula. We parked our van outside and took a photo with Johnie on the van roof. We had little time to venture inside as we were on a mission to get to our destination before evening. Driving in the dark would be difficult and we were eager to sleep somewhere warmer that night.

We were starting to get into familiar territory and my heart was racing. After managing to find some dinner in the familiar Suceava, we rolled into the lower part of the village and went straight to Mama Puiu's. What a welcome back it was! Volunteers Jon, Mary and Di were there to celebrate, as were the whole Puiu family. I had left there in November as the weather cooled and now here we were in early April as the snow was melting.

Little Daniella and Mihai-itsa were most excited to see me back. While I was itching to head up to the orphanage the very next day, we had to hold off due to some inspection taking place; but managed to recoup some of our energy from the long journey with a lie-in. We didn't waste any time, though, and by that afternoon we were invited to a psychiatric hospital in Botosani (Spital 4) for their regular weekly music and dance therapy session. Bob played his guitar and we all danced till we could dance no more; it was exhausting. What a hoot it was... dancing with the patients in their dressing gowns, some of whom had been coaxed out of their beds to dance with a clown. I had never visited such a hospital and it felt like we were part of a Romanian version of *One flew over the Cuckoo's Nest* and Johnie was our Irish version of Jack Nicholson.

The very next morning we were invited to perform a clowning show at little Mihai's school, nearby in Virfu Cimpului.

102

The show was something that we hadn't rehearsed, as we had been so busy just getting there, but we were safe in the knowledge that Johnie knew what he was doing. Somehow clowns speak a universal language of blah, blah, blah that all children and adults understand. For this first show he was wearing his dungarees with patches and a wide-brimmed hat. His face sported a huge painted smile and red nose and not much more. His expertise excelled and the unicycle and juggling clubs were favourites as well as a beach ball that bounced into the crowd. I don't remember much else except very happy children, mostly wearing hats indoors for warmth and keen to participate when the clown asked for volunteers to try juggling.

They would get a huge round of applause for trying, even though they dropped the balls, as that was one of Johnie's messages: We don't always get it right straight away in life, but it's important to keep trying and learning. With many of his tricks, he would try and fail on numerous occasions, mostly on purpose, until at last he would succeed. Bob brought out his guitar wearing another of Johnie's spotty costumes and Caroline and I wore brightly-coloured shirts. Caroline made sure she was there to hand Johnie the various props needed, while I felt decidedly unsure of my exact role in the show at this point. That was yet to come as the show was developing 'in the moment' and we were quickly finding out what we could and couldn't do. Essentially, the slapstick humour prevailed. Johnie was a fan of Charlie Chaplin and it showed. However, this was a crowd of appreciative school children and it would be in the evening that we would make our first visit to the orphanage for severely disabled children at Ionaseni. These abandoned and severely deprived children were our target audience for this project.

Before heading up to see them though, we also travelled back to Suceava to telephone the London office, confirming our safe arrival, and to fulfil a few other tasks such as refuelling and stocking up on some fresh supplies from the market. We also needed to let some of the other organisations working in orphanages here know that we were ready for action.

The translator we had lined up before leaving was no longer available as she had disappeared off to Bosnia to join Moona. Bosnia had certainly attracted a number of my friends. However, another organisation we were working with, The Romanian Orphanage Trust, could maybe help us out. Phones were not commonplace, unlike the mobile phones of today, and so we were dependent on the Post Office and Telecommunications buildings in major towns.

Finally, after all this was completed, we were able to turn up at the orphanage and see the excited children who remembered me from the bus, and were delighted to meet the newcomers. What a relief to be back at last. Those that could speak a few words asked about the 'Masina Mare' but I am not sure they fully comprehended my attempt to describe it breaking down in Moscow. At least our van was equally as colourful and Johnie captured their imaginations by arriving and leaving either standing on the roof or hanging onto the roof from the bumper. It was just the sort of thing a clown would do. This was the orphanage that had stolen my heart and where we were best known.

While for me this was familiar territory, the other three were deeply moved by the plight of all these children. They had only ever seen situations like this on TV and the smell told its own story.

Mama Puiu rewarded us with some yummy soup. I remember Johnie wanting to know what type of soup it was, to which she replied vegetable soup. 'Then what is this then?' he asked laughing, and held up what looked like a miniature penis from some unfortunate small animal. Before we could closely examine his astonishing find, Mama Puiu snatched the wee willy and promptly swallowed it, removing all evidence and trace of meat in her vegetable soup. The soup certainly took on a different flavour after that as we pondered what it could have been? We women slept well that night in the warmth of the Puiu's house, with Johnie and Bob on guard sleeping in the van.

The following day we were eager to get back to the orphanage and slotted in with the programme in the bungalow school run by Di Hiscock, along with various local staff. There were boys in the morning and girls in the afternoon. Both groups were aged 10 years or up and were fascinated to be face-painted. Bob played his guitar and Johnie did a few tricks. He had us all fooled opening the door and slamming his nose into it. What looked like an accident was actually a great prank and had everyone in stitches, including the director of the orphanage. Many of these children were unable to utter more than a few words but they were communicating through Makaton, the simplified sign language. They were capable of understanding humour, however, and they laughed a lot.

The next day we focused on taking the very small children from the Copii Mici wing for 'walkies'. It was the weekend and if we weren't there, the children would have remained seated on their little white chairs or in their cots. Not all could walk, but those that had some balance still needed a helping hand to get them moving around. With a shortage of staff, especially at the weekend, this was already a difficult task. You could see how the children could easily never learn to walk, even not entirely due to disabilities, which certainly some had. It was purely through not being given the opportunity to move or even the encouragement to try. For some of the staff it was easier if the children just sat nicely rocking on their chairs, not even playing with each other. This was nevertheless an improvement from the days of them lying half naked in their own excrement, tied to their cots; but these were mostly children that could not speak or interact due to lack of stimulation.

Once again little Adriana seemed to remember who I was, as she clutched at my familiar circle-shaped necklace which provided some form of object to scrutinise and play with. She looked at me with her big questioning eyes. There were so many children and our small action felt like a drop in the ocean.

On the accommodation front we would need to move elsewhere for the following days, but one of the workers from the orphanage had a spare room in the upper village, so we moved to Rodica's and Radu's that evening. The room was freezing cold and the Soba heater didn't work, or we didn't know how to make it work. Unlike Mama Puiu, who was available to fuss over us like a mother hen, Rodica was a working mother with scarcely enough time to see her beloved husband. He was unable to work due to illness or some work accident. There was no social security to help these poor village folk, and Rodica was lucky to have work at the local orphanage, even if it was poorly paid and very hard-going. A few extra dollars per night, for providing us with shelter, would certainly be most appreciated. We remained fairly independent on the whole, however, and used the room more as a base for the night, visiting various friends all over the village or elsewhere by day.

I was getting accustomed to drinking my fair share of the local moonshine or fire-water, named Tuica (stuica) and made from sugar beet. This was home-made and offered to visitors frequently. For various reasons the other three usually chose not to drink; I would accept, partly for fear of looking rude, but partly because I had acquired a taste for it too. We would raise our glasses and toast 'Noroc' (good luck), 'sanatate' (health), and jokingly also to a 'casa de piatra' (house of stone) although this custom was usually reserved for weddings. It was a moment of connecting with these hospitable people and of showing mutual appreciation.

After so many years of surviving under Ceausescu's communist regime and with little contact with the outside world, this was a moment to herald new beginnings and an opening up to the outside world. In the few houses where there were black and white televisions,

105

they were even screening the soap opera *Dallas* with subtitles, much to our amusement. I'm sure some of them believed we all lived that American life of luxury where we came from, and maybe it gave them a false sense of what to hope for. Still, here we were travelling the world in a vehicle we owned, with the freedom to come and go. I guess it seemed that we really did come from some more privileged backgrounds compared with their simple country life, working dawn to dusk on the land.

Monday arrived again and this heralded the third week of our project. We were back in action at Ionaseni dancing with children and helping with the lunchtime feeding. Bob's guitar was enjoyed, particularly by a blind boy named Florin, who was up close touching the guitar and adoringly feeling the vibrations as Bob strummed. Johnie helped Di with some physio activities and also painted some lovely big coloured shapes on the tennis courts. Miraculously a phone-call was received saying our translator would arrive in a couple of Mondays from Bacau. How reassuring, although we were funnily managing okay without one for now. In fact it would be another month before we finally hooked up with her before we went South.

For now, our project was concentrating on the north-eastern part of Moldova and we had a show to rehearse. Johnie had come up with a story to hold all the action of the show together. Drawing on the universal appeal of animals to children, the idea was that three of us would be dressed as a mouse, cat and dog. We would appear, one by one, as part of a story. This started with an old man (Johnie) who had nothing but one loaf of bread. He fell asleep on a chair hugging his loaf of bread, snoring very loudly. Along came a little mouse (Caroline) dressed in pink. She was very hungry and set about stealing the bread, slowly managing to prise it from his grip and running away with the bread. Then of course a cat (myself), dressed in colourful yellow shirt and tiger-like face, arrived on the scene and chased the mouse as she was very hungry too. Then the dog (Bob) followed in hot pursuit. The old man awakens, and joins in the chase to get his bread back. When he finally catches them all, he sits them down and teaches them tricks. They will work for their bread rather than stealing.

First the mouse learns to juggle; Caroline had managed to pick up this skill. The cat learns to skip with a rope (as that is what I could manage), and the dog learns to play the guitar and sing, as that was what Bob was good at. In return for these tricks we all received our own share of the bread. I'm not sure we had intended to have such a moralistic story but it certainly provided a framework for us to work together and get the children up moving and dancing at the end.

Johnie still opened the show doing various clowning tricks and getting children to participate before we began this interactive story. We didn't have long to rehearse, as we were invited to perform at an orphanage school for slow learners in Agafton the very next day and another similar school in Zvoristea on the Wednesday.

With our hearts beating wildly with nerves, even including Johnie, who was used to performing, we premiered our first rendition of this show. By now Johnie had a few Romanian phrases to greet the crowd and fool around with. For example, instead of saying 'multumesc' (thank you) he would say Mickey Mouse and instead of 'cu placere' (with pleasure) he would say 'couple of cherries'. He often reverted to speaking his blah, blah, blah language as well.

He did juggling and unicycling tricks, then offered the chance to volunteers in the crowd to give it a go. He encouraged the crowd to chant their name and then once they tried, they would get a huge round of applause. After building up a sweat, he announced how thirsty he was and ask for 'apa' (water). Before anyone in the audience had a chance to produce some water, Caroline carried on a heavy bucket of water and a cup. He scooped a cup of water from the bucket and embarked on a long gurgling session, finally swallowing the water followed by a huge burp. The children loved every move he made and relished every noise.

Then he asked if anyone in the crowd wanted water too. Many put their hands up, hoping the clown would pick them. Then Johnie teased the crowd by rushing towards them with the bucket, ready to throw water, but then changing his mind and heading towards another part of the crowd. By this stage they were flinching as he finally threw the contents of the bucket on the crowd, their faces aghast, except the bucket was full of confetti paper rather than water. How had the clown tricked them and transformed water into paper?

Then there was his balloon trick, where he would blow up a balloon as large as it would go, encouraged by the children screaming in unison 'mai mare, mai mare, mai mare' (bigger, bigger, bigger) and eventually it would pop. The explosion pushed him backwards onto a chair, which then fell over with Johnie landing on his back, still trying to blow up his balloon. It amazed me how he managed to fall over on his back like that without injuring himself, but he reassured us that he had been trained in the circus in such physical feats. Soon after that, the multi-coloured beach ball came out and was pushed into the crowd, who in turn would try and keep it in the air, if they weren't trying to hang onto it for dear life as some eager children were prone to doing.

This part of the show was a miniature circus-styled show and then it was our moment to shine as the story began with the old man and his loaf of bread. A local teacher was called upon to narrate, reading from a script someone had helped us write. Then out we came making our various animal noises in Romanian. It was 'chit' (pronounced 'kits) for the mouse, 'miau' for the cat and 'ham-ham' for the dog. So there weren't long lines to learn and we just had to play the parts.

I remember the first few shows were quite civilised, with the children watching from a distance, but later on in the tour there would be times when we chased each other through the audience.

The Scottish group based at Ionaseni also had volunteers working at the infamous adult psychiatric institute of Podriga. I had heard the frightening stories from when the bus had visited the year before, while I was organising visas. They too would like us to visit and cheer things up. We bumped over pot-holes and avoided horses and carts on our journey east to Saveni, near the Moldovan border. As we travelled, Johnie, egged on by ourselves, hatched another plan to fool the volunteers. He would go into his dim-witted 'Brian Melley' character, wanting to help the children of Romania. We would claim to have picked him up on the way, hitch-hiking to Podriga, after Ionaseni volunteers had sent him in that direction for obvious reasons.

We hadn't even got to Saveni, when we saw two foreigners drinking at an outside café/bar on the side of the road. They seemed to hail us down so we obliged and stopped. Here we met with a couple of Paddies, both named Patrick, one with shoulder-length ginger hair and the other with a Mohican. 'Brian' stumbled out of the van to greet them, once again his trousers pulled well up, his crazed eyes behind the thick glasses and his green hat with flaps keeping his ears warm. We explained how he was a 'surprise' volunteer we found hitchhiking in the middle of the road on his way to see them. While they looked genuinely happy to see to us, you could see their eyes starting to roll when they realised what they were in for with Brian, having heard about the Romanian orphans on the radio and wanting to help with painting, yes, painting his little duckies on the walls. How could Rupert, from Ionaseni, play such a cruel joke... they would have to send this guy back somehow. But 'Brian' wasn't completely innocent. The sight of a cockerel started him off singing a rude ditty about a cockerel waking its owner up in the morning. On top of that, after guzzling a local beer down, he proceeded to show them how he could flip a bottle between his fingers, like a cowboy does with his gun in a good old Western with John Wayne. All the while, Johnie kept his dim-witted Brian persona going. Once refreshed, we all climbed aboard the Clowntown express and sped further along to the institution, Podriga, to link up with some other volunteers.

What a beautiful grand structure the building seemed, although it was painted bright pink. There was no running water and we could see an open-air bathtub outside. A crowd of mad-looking patients half-dressed in assorted clothes greeted us and took us inside. One was keen to shake my hand and slipped me his willy instead. How repulsive, and how naive I was not to see that one coming. We soon linked up with their volunteer co-ordinator, Andy from Scotland. As Brian expressed his desire to paint duckies on the walls, it was lucky Andy was in on the joke, having met us the week before, as one could sense how he could easily have been tipped over the edge, in an already stressful situation. The smell in this place was so overwhelming we were out within minutes and felt sure our show would need to be outdoors.

Johnie persisted with his character until we returned to the apartment the volunteers shared in a neighbouring town; then he knew his game was up. What a relief for them. This was followed by an evening of exchanging stories and plans. We were told how one of the patients was nick-named Mashina, and was known for swallowing small live animals whole including a bird chick and a kitten. How mad and gruesome it all sounded. We hadn't seen anything like that while we were there.

We were up the following morning, raring to go for our show, when disaster struck. Bob was fumbling with the gears to the van, as he had done on various occasions, when there was a strange, foreboding, metal-breaking sound. No matter how hard he tried, the van would not engage into gear. We were going nowhere! Well at least not in our van. Hopefully it wasn't anything too serious.

We hung onto the hope that someone mechanical could quickly fix the van and we would be on our way, but this was not the case. It was starting to look more serious and was possibly the gears. We would need to be towed all the way back to Botosani and Ionaseni. What a serious bummer. My world seemed to come crashing down around me as I imagined the worst. Was this another re-run of the bus in Russia? Would we be able to continue with the project? Was this the end of the road and the shows?

We would definitely need to wait for a strong enough vehicle to tow us and with the volunteers already in action for the day, we needed to wait till the following day, a Saturday, which just so happened to be my birthday, April 17th. It certainly didn't feel like any cause for celebration and I was on a serious downer that day. The way I felt then, the project was doomed; and this was only the third week.

Fortunately I was travelling with an up-beat team and we were with people experienced in facing trying situations in Romania, but our future seemed to hang in the balance.

I was wakened early to Caroline exclaiming 'surprise Simone' with her hands filled with gifts. I was amazed that she had managed to find something in a shop somewhere. There was some local strawberry hand cream (not quite up to Body Shop standard mind you) and bits and bobs, plus a bottle of local sparkling wine.

Meanwhile the van was attached with a fairly thin and fraying metal rope to a Toyota Hilux and we didn't waste much time hitting the road. We had a fairly long journey ahead of us which would take a good couple of hours and we weren't even sure the rope would hold out over all those pot-holes. To minimise the weight being pulled, we two women decided to travel up front in the Hilux and left Bob and Johnie to travel in the combi behind.

It felt luxurious to be in the more modern vehicle driven by Andy, with the two dogs, Smecki and Nipper for company. Seeing it was my birthday, we decided that the party needed to happen right away. What could have been a highly depressing situation turned into an unusual birthday party as we cracked open my bottle of sparkling wine and started to celebrate. Meanwhile Johnie hopped around the combi van pulling funny faces at us every time we turned to look back clinking our glasses.

Of course, Andy concentrated on the slow drive and the two little dogs yapped excitedly.

We crawled in to Ionaseni and pulled up outside the volunteers' apartment. There was little we could do with the vehicle for now, as it was Easter and things were on a different rhythm. In fact, things were on quite a different rhythm indeed, as this was the beginning of Easter according to the Romanian Orthodox church, which meant it was a week later than in Western Europe. I was excited to discover on a hanging wall calendar, that my birthday was even the same day as St Simeon, the martyr and Bishop of Persia. Somehow this coincidence made the day even more surreal, as I danced around wearing an inflatable cake with candles on it, on my head. Only a clown would pack such a useful item. The big surprise of the day, however, was when Caroline and Johnie announced to me that they were actually romantically involved. In Ireland, they were an unlikely couple being from quite different backgrounds: Caroline a Protestant and Johnie from a Catholic family. Caroline had studied at Trinity College; Johnie's education had been on the streets of Dublin and at the Blackpool Tower Circus. In my naivety I had not realised that they were 'together'. They certainly seemed a very happy couple and relieved to have broken the news to me.

Easter Sunday arrived and that meant a visit to Mama Puiu's and her family was in order, along with some tasty Romanian food.

En route to Virfu Cimpului, instead of the usual 'buna diminiata', we were greeted with a 'Hristos a inviat' (Christ has risen) and were told that the traditional reply was 'e adevarat ca a inviat' (it is true that he is risen). How amazing to think that under communism the Christian traditions had managed to exist in the villages, unlike in the cities. Late afternoon, we wound our way back up to Rodica's, greeting all that we met in this new-found way and then enjoyed going to the Ionaseni Ball that night. There we danced like idiots to local music in the community hall. The worries of the van repairs seemed to disappear for a moment; we were told that a volunteer named Richard was looking into things for us.

Within a couple of days the gear-stick problem was seemingly fixed. Apparently we didn't need to find a spare part, as in this neck of the woods people were used to making or welding something to do the job. Phew!

There were exciting things to look forward to, including a carnival a couple of days later.

This involved getting into costume, with the children using face-paints and hats, and then a parade to begin the carnival festivities in the morning. There were various sports activities, music, gumboot throwing, wet-sponges to throw at people in stocks and some Treasure Island game. Our show kicked the afternoon event off, followed by a disco in the dining room with a local music group providing dancing for all till 6 pm. It really was an action packed day where everyone let their hair down and expended lots of energy. Contact was made with someone visiting from a huge institute on the Ukraine border in Siret, where we would be welcome to visit the following week. We busied ourselves sorting out the itinerary for the following week, various musical and walking activities with the children, administrative tasks and the festivities of St George's Day. I was amazed how serious everyone was in celebrating this patron saint of their village. We enjoyed a huge feast at our host Rodica's and later danced the night away at another Ionaseni Ball in honour of St George. The 'diddly, diddly' local folk music strangely was starting to grow on us.

I was relieved to speak to my mechanic cousin Grant from the post-office in town and describe our van issues. Calmly he reassured me about the gears problem but he encouraged me to source spare parts if needed again. This would be a constant challenge during the project.

We now had our chance to return to Podriga to finish what we had set out to do one week earlier. One of the local educators, Costel, joined us for the trip and was not shy to get into costume for the show as well. We made our grand entrance in the van with Johnie swinging from the door and a crowd quickly formed around us, happy to see us again.

I don't know what possessed Caroline to be so brave, but she was quick to embrace one of the residents that approached her, for what she thought was a hug. She was trying to be warm and friendly. Much to her horror the woman, wearing rags and with a small shaven head, plunged her teeth into her chest area and bit her hard enough to draw blood. What a shock for us all, most of all Caroline. We laughed about this later, as this was the person who was notorious for eating small animals; Caroline was prancing around dressed as a mouse!

Despite this set-back and with Caroline hiding her tears, we gave the best show thus far, in the lovely spring sunshine. I remember wondering if the group of giggling women sitting on a bench, trying to blow up balloons, were actually staff or residents; they all seemed to blend into one. But what was essential was that it was a funny day for all to remember and a serious break from their routine.

We awoke the following morning to hear that the beloved dog Nipper had been poisoned. A vet was called urgently to tend to him, and several hours later, he made a splendid recovery. We savoured the remaining weekend hours by visiting a nearby lake with our friends to soak up some sunshine, before the trek back to Ionaseni.

That week we performed in two Camin Spitals (Sasca Mica and Siret), and for two Dorohoi schools combined in an outside stadium. We also discovered a leaking oil problem; a week wouldn't have been complete without some vehicle trouble.

It was the Institute in Siret that surprised us the most. We were shown around this home to some 500 children of varying abilities and it seemed like utter chaos at first. The programme here was intense. This was to enable shows and activities to suit all the different needs and number of children, all in the space of two days. Thank goodness this one had been sorted out in advance.

Their 'school children' were very alert and receptive to the show, while those in the Therapy Salon were more suited to gentle bouncing of balloons and music. The rooms ranged from the dining room hall to the little kindergarten rooms. I remember the younger children with extremely cute faces, tapping their hands in unison with Johnie on the little tables and screaming 'Ya-oo' along with the clown. Kids just love to mimic and here they were being given the licence to bang on the tables as part of the show.

You would have thought that was enough for the week, but we finished it off with a Saturday show for the locals outside on the main street in Bucecea Village. We had to adapt the show to make way for various horse drawn carts (carutas), the local police and even the local priest, as they passed by. After much amusement, we even managed to get the excited children to help clean the van with water from the well. Many of the village roads were not paved so the dust and mud covered the bright colours of the van.

Later that evening we got together with the volunteers from Ionaseni and Podriga to celebrate Costel's birthday. Sunday was a well-deserved rest day.

A new week was upon us and another Costel (popular name in these parts), the handyman, soldered the leaking oil gauge of our van before we charged off to the market for provisions. We were also collecting a spare part needed for the correct gear repair. On our way back we discovered there was a red light on the dashboard. Oh no! We stopped to check the oil but there was no oil problem. We continued on our way with the red light persisting, but several kilometers later we lost power and broke down on the side of the road, in the middle of nowhere. At this rate we would be hitch-hiking back or walking. Life was never dull in an older vehicle.

Unbelievably, after some time contemplating what to do next, another VW appeared on the horizon. We flagged him down; he seemed to know these vehicles well. How about that for synchronicity? He tried a few things, including cleaning the points, and almost by magic the engine sparked back into action. We were on the road again and made our way back, counting our lucky stars as night fell.

'I'm jinxed,' Johnie mumbled under his breath with a certain resignation. It was a wet day and we had awoken to discover that our wing mirror was missing. He somehow felt responsible for all this vehicle trouble. I guess someone fancied it as a mirror or might try to sell it at the market. With rain persisting, we also needed to arrange for the gears to be repaired by Costel, in some alternative garage undercover. It would take longer than a day but we were just grateful he could do the work. The rain had put an end to any chance of a show at the local school in Ionaseni. The dampness seemed to reflect our mood, which was influenced by the state of the van.

Thankfully the next day brought sunshine and a fresh start. We managed the show at the nearby local school and then discovered the van was ready just as a thunderstorm seemed to strike the area. We were able to help Di do some home visits in Bucecea. I think one of the families she was checking on had a little deaf boy. Di had been busy processing the necessary paperwork to try and place him in a more suitable place, where he could at least learn and attend school. This child could have easily ended up stuck in the orphanage for the 'irrecuperable' with no chance of a future. He was lucky Di was there to fight his corner, as the mother had little chance of knowing what the options were and how best to seek them. At one of the houses we visited, we managed to buy some tapestries off a woman who had nine children. I wondered when she found the time to make such beautiful and intricate tapestries with nine children to care for?

Our work in the area was complete, the van was repaired and we were just waiting on the arrival of the long-awaited and promised translator to turn up. Two women arrived the next day for good measure. We were unsure how two translators would now fit into our close-knit team.

After a few awkward introductions at the orphanage, we were scheduled to take the little children for 'walkies'. It was also time to say farewell to the children, and after lunch we slotted in a longer walk into the forest with the boys from the bungalow. I never enjoyed the goodbyes.

Admittedly we were running out of time if we thought we could get on the road that same day. Almost as an indication not to rush things, we discovered another puncture in a tyre. We had to wait another night.

Once we had repaired the puncture and packed up, we had the huge farewell from children and friends alike. 'La Revedere! Drum bun!' they all shouted or waved. We couldn't be sure when we would meet again and I always found leaving this place with familiar friends and children a big wrench. It had become our comfort zone and my favourite part of the world.

Fortunately we were welcomed with open arms at our next destination, where the bus and original team had also been before. Hirlau was a huge institute for adults and children (aged 3-93) and this time World Vision hosted us in their comfortable house with its modern appliances. Their person on the ground, Margaret, was from Australia and it was lovely to connect with another person from Down Under and be able to cook in their kitchen. I was familiar with the organisation since sponsoring a child in Africa with my family when I was growing up. We had exchanged many letters and photos with Tobias, a friendly boy whose family had been left fatherless. At high school we'd even participated in sponsored 24-hour famines, to raise money for World Vision and it was meaningful to actually meet one of their staff. I just hadn't expected to see them in Romania.

After a much-needed rest the following morning, we were ready for action and a well-received show outside that afternoon. The thing that stuck in my memory was that half way through the chase one of the residents actually 'stole' the loaf of bread. It must have been too tempting for some hungry soul to join in the chase along with us. We managed to retrieve a small portion to finish our story nonetheless. There were also many residents who hadn't made it outside, so we were asked to return on Sunday. It was not in our vocabulary to say 'no' to a show.

While my heart was willing, I awoke that day with a serious cold and a bad case of asthma. The happenings of the previous six weeks were catching up with me and we had slept in some damp and dusty places, which probably didn't help. Margaret was only too happy to stand in for me as the cat for a day while I rested in bed. This was an enormous relief.

The quieter day served me well and we were rewarded that evening with a meal out in a fish restaurant, where local farmed trout was on the menu.

Off we set the next day, this time with me at the wheel. My patience had been tested at times with Bob as our only driver and I had decided it was time to pluck up my courage and drive in these hazardous conditions. The tension was mounting a little with six adults in the van. It was too many for our small space and we couldn't understand why we had been sent two translators, though we were grateful for this assistance from The Romanian Orphanage Trust. They had also provided us with a loose itinerary of sorts.

I only drove as far as Tirgu Frumos, some 30 km down the road, but after a few close shaves with various vehicles, pot-holes and carutas I gladly handed this role back to Bob. I had a greater appreciation for his driving ability after this, but it was good to know I could drive if needed. When we finally got to Piatra Neamt we had time to arrange somewhere to sleep and a few shows for the following day. Then we even managed a visit to one of the famous monasteries in the forest.

The teeny children we saw the following morning in two Leagans (nurseries) were so young, we had to quickly adapt our approach. We needed to proceed quietly after they were initially startled. They were more fascinated by the animal characters and a 'gentle' Johnic for a change. This was followed by a performance in the playground of the Casa de Copii no. 3 where some of the older children remembered us from a previous show.

115

Meanwhile the translator dilemma seemed to work itself out naturally. One needed to go down to Bucharest; the other one just disappeared.

Through a young teenager, we were put in touch with the local high school and performed there the following day.

This was quite a different audience of older, normal adolescents. When we got there we realised that there were some 500 children. The school director was there to provide some authority and the children formed a huge circle around us in the courtyard, almost like in a circus. The crowd roared and it was great to see that our show could be adapted to almost every situation. Somehow in the commotion of it all, the other wing mirror went missing. Seems they were too tempting a target and fairly easy to unscrew.

It was time to make our way to Pastraveni orphanage, where the director gave us permission for an outdoor show; one of the children performed a fantastic song for us at the end. It was precisely this type of response we loved and it was one that came naturally for some.

By the time we arrived in Bacau where the Romanian Orphanage Trust had an office they were already closed up for the day. We decided to sleep sardine-style in the van.

We were there bright and early to start organising the next five days of shows and miraculously the translator named Marina reappeared from Bucharest to help us organise and translate. There followed a couple of shows and a night out with the volunteers, who were always intrigued to meet us.

I even tried phoning the London office to touch base and managed to speak with Nev but there was no real news and I felt we were worlds apart. He explained he wasn't usually there, so had no idea what was going on. Mind you, it was the weekend. Christopher was at some football match, which was one of his favourite activities when he wasn't wishfully talking about meeting a 'babe' somewhere. He didn't usually go out much as he was so dedicated to holding the office together.

We heard about the local Puppet Theatre and on Sunday we trotted along for their 11am show and even went backstage to introduce ourselves. They said they would love to meet up with us again the following day, which we did. The director was fascinated to link up, and we discussed the possibility of performing on their stage that Wednesday and Sunday. A real theatre stage for us: now that was a first! They even had special posters made up for the occasion, which were plastered around town. 'MANIA PENTRU ROMANIA cu TRUPA 'The Serious Road Trip' (ANGLIA) in Distributie: Johnie,

Caroline, Simone si Bobby' We had to laugh about Bob being called Bobby as this was no doubt some reference to the Bobby from Dallas! It was nice to be seen as some international troupe on tour by the professionals.

For now we were intrigued to see another puppet show: once from the audience seating, and then again from backstage, to see how it was done. I had performed fairy-tales as a child using an old Punch and Judy styled booth, but this was a full length theatre devoted to puppets.

It was a privilege to meet the puppet-maker responsible for creating the hundreds of puppets. I was drawn to these puppets; they provided some link with fond memories from my own childhood. My Auntie Carol, who was an art teacher, had created glove puppets with her theatre students for our very own 'Little People's Puppet theatre'. Under her guidance, my brother, cousin and I had given performances to kindergartens and hospitals. By comparison, these were enormous puppets; many had limbs attached to rods, and big round heads. My favourite was a long, hairy, sausage dog that was able to mimic the movements of a real-life dog. You couldn't get the same effect with a glove puppet, plus this one was the same size as a dog. It was amazing to see the possibilities of different styled puppets. What a highlight this all was for me!

Mind you, as with everything there were the ups and the downs. After a couple of successful shows slotted into that afternoon, the van gears slipped again. It was so frustrating! To add insult to injury, while we met with a few folk in a local bar, not far from the immobile van, it was broken into from the other side. The curtains had been pulled shut to stop prying eyes, so we hadn't even seen it happening, as we sat just metres away. They had pried the lock open with a crowbar and Johnie's special spotted boiler suit and other costumes were taken, as well as face-paints and a huge ghetto-blaster. It was heart-breaking and felt like we were being kicked in the teeth, when trying to help. Our colourful van was just too tempting and stuck out enormously.

'I'm jinxed!' Johnie continued to mutter.

The police and local newspaper were alerted but we never did get to the bottom of what happened and the stolen goods were never retrieved. The flip-side was that a small piece in the local paper gave us extra publicity for the shows, and probably left the readers wondering what Johnie was going to wear for the show? At least he still had his dungarees!

We were relieved to see a mechanic appear early the next day to fix the gears and weld a piece in the engine, although we were still unable to lock the vehicle.

The swift repair meant we were only slightly late for the two back-to-back morning shows.

Some volunteers from a Camin Spital in Ungureni met us at the ROT offices and guided us to their institute for what turned out to be a rather disorderly show with a wide stage area. The audience was of many levels of disabilities with lots of very handicapped children in wheelchairs. What struck me were their legs: they were so thin they resembled spider legs. This was probably from being cooped up in cots all their lives until recently. Some of the children would have just sensed the colour and music, while others followed the story from start to finish and didn't miss a moment of Johnie's and our comedy. The sparkling eyes and giggles rose above the din and Bob stood on a chair to play guitar to enable the vast audience to see and hear him.

That night we had a rare opportunity to further share our goals with a group of students at an English language evening class. We wanted to convey how simple it was to stimulate the children in the orphanages and we asked them if they would one day do the same? Johnie was in his element clowning away in English with an audience who understood.

We had utilised every moment of that day from start to finish and exhausted, slept soundly.

We needed the rest in preparation for the high energy show in the packed Puppet Theatre. It was wonderful to be on the stage with such a wildly responsive audience. The chase of the animals went through the seated audience, which they loved, and we were happy to receive flowers at the end of the show. We met with the local actors afterwards and they had loved it too!

We would meet up later with some of them but for now we had to rush on to the next performance in a rather modern housing project. Here we could see that foreign assistance had enabled this institute to replace its older building with very modern homes with UK designs. The foreign assistance here enabled a whole other standard of living; we almost could have imagined we were in England rather than Romania.

That evening we were invited back to one of the puppeteers/actors' family apartments. His name was Puiu and he was a tall lanky chap in his thirties. He and his father both shared a passion for puppets, although Puiu explained that under communism he hadn't been able to pursue this as a career. With his father employed by the theatre, Ceausescu's regime didn't allow for a son to master this craft as that would have given the family too much power. For this reason it was only with the fall of Ceausescu that Puiu had been able to pursue this pathway. It was amazing to see the love of puppets that they shared and to meet Puiu's wife and young son, who also shared this passion. They proudly showed us their home-made puppets. It made me aware of the freedom to choose our own pathway that we took for granted in our society.

The rest of the week took us elsewhere, including the Moldovan border village of Falciu. There we performed for young kindergarten children in a lovely family-type atmosphere. Most of the little children seemed to be wearing little sweatshirts with the initial J on them, although in many different colours. Had some warehouse not managed to sell this particular letter and shipped the sweatshirts off to Romania; maybe there was some other significance?

Another Camin Spital, similar to Ionaseni, beckoned us in Giurcani. There was a lovely atmosphere, such as in Ionaseni, and we were invited to eat with the children afterwards as a 'thank you' for the show. There was huge excitement in the canteen with us being international guests, and Johnie got the children to tap in unison on the tables with their cutlery while we waited for our supper. I'm sure they wouldn't normally get away with this, but with a clown in town this was 'acceptable' and taken in good humour.

The cabbage broth with noodles was actually quite tasty.

It was Friday evening and with a 24-hour gap in the itinerary we decided to take a break from the orphanages and drive to the beautiful city of Iasi. This second-largest city of Romania had once been the capital of the principality of Moldavia (1564-1859). It was the capital of Romania for a much shorter period during WW1 (1916-1918). I remembered this grand cultural city from previous visits and we were astonished to find that the grand Hotel of Traian was not as expensive as it looked. It had been built by the famous Gustave Eiffel in 1882, giving it a certain French feel. It was on the main Unirii Square in the centre of the city.

The rooms were very spacious and elegant with tall ceilings, large windows, balconies and classical furniture including four-posted beds.

We really felt like kings as we dined that evening in the restaurant; Bob even ordered champagne to celebrate. It was a far cry from my last experience drinking Moldovan sparkling wine in the wee hours of the night at the border's train station with a few friendly black-marketeers just under a year earlier, or sleeping cosily in the van with no room to move.

The breakfast was also a treat and with a sunny day to top it all off we were able to sit on the terrace in the morning sun and catch up on writing postcards and our diaries. What a luxury for us to have some 'free' time and such a comfortable sleep.

The Sunday show back at the Puppet Theatre in Bacau topped the week off nicely. There was just one more show in the area in Buhusi at a dystrophic ward. We were welcomed by Sally (UK), two volunteers, local staff and 35 young shaven children. Once again Caroline was bitten by one of the residents, although admittedly a child this time. There was some mild panic, when we realised that 75% of the ward were HIV+. Her wound was bathed with disinfectant and fortunately our alarm was no more than that.

As we left the Bacau area we bade farewell to our translator Marina, The Romanian Orphanage Trust and our dear friend Puiu and family. It was raining as I drove towards Nicoresti. There was a nice warm welcome from an Irish co-ordinator named Jean. We would base ourselves here for the rest of the action-packed week.

Next we drove south to the big city of Bucharest. We had meant to connect with TROT but it was late so we ended up resorting to EquiLibre for accommodation rather than staying in the van. I remembered where they were and fortunately their cook remembered me from the previous year. We dined to our content, before being shown back to the peaceful 'maison de passage' to sleep. We seemed to be the only ones staying for now. The following morning, the co-ordinator and his wife, who also remembered our group from the bus visit, confirmed that we were welcome to stay in return for a small fee. This was a relief, as here we were comfortable and extremely well fed.

It was June 1st and we had a mid-morning meeting at The Romanian Orphanage Trust's offices. We were informed that it was International Children's Day and were asked to perform on the steps of the Athenaeum (concert hall in the centre of Bucharest) alongside various other acts to mark this occasion. Just as well we thrived on being spontaneous as this seemed quite a big deal.

The stage was set before the domed, circular building with its Greek-styled pillars out front. This building was recognised as a symbol of Romanian culture, and there we were outside it with banners 'Pentru Copii Nostri' (For Our Children) advertising The Romanian Trust's slogan. There was a giant inflatable Pepsi can to attract attention. There wasn't much advertising of this nature in the country yet, so this was a huge contrast with what we had seen thus far.

First up were midgets from Moscow posing as the Seven Dwarves, followed by a 'pathetic' fire-eater (according to Johnie) and then a TV presenter with some games for children. We were the final act and

'Rebel' truck on convoy.

Bananas 4 Split show with Simone, Johnie, and Caroline. Croatian coast, 1993.

Juggling scarves. Refugee centre in a hotel on Croatian coast. Johnie and Victor.

Child after show with face painted. Obonjan Island, Croatia.

Relaxing over a pint in London: Penny, Simone, Pip, Meni and Christophe's eye.

Allan and Christopher in the London office.

Leaving London from Charlie's Yard. The bus and many Serious Road Trippers. (Bananas Split II, 1994)

Passing through Luxembourg. Simone snatching a moment with her sister, Ingrid.

Riding on top
up front.
Christopher,
Simone,
Raphaelle and
Paul B.

'Tessa' the Land Rover
at Tessa and Wolfie's in
Bavaria, with
Christopher and Jerry,
1994.

Drivers and
clowns, Allan and
Yoyo, with
Bananas 4 Split II
bus in Croatia.

Sveti Kajo,
refugee camp in Croatia.
Bananas 4 Split II.
Sniejana, Yoyo, Mirella
and Paul B.

Yoyo's Velcro hat trick.

Allan flies over chair backwards for show.

Child attempting to juggle splats. Paul B., Christophe and Yoyo. Croatia, 1994.

Bus in East Mostar, Bosnia.

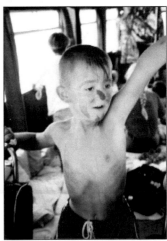

Fun on the bus.

Graves in East
Mostar garden,
1994.

Children in
East Mostar.

The Serious Road Trip
office in Unis Tower, Sarajevo,
Bosnia.

Filling water containers,
East Mostar.

Outside the office in Sarajevo, near Holiday Inn. Trucks: 'Jabba' and 'Meni-Mog'.

The Serious Road Trip convoy at Gorni Vakuf, Bosnia, 1994.

Convoy in Bosnia. Tony G. and Vince.

Handing out
chocolate,
medical supplies
and crutches in
Zenica, Bosnia.
Roger and Tony.

Clowning in
Mostar, Bosnia.
(Christophe,
Paul Brett and
Simone.

Face-painting in
Mostar.
Simone in
spiky hat.

Simone during tour in Mostar, Bosnia. Without face-paints for a change, 1994.

In the bus with everyone blowing up balloons. Paul, Anna, Pinkerton, Trevor, Pierre, Graeme.

From top left: Paul B, Phil, Roger, Pierre, Christophe, Tony, John P, Trevor, Mike, David, Simone, Peter S, Christopher, Graeme. On 'Tessa' the Land Rover.

proceeded to steal the show, getting everyone up dancing at the end. I remember my heart had been pounding; I had to step up to the microphone as the narrator for our story in Romanian, before entering the stage as the cat. Thanks to Johnie being Johnie, it was a total success and to add to the excitement Television Romania was there and Caroline and I ended up being on National News that night.

We even got invited to attend a Beethoven music performance there later in the week. What an opportunity.

TROT was very happy with how it all went and wanted to discuss a performance on Saturday in the big park in town. They would also help with visa extensions through the Ministry of Health, which was a relief: our 3-month limit was soon to expire. While Caroline and I worked on this, Bob went off with someone to try and sort out the gears and brakes of our trusty combi. What a juggling act it all was with sorting out paperwork, permissions for shows and co-ordination of itinerary, fixing our vehicle, finding petrol or food and lodgings wherever we went. Bob was outraged when he was ripped off by a street hustler while changing some of his own dollars into local currency, but I guess he was an easy target. Meanwhile Caroline was always finding it hard to change the traveller's cheques she had brought from Ireland. It was never worth changing too many at once either.

The next big show that day was at Orphanage number 1 where Michael Jackson had made his mark with a beautiful playground for the children. As part of his 'Dangerous World Tour' he had performed in Bucharest on October 1st the year before, in 1992, just a couple of months after our first show. It was sponsored by Pepsi-Cola and all profits from the tour were donated to various charities including his 'Heal the World Foundation'. He too had been moved by the plight of the orphans and this amazing playground was certainly a big gesture and his concert had undoubtedly put Bucharest on the world stage.

We didn't have the same superstar status but did have a brilliant response. One of the climbing structures provided an interesting stage for Bob to sing from whilst some of the little toddlers tried to climb up to see him.

We celebrated that evening over a meal with the French staff at EquiLibre's canteen. They explained that there were now only 13 staff compared to the hundreds from the year before. Their huge plumbing project throughout the many orphanages had come to an end and the needs had also changed. I guess the needs of Bosnia had also attracted a fair bit of attention and funding.

f

We thoroughly enjoyed hearing Romania's world renowned pianist, Dan Grigore, play Beethoven at a superb concert in the amazing Athenaeum, with its ornately decorated dome ceiling. He was amazing to hear and with it being a full house, we were happy that they had managed to squeeze us in behind the violin section. What a wonderful opportunity. Such a contrast from our daily activity… especially when you think we were entertaining children with Aids (and HIV+) at the Victor Babes and Colentino hospitals the following day.

We just couldn't understand how so many children had developed Aids. It was explained to us that when administering antibiotics to children in orphanages, the staff had been reusing dirty needles. We were extremely saddened that these children's futures had been blighted by this lack of knowledge and supply of needles. To think that by treating a routine illness, they had contracted something far more serious.

The big show in the Herostrou Park for The Romanian Orphanage Trust was similar to our earlier one with the same giant Pepsi-cola can and banners advertising 'Pentru Copii Nostri'. This time, however, there were very rudimentary Michael Jackson lookalikes along with the same pitiful fire-eater. Being a professional clown, Johnie had an eye for all this. Various student groups performed, there were games such as sack races, and our show was saved for the finale so the event finished on a high note. Johnie had a way of really building the audience up to a fevered crescendo.

The director of TROT, Jeremy, was most impressed, and invited us to dinner at a fancy restaurant 'Premiere' behind the theatre.

I remember him asking Caroline and myself if we were involved with TIE back in the UK. We didn't know what he meant, but when he explained it stood for Theatre in Education it seemed to make sense that we could have been. 'No, no,' we explained that we just wanted to make a difference to the children's lives and change attitudes towards disability. Our show was for everyone, neither of us was involved in theatre back home, although Johnie was a professional performer. I explained how the show had been developed almost by accident the previous year when visiting with our bus.

The week included shows in various orphanages in and out of Bucharest as well as one in a park for the street children and any other passers-by.

Here I finally managed to catch up with Vali from the year before who was pleased to see us again, although we didn't manage to see the children from the previous year. I was able to explain all that had gone on since we last met. He thought he had seen us drive off into the sunset on our way to NZ!

After almost two weeks in the capital it was time to say farewell to Bucharest, and in typical style, as we were about to leave, the van gears went. Somehow we needed to find a screwdriver to accomplish some mechanical manoeuvre and, by a stroke of luck, Caroline produced some toy key-ring screwdriver that was just the right size to do it. Talk about lucky.

We were on our way to the last shows of our itinerary near the border with Bulgaria on the Black Sea and planned to spend the weekend there catching up with a contact from TROT. After driving to Constanta we then made our way towards the border town to discover that our friend had not come after all.

We were so close, however, so we walked up to the invisible border with Bulgaria and joked about the fact that we had one foot in Romanian sand and one in Bulgarian sand and no need for our passports as there was seemingly no border patrol on the beach.

We found a suitable spot nearby and decided that we might as well sleep on the beach under the stars. How idyllic it all seemed.

Of course the reality was NOT. There were all sorts of mini-beasts pestering us all night and we awoke after very little sleep to the many noises outside such as tractors, donkeys, those too familiar roosters, the sun and, of course, loads more beasties. We headed for the water, also pestered by insects, only to discover that the water was bitterly cold. I'm not sure the 'perfect' resting spot had been worth it after all.

We ventured further up the coast to the port of Mangalia, and the seaside resorts of Neptune and Jupiter. We were relieved there were no insects and the water was marginally warmer, but still cold. I guess we had been hoping for a mini summer break, but it was still only early June.

After a round of crazy mini golf for a laugh we found some nice but cheap accommodation in the Jupiter area near the water. But what we saved on the rooms, they made up for by overcharging us at dinner.

Monday morning we drove back to the border area to Negru Voda where we were welcome to stay with the volunteers. They lived in rather cramped quarters, but still managed to find space for us that night.

The afternoon was devoted to working with little children who were severely disabled. The dining room provided us with space to get out our balloons, music, juggling balls and scarves. The highlight was the blanket rides we managed to give each child. This required two adults holding the corners of each end of a blanket and an excited child to be carried or swung, almost as if it were a mobile hammock. I wish we had thought of this activity earlier! There were so many children we'd previously entertained that would have loved it too.

123

The following day we performed three successful shows in the area and were pleased to rest that evening with the volunteers for company.

The final show was in Constanza the next day in the hospital where there was an Aids ward. There were many children as well as their mothers present. The main difference for this finale, was that Caroline and I swapped roles. What a change it made to be the mouse instead of the cat! It seemed to give us the final surge of energy we needed.

We were ready to collapse after our intense tour and needed a few days' break before the return journey. We made our way back to Jupiter, checked into the same Mercury Hotel and slept like babes.

We were keen to map out our return journey before truly relaxing on the beach and were excited when it looked like we would indeed travel via Ionaseni.

The clouds did not co-operate and hung tightly above the beach, so although we looked forward to our beach day, it ended up more of a beach walk.

The next day was not much better, with a clap of thunder greeting us as we arrived on the beach. We only just got back to the hotel in the nick of time before the heavens opened. This didn't stop us swimming in the warm hotel pool under the pelting rain, until lightning struck particularly close by, frightening us to shelter inside. It was an electrical storm and we watched in awe as the intense lightning lit up the entire area and glistened on the water of the Black Sea. Meanwhile the rain was relentless. There was something relaxing about listening to the sound of rain on the roof, but not only that: This was a thermal area and the familiar smell of hydrogen sulphide or 'rotten eggs' permeated our senses. I had grown up in Rotorua (NZ), also known as Sulphur City or Rotten-rua, famous for the mud-pools, geysers and hot springs, and this smell made me feel almost at home. Not so for the others, however. Something about the rain made the pungent smell more intense.

The rain cleared by the following day so we made a beeline for the beach. The swimming may have been brilliant at last, but with the sun only making a few entrances from behind the clouds, we felt we needed to stay just one more day in the hope of glorious sunshine.

We were not disappointed. By now it was Sunday and the sun was here at last.

We truly relaxed on the beach, basking in the sun. The warmth seemed to wipe away the aches and stresses of the tour. Of course, that didn't stop the jelly fish from arriving and making swimming not quite so enjoyable!

The departure the following morning wouldn't have been complete without some vehicle delay and the combi did not disappoint us. This time it was a flat tyre.

Once we were on the road we made our way through the Danube Delta area in the soaring heat. The drive was extremely hard, with more horses and carts than we had experienced further north, as well as general traffic.

We broke the journey by staying in Nicoresti before making our way up north. After a close shave with a truck, we were relieved to get back into the familiar territory around Ionaseni. We arrived there in good time to surprise everyone and had a flat tyre on arrival.

It was lovely to see everyone again and hear their news. Costel was just back from a training trip to England. Andy was celebrating his birthday that Thursday and we were all invited to the surprise party. Rupert had just returned from a trip to Croatia and had seen The Serious Road Trip crew down there. He was most impressed with our work and was convinced we would be needed there. We rang the office to let them know our whereabouts and I heard that my sister Ingrid had arrived in Europe. This was big news for me.

We tried to ring the Croatian base to suss out the possibilities, but were unsuccessful after two hours of trying. There was a small glimmer of seeing Moona again after all, but it was not meant to be. Our energies couldn't have lasted another big project just yet anyway.

There were a few mad days of joyful reunions with various local friends and volunteers as well as Andy's late night birthday surprise. Johnie's Brian Melley did an amazing presentation to him with a hilarious 'Ode to Andy' before we crawled into our sleeping bags at 3.30am.

Back at Ionaseni, we visited the children and feasted at Rodica's and Mama Puiu's.

This time I left without saying a goodbye to the children. It was too sad; I had already done this enough times.

We distributed some of the supplies that we didn't need any more as well as a few presents and then it really was time to head back to the UK.

There were a few mishaps along the way such as queuing for ages to get petrol in Bistrita (Romania) and a spectacular puncture on the German motorway.

It was exciting to meet up with my sister in Luxembourg and scoop her up into the van for the final leg of the journey. She donned Johnie's straw hat and with a big smile on her face, seemed to slot right in to the jubilant atmosphere of our little troupe.

While it was sad saying goodbye to the group in London, I was pleased to have my little sister around. Ingrid had studied French like myself and was keen to use this language. She felt drawn to working with children and set about finding an 'au pair' job in France. Having cystic fibrosis, her health wasn't suited to the ups and downs of The Serious Road Trip projects and coming to Europe was already a feat in itself. She ended up landing a job in Grenoble caring for two little ones.

Chapter 13

London
– Croatia Beckons

The office was busy with a new project, one that captured my heart as well. The Anne Frank Educational Trust in conjunction with The Serious Road Trip, had launched an appeal for letters from school children to be sent to the children of Bosnia. The inspiration for this appeal was drawn from letters sent by schoolchildren in Zenica, Bosnia to the Anne Frank House in Amsterdam. The children asked not to be forgotten, comparing their situation with that of the tragic wartime diarist, Anne Frank, who had to hide from Nazi persecution and later died in a concentration camp. This story had really moved me as a child and my parents had even taken me to her house in Amsterdam. My brother (eight) had fainted there, when confronted with some horrific photos of the camps. Now our office was swamped with thousands of letters and a truck was organised to take the letters overland. The truck had left, but the letters kept rolling in.

On top of this, the charity sharing premises with us, War Child, were teaming up to send a portable bakery to Bosnia.

Their logo included a photo of a tragic child victim of the war. Suffering was written all over the child's face. I knew this image would pull at the emotions and bring in the necessary funds, but I much preferred our image of an exciting magic double-decker bus coming towards you from around the world. The energy evoked in this image said it all to me and would keep things positive for the children

127

at the other end, where life was desperate enough as it was, without having the look of misery rubbed in your face.

The U2 Zooropa tour was also occupying our minds, since an American journalist, Bill Carter, had joined The Serious Road Trip for a few months and had established various contacts with key people we knew at the television station in Sarajevo. He'd come up with an original idea and had persisted in trying to link up with the band on their tour of Europe. U2 had been taken by what was happening in Bosnia and had hatched a wild plan to raise awareness of the plight there. Their live link-ups by satellite phone with the war-torn capital while on tour, had thrown light onto the plight of the people of Bosnia and in particular Sarajevo.

U2 were performing at Wembley Arena and had offered a few free tickets to The Serious Road Trip. A small group of us were going and were rather excited as under normal circumstances this was a luxury we could barely afford. I was thankful for some female company amidst the convoy and regular office trippers. Carine Mandere, a young French journalist who had covered our story when the original bus had passed through Orleans in France, was in London. It was good to rekindle the friendship and enjoy the concert together, although the huge sea of people and the music is somewhat of a blur.

What I remember most about that time is that within hours of arriving in our midst Carine had learnt to juggle, which gave me good reason to give it a proper go. After all, I had been with The Serious Road Trip a couple of years by this stage. I had been envious of all the others juggling, but I still hadn't put in the proper effort to learn myself. To think that someone had just picked it up that quickly in a matter of hours. I was determined to do the same and much to my surprise I progressed quickly from one ball, to two balls then three. It was important to get the technique of passing the ball from one hand to the other in an arch-like motion in order to succeed before adding a second then third ball. Once I had semi-mastered the basics after a couple of days persevering, it felt like I had overcome a major hurdle. Now I felt ready to face more!

Christophe had heard of our successful clowning tour and persuaded me that the children in the refugee camps around Split (Croatia) needed our shows too. 'Don't worry,' he reassured me, 'It's much safer than you imagine.' We didn't need to venture into Bosnia, like the trucks, to bring a smile to the thousands of refugees that were housed in hotels and barracks, all over the coast of Croatia.

We had just finished writing a report of the project and were still catching our breath from the intense three months in Romania. After a

128

good discussion with the team, it sounded like we were all up for it. Even Johnie and Caroline's fundraising companion, Kennedy, set out to help with pub quizzes in Ireland once again. There was not a minute to lose as we had less than two months till a possible start date and we needed to get there before the colder weather set in.

And so the 'Bananas 4 Split' tour was born.

The name came up as a natural response to the city named Split. What a funny name for a city we thought. Somehow bananas seemed to be the word to go with Split and conjured up happy memories of a tasty treat. Besides, bananas were as good for you as the humour and energy that the clowns would bring to the fun-starved children.

At this stage, I don't think I was conscious of the children's television programme that had screened in the 70s, featuring the Banana Splits, but in any case we were onto something as the name seemed to be so apt.

I wrote to a children's group named Sunsocret, based in Zagreb, working with children in refugee centres, to tell them of our intentions. They were very enthusiastic about our project. They said they could tell we were an organisation that really wanted to do something for the children. Our 'Bananas 4 Split' name said it all.

Bob then announced that he was no longer able to come. He had a new life with a job, a girlfriend and a new flat. Things were going so well for him now; he felt he had too much to lose by going away again. But what were we to do without our 'music man' and driver? It was a blow, but we felt sure the right person must be out there. And so the search for a guitar-playing driver began... the word went out in Ireland and the UK.

Hallelujah, shortly afterwards, Johnie and Caroline seemed to find the perfect match. He was from Ireland and was up for the trip. And so Victor joined our tight-knit group. On top of his entertaining skills he was a photographer and journalist and was keen to embrace a very enticing opportunity to document the high-profile war crisis. How perfect for us! Or so it seemed.

Amidst all the preparations for our tour, fresh images of the situation in Bosnia emerged. They showed thousands of Bosnian Muslim men behind barbed wire fences. Many were poorly clothed; you could see gaunt bony faces and torsos. 'Surely not in this day and age,' I gasped. The faces of these men from the Omarska and Trnopolje concentration camps were haunting images, reminiscent of the camps during the Holocaust. I knew there was a war happening, but I had not imagined this type of scenario could ever be possible again.

As a youngster I had devoured stories about the WWII holocaust and in my teens I had even visited the concentration camp in Dachau, as part of a German government PAD (Pedagogical Exchange Services) student scholarship to visit Germany. For five weeks I had travelled with 80 students from all around the world. I could still recall the poignant International Monument in Dachau. It consisted of a giant bronze sculpture showing barbed wire hands, on which skeletons are hanging with their heads dangling sharply. It symbolised the emaciated bodies of the prisoners who died of starvation and disease in the camp 1933-1945. The monument was designed by Nandor Glid, ironically a Yugoslavian artist whose parents had died at Auschwitz. The monument and museum served as a reminder of what had happened during WWII and the poignant words 'Never Again' had been translated into five different languages and inscribed on a wall nearby.

I couldn't believe that such an atrocity could ever occur again, but here was proof in the world's news that such barbarism was actually happening less than 50 years later, in the backyard of Europe. It was heart-wrenching stuff and I was extremely moved. I certainly hoped we would not be venturing into such areas.

After many quizzes, raffles, sponsored activities and pleas for sponsorship and donations we had most of the funds needed and were raring to go from London. We found a fresh supply of face-paints, balloons and juggling balls from More Balls Than Most. The combi van had had a full service, thanks to my mechanical cousin Grant. The costumes from Romania were revived and Johnie had a few new props. Midge, an artist we knew from London, had started a new design for our van; it looked slicker than the spray-painted decorations hastily done for Romania. Midge used bright red, yellow and green stripes and enormous yellow bananas with The Serious Road Trip logo in the centre. While we were not travelling in the red bus any more, we were still very proud of our original vehicle and the movement and energy the logo embodied. On the other side he sketched the outline of Tom and Jerry which we would have to colour-in later. Midge had been responsible for decorating various trucks as well.

The paperwork and passports were ready and Christophe was eagerly awaiting us at the other end, along with the many children crammed into refugee camps and centres all along the coast of Croatia.

Chapter 14

Bananas 4 Split Tour
(1993)

The local media covered our departure for Dover. We made our way to the ever-generous friends in Luxembourg, enjoying a stopover to see friends (notably Cynthia, Susan and Chris) from my days in the financial services, and do some last-minute fundraising at old haunts such as the White Rose and The Harp.

We also made a stop in Bavaria in Übersee am Chiemsee to stay with our friends Tessa, Wolfgang and family. A Land Rover had even been named after Tessa, such was her importance. Her mother and uncle being escapees of the Nazis as children, she was a huge supporter of our endeavours. She also provided shelter, food and some paid work to the various 'lost souls' that found their way to their huge home.

We had been told to head to Rijeka in Croatia and then to take the ferry to Split, since the road along the coast had become rather dangerous. Not quite as safe as I was hoping after all. I did an internal gulp.

That night we boarded the enormous ferry with hundreds of other passengers, lost in the giant boat crammed full of people. Our feet and wheels were not firmly on the ground. The ferry rose with the waves of the Adriatic Sea as we travelled through the darkness towards a war zone.

What could we expect at the other end?

My thoughts drifted... it had been a long time since I had been in this part of the world and here I was heading back in a similar vehicle, but under different circumstances of course. Back in 1977, my parents had

131

embarked for several months on a European working holiday from NZ with their four children in a blue VW campervan. My mother and father were intrigued enough about how it would be on the other side of the Iron Curtain that they had chosen to visit Yugoslavia. We had even ventured as far as Belgrade to collect some letters from NZ via the American Express Poste Restante service. I remember many pot-holed roads and the vehicle shuddering along on roads that really were not of the standard we were used to. My biggest memory, however, was staying in a camp-ground north of Rijeka. The beach was of rounded pebbles rather than the sand I was used to in New Zealand. It was here that we almost lost my father in rather strange circumstances. Camping in one place for the week, we had befriended a German/Japanese family and their children. They had a rather modern inflatable boat, with a mast for sailing and we had enjoyed various outings at sea in the glorious summer sunshine. Then one day, they decided to make a day trip inland, and asked us to keep an eye on the boat, moored with another similar boat. That day the weather changed dramatically, as it was prone to along this coast. The wind whipped up rather abruptly and all of a sudden dark clouds merged ominously above. A retired German man approached my dad and pointed to the two yellow boats, bobbing upside down at the water's edge. He didn't speak English, but it was clear that he was motioning my father to come and help bring the boats to safety. They hurried down, wearing not much more than swimming trunks, waded a few metres to the boats, turned them over with difficulty, pulled up the anchor and set about rowing them ashore. This was to prove a seriously naive move as the masts had been holding them in place and no sooner had they freed the boats, than the strong wind caught hold of the light boats. At top speed they were blown out to sea with such great force that no rowing could ever counteract this mighty wind.

Within a few short minutes we could barely see the yellow dots, bobbing dangerously on the waves of the Adriatic. How could they ever get back? What were we to do? How desperate my mother must have felt with four young children, seeing my father slipping out of sight. The wife of the German was panicking, but made her way quickly down to the Harbour to see what could be done. She alerted the authorities, but the Harbour Master said they would not venture out to sea to rescue some foreign 'joy-riders'. We paced along a pathway overlooking the sea, trying to see if we could catch any glimpse of them, but to no avail. It was useless, they were lost at sea and the storm looked like it was intensifying. The only thing I felt I could do was pray with all my might. I was too young to lose my father; my youngest sister was only three.

We waited and waited, wondering about what might happen. The German's wife returned again to plead with the authorities, but they said it was too dangerous to set off and, in fact, anyone who did so would be breaking the law!

Meanwhile, out at sea, my father and the German, neither speaking the same language, were clinging to each other for warmth as the cold wind and seas battered them relentlessly. Neither was wearing a life-jacket and they had lost sight of the shore a long time before. By this stage they were starting to suffer from hypothermia. They were certain that these were their final moments and were saying their final prayers, when almost by miracle a tiny fishing boat approached them with a little old fisherman and a companion aboard.

They were helped aboard the tiny boat, where they were wrapped in warm blankets. The little fishing boat battled against the winds of the storm to bring them all back to safety; even dragging the two yellow inflatables with them.

Back on shore you can imagine our relief on their safe return. We were invited back to the German's caravan to drink Schnapps and warm up. Once again, we found ourselves unable to converse much, but somehow the essential stuff was communicated. They were both extremely lucky to be alive. This had been a very close shave. To think they had almost lost their lives in their attempt to save the boats.

This did not stop the Harbour Police wanting to cross-question them both the following day for their involvement in breaking the law, but as for the little old fisherman and friend, they had just disappeared into thin air, no one knowing where they had come from or where they had gone.

Fairly traumatised from this near-death experience, my father was not up to facing police questioning in a foreign land and in a foreign language. Instead, the owner of the boat had returned and would speak on his behalf.

With the carefree sunny weather over, we packed up camp and carried on with our journey, back towards the more familiar West.

So here I was again on that same Adriatic coast-line for a second time, with much uncertainty ahead. Had it not been for that little old fisherman, maybe my life would have taken a different turn. Had it not been for the German wife communicating in German or Croatian with the locals, our plea for help might not have been heard. Maybe on some level I was here to repay that fisherman's good turn and bring some laughter to children and their families in their time of great need.

In any case I had not set out with this intense desire to travel to a war zone. Far from it, I had tried to avoid it. It was something that had come up for us and we responded to the situation and needs.

The ferry reached Split harbour as dawn broke to a beautiful, calm and sunny day. How different the world seemed in daylight and how reassuring to find my dear friend Christophe at the other end as we disembarked. He was equally excited to see us. He knew Caroline from her student days in Tours (France), when I was teaching in local schools as an English Assistant Teacher.

He had been piecing together an itinerary for us with the help of UNICEF. There was a long list of refugee centres to visit all along the coast, including on some of the islands.

We made our way along the coast road to Podstrana, where The Serious Road Trip had found accommodation at Magda's Pensione right on the water's edge. Under normal circumstances this whole coast would be brimming with tourists, but now the hotels, pensiones and holiday camps were brimming either with refugees or displaced persons and humanitarians. Right next door there was a small holiday camp overflowing with 30 or more Bosnians who had escaped the horrors of war.

The Serious Road Trip would later park their colourful trucks outside their building between convoys into Bosnia, but for now that space was empty. We had just missed the convoy drivers who had left a day or two before for Sarajevo. We had Christophe to show us the ropes and be our guide. He was eager to check that the trucks had arrived safely in Sarajevo, so while the others rested, we headed over to EquiLibre's headquarters nearby.

This better-equipped NGO had daily radio contact with Sarajevo and could signal whether the SRT convoy had arrived or not. One of their team had even lent our convoy leader, Tony Gaffney, a radio to maintain some contact. Not only had they not seen them arrive in Sarajevo, but there seemed to be no radio contact possible with them at all. We tried not to be too concerned at first, as delays were not unusual in these circumstances. However, our thoughts drifted back to a recent convoy our crew had undertaken that had been ambushed, resulting in three vehicles being stolen by Croatian irregular soldiers. The international team had been lucky to escape with their lives, but the fate of the local guide was uncertain as he had been led down to the river and shots had been fired.

I tried to remain hopeful, but we were in such a volatile environment compared to where we had come from; I didn't really know how to respond. Christophe seemed fairly casual, perhaps because he had been working in this war-zone for a good year now and he had become accustomed to these situations. After his scary time in Sarajevo under siege, this was relatively peaceful. I was not ready for the emotions I felt when I realised how precarious things were for my friends driving convoys into Bosnia. It was stressful to say the least.

We touched base with people from UNICEF, American Refugee Committee, International Federation of the Red Cross, SOS Balkanes, and Suncokret. They helped us contact refugees along the coast. An itinerary of performances at refugee centres had been drafted up for the following week in Split and surrounding areas such as Solin and Stobrec.

Our group naturally met with other humanitarians renting rooms from Magda, including two Austrian women called Jutta and Doris. They were working for a group called MIR and with a different type of refugee: the mentally and physically handicapped people from a centre that had been evacuated in Croatia. We were familiar with the institutions in Romania and the stressful situations, but Jutta, Doris and their team were dealing with the added dimension of their charges being refugees. We felt compelled to do something, so we set about slotting in some light relief for these people. We performed our first event at the Zavod Vrilika Institute for handicapped refugees, and at the similar Juraj Bonaci Institute the next day in Split.

Johnie's slapstick humour went down a treat as per usual and it was a relief that we met with the same smiles and giggles. Once again I donned my yellow/orange shirt and cat/tiger face-paint and Caroline made an endearing pink mouse. Christophe made a great yapping dog and our new driver, Victor, made a very hairy bearded monster. The story of the old man who loses his last piece of bread to the hungry mouse, then cat, followed by the dog endured and we all had to learn the different noises for our various animals. Mine was simple as Miouw seemed to be universal, but the mouse made a 'Mis' sound and the dog a 'Vau' noise in Serbo-Croat.

Meanwhile we were starting to get rather anxious about our friends driving the yellow Bedford trucks into Sarajevo. Christophe and I touched base through the radio contact at EquiLibre, and still there was no news. It seemed as though the trucks had disappeared into thin air. Christophe even went to the UN briefings that took place in Split each morning to see if any of the organisations there had seen or heard of their whereabouts. The trucks were seriously conspicuous, being bright yellow and emblazoned with cartoon figures, and yet no one seemed to know where they were. Had they been kidnapped and would we be expected to pay some ransom beyond our means, or had they met a more serious fate? By now even Christophe was so worried that we stayed up all night with two EquiLibre friends waiting for news by the radio.

We also heard how Split might be about to be bombed and I was thankful that our base was a little further out of town in Podstrana.

Finally we got an answer regarding the convoy. Someone from the British Battalion had seen them in the small town of Kiseljak, some 35 km from Sarajevo. They were alive, which was an enormous relief. We later found out that they had been held up getting permission from the Serbs to travel into Sarajevo. This usually meant that they had to negotiate giving a portion of their aid to them. Of course, there were other issues that had arisen on that convoy, but for now our minds were put to rest.

Not far from Magda's pensione, we were reminded that Scottish European Aid also had their base there and Moona was spearheading that mission in Bosnia. My heart was beating wildly, wondering how it would be to see him again after our parting in Ireland. I heard he had visited London while I was there, yet he hadn't managed to touch base then. I didn't hold much hope. After all, I had travelled from Romania to Scotland and he hadn't managed to find his way across London. Yet the optimist within wondered if a new scenario might bring a happy reunion.

I walked along the footpath next to the Adriatic's edge in the direction of SEA and the water lapped against the concrete, as I came closer to finding out with every step I took. It was almost a year since we had seen each other and I had found myself daydreaming about our happy times in Romania…

What a relief to see him again and yet he didn't look so happy-go-lucky now. I think he was surprised to see me in this corner of the world, especially as I had only recently been in Romania.

It was wonderful to see his familiar face amidst this new world of turmoil and yet we maintained a certain distance. There seemed to be a mutual attraction of sorts, but his words came tumbling out to the contrary. He explained that he and his translator friend Monica, from Romania, had finally decided to become an official couple. Moona didn't want to hurt anyone further and came clean with his admission that there was no possibility for us now as he was already spoken for.

The truth cut like a knife in my heart, even if I tried to maintain my calm exterior. I didn't hang around for more pain.

Thankfully I was able to join other members of the Scottish team at a nearby Taverna to take my mind off this emotional rupture. A new director of operations from Fife, Mike MacKenzie and an engineering geologist from Dorset, Mathew Stogden had just arrived in preparation to work on a project involving the water supply to some Bosnian cities.

Nan Owen, a lawyer from Norwich, had made her way out here, originally with a Serious Road Trip convoy in the hope of rescuing an orphan, as she longed for a child. She had been on that fateful ambushed convoy, so this plan to adopt hadn't worked, but she had remained here to help in the interim. Luckily she had found herself a place in the office of SEA and there was an instant connection between us. Maybe it was two women searching for love (her a child and me a companion) in a very unlikely place that drew us together. There was so much to share and close bonds were forged quickly in this environment. Life was to be seized with two hands (and a few local wines went down a treat). You never knew what the next day might bring.

Several days later, tragedy struck our small group of humanitarians on this coastline near Split, but for now we were bringing some much needed laughter to the refugees, children and adults alike.

One place we visited was a hotel filled to brimming with so many people. One man saw us arrive and scornfully asked us why we were there. My explanation of our show did not meet with his approval. He had lost his whole family, his wife and children, not to mention his home and country. What was there to laugh or smile about? His life was over as far as he was concerned. His reaction did make me question our role in such dire circumstances, but I asked him to come to the show and see what we had to offer. There was so much the people we met had experienced and lost.

Nonetheless we resolved to fulfil our intention and so our simple but dynamic show took place, with the help of a teacher who narrated our story in Serbo-Croat. With no stage, we sometimes found the children creeping forwards till there was no space for us to perform, so we needed this help from someone local to keep the children seated.

Johnie's success never failed and we managed our small tricks of juggling, skipping and singing. The clown was always the centre of attention. He had learnt the appropriate words for Hello (Zdravo), Thank you (Hvala), What's your name? (Kako se zoves) as well as Water (Voda) and More (Jos) for the various tricks. I just loved it when the crowd would shout 'Jos' (pronounced Yosh) louder and louder as the balloon was blown bigger and bigger until it popped and Johnie would fly backwards over his chair still trying to blow up the remnants of the balloon.

The crowd responded as they usually did, but for a few little children the exploding balloon was sometimes too much. We couldn't help but think they had heard these types of noises before, but not in a safe context. For obvious reasons, Johnie's fire-juggling and knife juggling tricks had been cut from the show early on in the piece as these were too much a reminder of horrific experiences. He had plenty of other tricks to keep us all entertained. One of the favourite tricks was the Banana Split trick where Johnie would karate chop a banana, although the skin would remain intact leaving the crowd to believe his trick had failed. To everyone's amazement though, when he peeled the banana, it revealed that it had indeed been chopped on the inside. How was this possible? Of course we would never disclose how the trick was performed as that was the magic of it all.

But what about the man we had encountered on our arrival, we wondered? Thankfully, curiosity had got the better of him and he had managed to watch the show from behind the main crowd. His face beamed with the most enormous smile showing a few gaps in his teeth, but I could see his eyes sparkling. Our eyes met across the crowd and he seemed to be saying 'thank you'. We had done what had seemed like an impossible task. Somehow our small show and actions had reached him. We cared about the people's plight and even if for just that brief moment, we had provoked a smile in what had seemed like one of Bosnia's destroyed souls. This may have seemed like a drop in a large ocean of needs, but my energy and resolve to continue was even higher now, I was so over the moon, as were the whole team.

Another NGO we were introduced to on our arrival was Premiere Urgence from France. They were well known for their large convoys to Sarajevo under siege and their agency had sprung up at the beginning of the Bosnian conflict. They were a larger organisation than ours, with more funding, plus they had UN accreditation which entitled them to more protection, including armed escorts, and UN bases to shelter at en route. A strong friendship between our two organisations had sprung up and one of their drivers, Yoyo, had even swapped over to join our crew, though we hadn't met him yet. Christophe, being from France, was a natural link and introduced us all.

The fact that Caroline and I spoke French helped communication and everyone warmed to Johnie and his clowning behaviour and blah, blah language. After they saw how versatile he was at fooling everyone and sharing some of the same humour, one of the Premiere Urgence team approached us with a new request. Would we help them fool some new volunteers arriving a few days later? Of course we were up for this new challenge and thought it would provide some light relief for the humanitarians working under extremely stressful conditions.

Mind you, it was going to create some extra stress for two unsuspecting new recruits.

They arrived at Split airport, where they were met by Max, one of the Premiere Urgence drivers. Another of the PU group approached them 'undercover' at the arrivals hall, roughing them up and screaming abuse at them for being gun runners working for Premiere Urgence... They quickly made their way to the car where the radio had been set to create a static noise, as the car sped at top speed to where we all were gathered at Magda's pensione around a table in the courtyard below. At one end of the table was Victor (Guitarist/driver) and Paul Kirwan (our original bus driver, now working for UNICEF but keen to get in on the act) playing the role of Irish mercenaries, poring over a UN map of the Bosnian territory, and plotting their next round of violence. At the other end of the table were Caroline and I and maybe a few others in a highly anxious state. On the arrival of the two newcomers we asked them who they were. 'Oh no!' we exclaimed and explained how dodgy Premiere Urgence were. We reaffirmed that we didn't know who funded them and wondered if they were gunrunners. They were rather surprised to realise that they weren't at the PU Headquarters and we asked how they had come there and why had they volunteered for such an awful organisation. They were unsuspecting and fooled by the ruse.

They pointed up towards where the car was parked with their backpacks inside, but at that moment the car disappeared, speeding off with their luggage aboard. 'Merde', their possessions had been taken, but fortunately their passports were safely tucked in money belts. I started whimpering along with Caroline:

'We're planning to leave as soon as possible! It's so unsafe on the coast, we don't know who to trust and we can't take it any longer!'

They tried to calm themselves with cigarettes, when all of a sudden we heard what sounded like gunfire above us, but it was in fact Johnie popping some balloons in an apartment on the first floor.

We dropped to the ground hiding under the tables; meanwhile someone had turned all the lights out. We urged the newcomers to put out their cigarettes, for fear that the lighted cigarettes would give us away in the darkness; while Caroline and I tried to mask our giggles with exaggerated, frantic cries of fear. We were urged to keep quiet and were ushered into one of the rooms at ground level in an attempt to hide. We waited in fearful silence although we could hear the two new recruits whispering about how they planned to escape on the next ferry if they got out of this situation. Then the door swung open and in came Johnie dressed in black with black face-paint smeared over his face shining a strong torch on us all. He was playing some crazed Croatian irregular soldier, back from his tour of duty and wanting to know who these newcomers were. He tried to bluff it with a few foreign words to make himself sound more authentic and consequently he kept repeating some Romanian words he was more familiar with such as Copii Mici (little children). Johnie demanded passports and they fumbled to get them out of their belts. The torch shone on their faces, then back onto the passport photos. The war-crazed Johnie shook his head and shouted in a few simple words that this wasn't the same person. He demanded to know where was the moustache? The person in question trembled as he explained and motioned that he had shaved his moustache.

And finally our game was over as we couldn't maintain the serious façade. There was such relief on their faces, when we announced they had been fooled. The original welcoming driver, Max, reappeared amidst the laughter and asked them to accompany him to the true PU headquarters.

The story of this 'initiation' set-up inspired all sorts of sequels, such as make-shift sleeping quarters in the middle of their warehouse, made from wooden pallets and basic foam mattresses, appearing like they expected their volunteers to sleep rough in between convoys, through lack of funds.

It was all a little light relief amidst the trauma of real-life war, and all very plausible, especially for The Serious Road Trip living on a shoestring.

By now we had nearly completed our second week of shows and had ventured further down the coast towards Makarska, performing there and in Baska Voda, Tucepi, Podgora and Zivogoscu.

Life in the camps was grim and we met with mothers after the shows. One Sarajevan woman invited us for coffee and then burst into tears as she explained that she hadn't heard from her husband in 15 months. She and many other women in the centres were all in the same boat. Their future was so uncertain.

The long hours driving as well as performing a minimum of two shows a day meant we were fairly exhausted, to say the least, and we had more shows scheduled for the next day.

Our own convoy drivers were still eagerly awaited and after a day of shows in nearby barracks, packed full of refugees or 'internally displaced persons', we were truly exhausted. Everyone decided to retire to their rooms to catch up with energy and with other tasks, such as getting the props and face-paints in order. There were always sponges covered with face paint that needed rinsing and cleaning in preparation for a show, without mentioning holes in costumes to be repaired.

I, on the other hand, felt the need to connect with some other friends and see if there was news of our own convoy. I decided to steer clear of SEA, after the situation with Moona had gone so wrong the week before. Any notion of rekindling an old romance had died a sudden death. For now I wanted to venture up to see Premiere Urgence again. It was getting a little late by this stage, so it was already dark on the fast coastal road above our seaside haven.

Nonetheless, after some deliberation, I took to the wheel of our trusted VW combi and started out alone on the road along the Adriatic. I didn't get very far, maybe a few hundred metres, when I needed to slow down for some reason. I could see a police car ahead blocking the traffic. There was an eerie feeling as I wondered what was going on. The cars started backing up behind me. Before there was no space to turn around, I quickly did a U-turn and returned home. Christophe explained that this was not uncommon on the coastal road and it sounded like I had avoided being stuck in a serious traffic jam that went on to last hours. I collapsed into bed thoroughly exhausted and with not much else to do.

The next morning, we were awoken to hear that a serious accident had happened on the coastal road involving members of Scottish European Aid. Three of the group had been hit by a car that had veered off the road (possibly with the driver falling asleep at the wheel). They had been standing by the entrance to the restaurant we had visited earlier that week. Tragically, Nan, my new-found female friend, had been killed on the spot! How on Earth was this real? Their recently arrived geologist, Mathew, was critically injured and died several hours later in hospital. Meanwhile Mike, their new Director of Operations in Bosnia, was in a very critical condition and it looked like his leg needed to be amputated. He was in a coma and his parents were rushing to be by his side.

How could this be? We were relatively safe near Split and this was an out-of-the-blue road accident. A fourth person, Murray, had witnessed the accident and a French girl, Isabelle was also nearby. They were closer to the restaurant and explained to me some time later, that the victims had been intending to get me and other Road trippers to join them. But why had they stayed on the dangerous coastal road? If only they had used the safer promenade along the water's edge. If only I had gone to see them earlier without worrying about my current romantic rejection. I was plagued with the 'what if' questions that happen in such a tragedy, as if playing the different scenarios over in my head would make it go away somehow.

141

With our busy schedule ahead of us we were unable to be by their side straight away, as we didn't want to let down the children. There were those that questioned whether we could do anything to help anyway in such a situation. Nevertheless, when we finally did manage to venture down to show our support and share in the grief, it was awful to face this grim reality, but they needed the moral support. One moment they were there, the next moment they were gone and the lives of their families in England and Scotland were changed forever. I didn't know how to react in the face of such a black and white situation of life and death but it's amazing how a hug or just being there, can sometimes do more than words hope to achieve. The doctors were doing their best to keep the one survivor alive.

Nan's husband had just been out visiting her the week before. When Moona had made that most difficult early morning phone call to let him know the tragic news, he had almost expected a call from his loved-one unable to sleep. The unbearable tragedy was taking its toll on Moona as he tried to deal with the realities and next-of-kin that needed to be informed. The 'happy-go-lucky', exuberant skateboarding and adrenalin fanatic was taking a serious dip in the roller coaster of life. Isabelle helped support them through this process as she had actually been there, and they all tried to come to terms with this tragedy.

I was most fascinated by her story of how The Serious Road Trip had met her in the middle of Bosnia. There she was hitch-hiking a ride back to Croatia, when they were refuelling somewhere. She had arrived in Bosnia with a British group and had somehow ended up staying in the middle of the war zone for nine months helping various refugees including a pregnant woman? How brave she appeared to me. The Road Trip had magically appeared to help her escape the ethnic cleansing that was taking place in the area she had been based in.

Almost in answer to our prayers, as the timing couldn't have been better, our convoy finally arrived back from their lengthy trip to Sarajevo. They too were upset to hear about the loss of Nan and two others, ironically in the relative safety of the Split area.

To think I had feared we had lost them on convoy, but here they were safe and sound at last. It felt more secure having them there, rather than being in our smaller group trying to deal with very new and stressful situations 'alone'.

They explained how they had to wait to get permission from the Serbs to enter Sarajevo and this was a time-consuming negotiating process. Then they took a good week to deliver the aid personally to various centres and families. This personal connection with the people they helped was just as valuable as the supplies they brought and ensured the goods didn't end up on the black market. When they came to leave there had been fighting on the airport road, where you exit Sarajevo, so it had taken much longer than normal. It all sounded like part of the 'normal' reality of operating in a war zone and they couldn't quite understand how much torment their dropping from sight had created. I guess the same went for our families in NZ and Europe, but I didn't quite see it from this perspective at that time.

Far from being happy reunions with our friends and fellow Road Trippers, although for some this was the case, there were others that did not know us from London and did not welcome our arrival on 'their turf'. An American in our group, Josh, who reminded me of a big soft teddy bear, told me that we didn't understand what it was like in Sarajevo. We hadn't seen the death and bloodshed in the aftermath of a mortar in Sarajevo. We hadn't experienced the glazed look of starving citizens in Sarajevo trying to dodge sniper fire whilst rushing with water containers to some form of safety. We hadn't had to dodge bullets ourselves or deal with the thought that any moment could be our last.

Rather than withdrawing at these 'accusations' of things we hadn't experienced, I found myself gaining strength and rebuking him.

'Thank God I haven't experienced these things,' I retorted, as this allowed me to be there in a different capacity, bringing our colourful project to the children. 'Thank God I am not plagued with images of bloodshed.'

I had even been spared the horror of witnessing Nan's accident. Although surrounded by the psychological horrors created by a war zone, at least I didn't have the direct experience of living through what they had seen.

Already it felt as though I had faced some major challenge, getting as far as the coast of Croatia, without the added danger of dodging bullets, mines and mortars. Besides, the convoys were taking critical supplies into Sarajevo at a time when people were starving and so the risks seemed to be justified. The supplies meant the difference between life and death for some people. Our clowning shows were focused on refugee centres, some of which had been luxury hotels, although some were more like barracks, or even tents. While we saw the scars of war and the overcrowded living conditions, life was not as precarious. Although the refugees' futures were extremely uncertain, basic food and shelter were being supplied. There, it felt that our clowning shows were more appropriate.

Maybe this was the fact with which some of the convoy drivers were grappling. Our goals seemed slightly different, although it was an integral part of who we were. The convoys had colourful trucks emblazoned with cartoon characters such as Felix the cat and Daffy Duck; also part of our travelling clowning show. We wouldn't be there if it were not for their actions in Bosnia, and they wouldn't be there if it were not for the actions of the original team on the bus, including myself, which led to going on the Peace convoy to Sarajevo in June the year before.

There was also the initial rejection of Serious Road Trip women in their midst. On convoys, women may have posed certain distractions within the group, or at checkpoints; without mentioning the added risks or the rough living conditions the drivers endured. Generally it had been decided that it was simpler to remain an all-male convoy team. There were exceptions however, especially when Raphaelle (Fr) joined the crew and teamed up with Dougie (NZ). She was so level-headed and just fitted in with the team.

These initial reservations or barriers were soon wiped away with some active juggling lessons from Johnie. For those that could already master three balls such as Graeme (UK), Johnie also had clubs, knives (no longer appropriate in the camps) and some luminous balls for impressive night-time entertainment. The balls that really tested everyone though, were these enormous splats which weighed a few kilos each. You really had to have muscles to juggle them and it felt like some form of weight training where there was no gym in sight. Just what the drivers needed to challenge them in the relative lull after an intense convoy.

The unicycle was also proving a hit with the drivers and the concreted courtyard provided a very convenient practice ground for a few keen ones. One such person was Yoyo (Yoram), who had jumped from working with the more conventional Premiere Urgence, despite being a newly founded organisation too, as he preferred the more informal and colourful approach of The Serious Road Trip. You could see the way he admired Johnie and his expertise in clowning. Mind you, Johnie was a hit with everyone. I was amazed at how some seemed to master unicycling relatively quickly, but they definitely weren't afraid to fall flat on their faces in the process.

The drivers shared the stories of their base in Sarajevo which was in one of the Unis twin towers. The buildings were heavily damaged from gunfire and shelling but TSRT had made a base on the fourth floor (or higher if you counted the basement and garage), with Premiere Urgence on the third, EquiLibre on the second and Bosnia Press on the first. All other floors were empty, and from the 8th floor

144

onwards the tower was totally burnt out with no windows and only the concrete skeleton of a building remaining.

Yoyo even told us a story of a close shave when he had been playing a game of poker with the others in the Unis Tower. He leant forward to put a hand of cards down and at that very moment a bullet from a sniper came through the window, narrowly missing him and landing in a wall just behind where his head had been. Maybe they had been alerted by the light from the cigarette he was smoking, but the cards were certainly on his side at that moment, or his guardian angel was working overtime. Obviously there wasn't a working lift either, so every trip down meant taking the many stairs and then returning laden with water containers or provisions from the truck. Baked beans and baby food were regular sources of food for the drivers, who really needed a good dose of fresh vegetables too, but at least they had something to eat, which was more than many of the locals. How thankful our Bananas team was that we were not undergoing such hardships and dangers.

Our third week of shows focused on areas in close proximity to Split such as Kastel Stari, Trogir, Omis and Dugi Rat. We were really getting the hang of it by now. With Christophe as our dog character, Victor could focus on his guitar and singing. He was also taking a fair few photographs, which seemed to interrupt the show at times, and I did feel uncomfortable at his overtly taking photographs of the children instead of focusing on the performing. However, I did understand that what we were doing was worthy of documenting.

So much so that an American journalist, wanting to run an article on The Serious Road Trip for the *Chronicle of Philanthropy*, tagged along for a show in Sveti Kaja, outside Split, where there were Bosnian refugees from both Croatian and Muslim groups. They had originally arrived at the camp together, escaping the attack from the Serbs. In a twist of fate, the political situation in Bosnia had changed with the Croat-Bosniak war. The collaboration between the Croatians and Muslims living within Bosnia had fallen apart, resulting in open conflict. This meant that people who had previously been united in their escape to safety from the Serbs, were now at war with each other.

Before starting the show, we somehow realised that there were no Muslim children in the audience and discovered that the camp authorities had only allowed the Croatian children to attend.

We promptly stopped our show. Johnic faced off the burly Croatian camp director, who begged us to continue but steadfastly refused to allow the Muslim children to see it. Coming from Ireland, Johnie and Caroline were more accustomed to divisions in populations, and

145

Johnie wouldn't stand for it. Johnie threatened to leave if the children were not permitted to attend. The director even tried to get the children to persuade us to continue, getting them to cheer us on, but Johnie held firm. The director finally relented and then chaos followed. The Muslim children started to enter, but the other adults present were not happy with this decision and started shouting at the director and also began leaving the room with their reluctant children in tow.

It was obvious that we could not win this battle in the heated moment, so we decided to make a hasty departure, leaving behind the group of arguing adults and puzzled children. I wasn't sure what was worse: only performing for a selected group of children or not performing at all?

Fortunately the next day's show elsewhere was a huge hit and the children and parents responded well. One woman was even in tears at the end of the show and when I questioned her further, she explained that her tears were two-fold. There was no doubt that she had laughed at the clowning antics and there were tears of joy, however she was crying for the loss of her children's childhood. The show had highlighted just how much they were missing as children, without even mentioning an uncertain future caused by war.

In one kindergarten we visited, I remember the children had all drawn pictures to thank us for our show. These were just young four or five year olds who were being taught to draw their Croatian flag as a focal point in their artwork, alongside the usual animals and flowers you would expect from this age-group.

But this newly-found independence from Yugoslavia had come at a huge cost, with wars being sparked off.

Our next challenge came within our own group. Victor was keen to return to Ireland after a hectic September and found himself a flight from Split. On one hand I felt betrayed that he was abandoning the project a little prematurely, but on the other hand we couldn't force him to continue if he felt he had given enough. Maybe I had assumed that he would be with us all the way and he hadn't realised our project would extend into October. Fortunately, we had a team of convoy drivers with a little down-time between convoys who seemed keen to assist.

The initial barriers between projects and groups had disappeared; we were starting to feel like we were all one team. One of the drivers, Meni, offered to drive the combi for the remaining weeks, along the coast, and all the way back to Britain if necessary. Yoyo was proving to be a budding clown alongside Johnie and we had others joining in the fun. Isabelle or Jutta didn't mind running around in our animal-chase story as the dog. A French driver from Premiere Urgence, Manu, brought his own rendition of the Karate Kid to the show, which went down a treat as part of the Banana Split trick. He leapt through the air making all the right noises to karate chop the banana. Johnie would look bewildered, as the banana was still intact after this hugely exaggerated karate chop, but what a surprise when the skin was peeled back to reveal a chopped banana inside. They had everyone begging to eat a little piece of this magic banana and people of all ages were left scratching their heads, wondering how he had managed to do it without slicing the banana skin.

Every show was followed by a frenzy of face-painting, each of us taking a sponge and a different colour, managing to put a colourful blob on each eager face. For smaller shows we may have managed a few whisker streaks, but generally each child at least got a splash of colour on their nose or cheek.

We took a much needed day's break to buy some food supplies in Split and explore this historical city. I remember enjoying an amazing coffee in a café, and finding a hairdresser to give me a well-needed haircut. For the past seven years I had been very proud of my uneven hair style, with one side long and the other short. For some reason, I felt now was the time to even the sides up. We joked over coffee, how they should have only charged me half the price seeing one side was already cut short. It was good to be enjoying some sort of normal activity, after such an emotionally charged project.

Back at the base at Magda's the drivers inflated a giant yellow sea-monster toy, decorated with colourful spots, much to the delight of the refugee children next door. The water was cold now and many could not swim, however a few adventurous ones clung to the monster and set off into the sunset to some imaginary faraway land for a few moments of fun. We all needed our own down-time, even if it was short-lived.

By now our tour was taking us further up the coast towards Sibinik where we even ventured out onto the small island of Obonjon. What an idyllic setting with the water so blue and the scenery so picturesque. To top it all off, there was even an ancient amphitheatre, not far from the water's edge where we managed to perform our show in gorgeous sunshine. The refugees here were quite cut off from everywhere, which obviously had its drawbacks. This had been a former scout camp and they were lucky to be far away from the intense fighting inland, but were very isolated as well. The boat that connected us with the mainland was rather small and infrequent. Thus our show was a welcome break for them in this unique and peaceful setting, and an appreciated link for them with the outside world.

The next island we visited was Brac. This was the largest of the islands off the coast. We would need a good two days for this stretch of the trip. These would also be some of our last shows. The ferry was large, so we could take our combi over and use it for sleeping. Once again we were struck by the beauty of the location and under normal circumstances this island would have been brimming with tourists. As on the mainland, the major hotels were providing refuge to women and children escaping the conflict and we visited the beautiful ports of Povlja, Bol, Milna and Sutivan. The waters were calm, the sun was bright, and the unique coastal villages absolutely oozed charm and history. How odd to be some of the only foreign visitors at such a time.

As we journeyed to do a small show in a kindergarten, our eyes were drawn to a poignant scene. There in one of the ports was an enormous ship. On board there were hundreds of soldiers all in uniform. On land their loved-ones were gathered to see them off, not knowing if they would return. They waved frantically for those final moments of farewell. I had never witnessed such a sight and it reminded me of documentaries showing brave NZ soldiers leaving for WWII and the like. I could sense the ruptures in relationships taking place and felt sad for the families being torn apart by this Balkan War. How ironic! They were leaving to make war with Bosnia and the very people we were trying to keep from starving. Here we were 16 months after our initial intervention on that Peace Convoy to Sarajevo in June 1992, where The Serious Road Trip had tried to stop the war alongside other NGOs. If only we had managed to succeed, then none of this heartache and suffering would be happening. Of course, we were no politicians, but we had at least tried to change the course of history. With another winter fast approaching, the need for supplies was even greater in Bosnia this year of 1993.

Back in Split the convoy team was all set to return to Sarajevo. The trucks were laden, the paperwork in place and the drivers itching to get back to where they were most needed. There was some suggestion that Johnie might like to travel with them to Sarajevo to provide his much-appreciated humour to the besieged children. For now he resisted the temptation, much to our relief, especially for Caroline. Besides, the weather was cooling, we were thoroughly exhausted from two hectic tours of Romania (80 shows) and Croatia (44 shows) not to mention endless fundraising in between and long distances covered. There would be another, more appropriate, moment for him to join in, he promised.

We bade our farewells to the drivers, wishing them all the best on their treacherous journey to Sarajevo. We didn't know when we would see them again or the dangers they would face. Some of those who had particularly warmed to Johnie's humour, such as Yoyo (France) and Allan (Australia) would take some of their new-found clowning skills on the road. In fact, these added activities would provide necessary stress-relief for everyone including themselves. Now, whilst waiting at checkpoints for clearance they could keep themselves, the border-guards and any curious children highly amused with various juggling acts.

We continued to interact with the local children from the neighbouring refugee centre and found out more about their circumstances. The building was called the 'Banjalucko Odmaraliste' which signalled a centre for Banja Luka (Serb-held territory) workers to come and relax by the sea during peacetime. However, someone had written 'BALIJE' over the sign in spray paint. This was a highly derogatory term for Muslims, which made their building stand out like a sore thumb on this road. The coastal road served as a link between Croatia and Bosnia-H. When Croatian forces returned from the front line in Mostar and elsewhere in Bosnia, they would shoot off their remaining rounds at the building housing those Bosnian refugees. How odd for them to be 'sheltering' behind 'enemy' lines. How safe were they here? This seemed a very complicated war to me.

One of the teenagers, Alma, explained that the living conditions were extremely cramped and they were sleeping on thin mattresses on the floor and there were some 33 people in one room. Their food was minimal, often a slice of bread with jam on it for breakfast and the same again at lunch-time, with nothing for dinner. She later told me that an elderly woman she lay next to had difficulty breathing using an oxygen bottle. One morning she awoke to find the elderly lady lying there, lifeless. She had died in the night. It was a grim existence as they were stuck there in limbo.

At least the comings and goings of The Serious Road Trip trucks, and now the clowns, provided some well-needed fun and laughter, or 'craic' as Johnie and Caroline would say. In fact, when the trucks were parked outside their building, their presence also somehow seemed to give the residents a level of protection while they waited in hope of being resettled elsewhere in the UNHCR Resettlement Programme.

As we lingered these last few days we were also hoping to catch up with some drivers we had befriended from Premiere Urgence, who were due back from Sarajevo. A convoy that should have taken under a week was now a couple of weeks overdue. One of these drivers, Max, had caught my eye and for some crazy reason, I was wondering if this attraction might go somewhere. They were due any day now so I didn't want to leave. Another plan emerged. There were some fire engines from Vienna delivering some humanitarian aid to Jutta's organisation; they were due to leave in a few days with Jutta on board. My group would make its way to Vienna and I would catch up with them a few days later by fire engine.

Needless to say, the waiting was in vain and this plan for extended time proved futile. Without the convoy drivers or my clowning team there, I could hear the cold winds ushering in the imminent arrival of winter. How lonely and aimless I felt.

I had delayed my departure as long as I could, but it really was time for me to catch my ride out of there. Jutta and I boarded those fire engines, happy to have each other for company and moral support. We had both experienced enormous changes in our lives and needed to head back to another reality. No doubt our families breathed huge sighs of relief, although I could not understand this at the time. The needs of the refugees seemed to block out all other attachments.

Back in the London office, several days later, French Max telephoned; he had finally made it out safely from Sarajevo. I forget the hair-raising details that involved helicopters getting them out safely. All I can remember was that we were now worlds apart, even if I was relieved that he was safe. He wasn't planning on coming to London and I wasn't returning to Croatia at this stage. If anything, I felt the pull of NZ. It felt like nothing was certain for now and maybe a trip back to my family would be beneficial. I certainly couldn't imagine spending Christmas in this office, where I was sleeping on a mattress on the floor.

To my dismay some things I had left, in a large striped bag for safety in the office, had become mixed up with aid collections of clothes, and disappeared. At least they had gone to a good home, maybe for some refugees who had nothing. I tried to reassure myself that this was the case, until I saw some new volunteer wearing my favourite burgundy-red boots. They were the ones from Nev.

'You're wearing my boots!' I shouted to some rather embarrassed woman. She explained that they had thought the goods donated were rather good, including some souvenir Celtic jewellery from Ireland, and wondered if it had been a case of some boyfriend throwing his girlfriend's clothes out after a break-up. She had no idea where the rest of my things were, but would return my boots if I gave her 10 pounds for the new heels and soles she had invested in. What a cheek! But I was so relieved to see my boots again that I parted with the cash. Within moments I was back with my rejuvenated old boots, which felt reassuring.

Life in the London office was far removed from the life out in the field on a project, but I busied myself with various media interviews and a couple of urgent trips. A group of us travelled up to Norfolk in the combi-van to attend a memorial service being held for Nan. It was in an old-fashioned English church with gravestones in the churchyard. Everyone, except ourselves, seemed to be dressed in black and it was a very sombre occasion. The tragedy of her death hit home again as we faced the friends and family, who continued to ask why such a giving and vibrant person had been taken so soon. Some familiar people from Scottish European Aid also attended and we caught up over tea and sandwiches. Moona's mother said I must have been a huge support to Moona at such a difficult time. It was true we had been some moral support as a team, but she obviously did not know about our rupture just before the accident.

While this tragedy was very unlucky and an incredibly cruel blow to all concerned, it perversely had attracted lots of media attention. The funds were rolling in to support their work in Bosnia and the much-needed water project in Tuzla.

Meanwhile, the surviving person in this accident had been transferred to a hospital on the outskirts of London. I was determined to visit him, so made my way there. His leg had been amputated and he was still very unwell. He looked like a ghost; I admit I felt unable to cope with the changes in such a strong man. I'm not sure he remembered me after all he had been through; I felt like a stranger in the wrong place. At least he seemed to be in good hands with nurses fussing around, and his family in the same country now.

The strain of it all was taking its toll and with my parents' encouragement and help, I made plans to get back to New Zealand before the airfares rose around Christmas. I was in dire need of some stability and hoped to find that there.

Chapter 15

New Zealand Interlude

A week later, touching down on the Auckland airport tarmac felt very familiar and the welcome home was reassuring. What a relief to be in my childhood home in Rotorua, surrounded by my parents, siblings, grandparents and a whole host of aunts, uncles and cousins. It was hard to explain all that I had done and seen; it was so far removed from their everyday reality. Conversations quickly reverted to more familiar, everyday topics, which felt trivial compared to the life-and-death scenarios I had faced. I had had similar feelings returning to the London office. I know that life goes on, but I needed some acknowledgement of what I had experienced.

The people that seemed to ask the most questions were local journalists, as they were keen to get a story from someone who had experienced first-hand some of the much publicised war in Bosnia, and to a lesser degree the orphanages of Romania. What a relief to be able to give my version of various events, and of the positive things our group was managing to do against the odds. Through the media, I did find an audience and communicated my experiences, and the plight of the people we had helped.

Some of the Serious Road Trippers from the original bus had made their way back to NZ and they invited me to join them down in Hawke's Bay for a brief stay. Belinda and Myles had even had a baby girl, Gracie, who had been conceived in Russia. It felt good to be reunited with them and a few others: Miles and Julie Dinneen, Damon and Amanda, Patrick and Seaton. With Damon's mother, Chris Hinton, at the helm, some of them were actively trying to raise funds for The

Serious Road Trip. With this aim we set up a fruit stall at a Mountain Rock Festival. This had been hugely successful at both Glastonbury and Phoenix Festivals in England; this proved to be a fun way to attract interest and create funds in NZ too, on a smaller scale.

Back in Rotorua, I needed to face the fact that my parents had just sold our family home much more quickly than anticipated. Even at home it felt like the rug was being pulled from beneath me. This was not the stability I yearned for, but at least I was there to help them pack up all our memories, sorting through all sorts of photos, ornaments and knick-knacks getting them ready for storage. I also had the company of my long-standing friend Dallas, which was reassuring. We'd been through high school and university together and there were many shared experiences. She'd even hooked up with the bus in France that highly emotionally charged evening, when we grappled with the decision whether to go on that peace convoy or not. What a relief to have her friendship, empathy and understanding.

The house my parents were moving to was not yet built, so they rented a small 2-bedroom Lockwood house on the other side of the lake. It was a wrench to have lost my home base. I needed to say goodbye to a house with so many happy family memories. I had to console myself with the thought that at least I was not losing my home under the same circumstances as the refugees.

Chapter 16

Bananas II by Bus Beckons
(1994)

The rental house was fairly cramped with four of my family there. Summer was drawing to a close, and I felt the call to return to Europe. My work in the humanitarian field was definitely not over, but I had recharged some of my batteries and raised some money for what was starting to look like a promising new project. One of the convoy drivers, Yoyo from France, was now in London to help prepare for the next clowning project, Bananas 4 Split Part II. When are you coming back? He asked by fax message. It was clear that Johnie had found a new clowning recruit; as Yoyo even mastered the unicycle.

Yoyo and Christopher Watt (in charge of the office and PR and now fondly known as Tito), picked me up from Heathrow in the familiar, colourful VW combi. It felt good to be back on track again, with plans to undertake the Bananas 4 Split Part 2. There were plans to resurrect the bus again and an unlikely romance was starting to blossom between myself and Yoyo. It was good finally to be heading off on a project with someone who had the same goals. It was clear the original bus, which had broken down in Moscow, was not an option, so needed replacing.

Excitement was in the air with the dream of getting the bus back on the road again. Maybe we would get to New Zealand by bus after all, but not just yet as there were other pressing needs.

Christophe was back in Podstrana after a trip to Zagreb, where he had met a new volunteer, Sneijana Majic, who was from a region right on the border between Croatia and Bosnia. She was now helping with the necessary paperwork and organisation for convoys. At last,

154

someone who could speak the language, was working voluntarily for us, and providing some well-needed female energy. With a romantic union there, they were also both keen to get the show on the road again and were starting to work on the itinerary.

Meanwhile Yoyo and I were trying to track down a second-hand double-decker bus. On our various journeys, we saw a few abandoned Playbuses in bus graveyards, but either their engines needed work, or the price wasn't right. They had all seen better days.

Finally we found what we were looking for. We named her BB... whether short for Beautiful Bus or BeBe (French for Baby) or some other name I can't remember. I'm sure we all made up a meaning for the name. She was a 'learner-driver bus' so had an extra seat for the instructor to sit, slightly behind the driver; this would be perfect for a navigator.

She was a Bristol Lodekka, not the traditional London RouteMaster. This meant she was 3.8m high: far more practical for passing under bridges 4m high. She was not bright red but yellow; a bus destined for a Bananas 4 Split project.

By this stage Allan (Oz) from the convoys, enjoying a welcome break from driving trucks into Bosnia, had also joined us. The three of us felt rather triumphant driving away with our new-found vehicle, led by the original Bananas combi. There was some debate over whether to keep the bus yellow or not, but with Metroline (part of London Transport) in Cricklewood offering to give the bus a red make-over, we opted to continue with the magical effect that red London buses seem to have. They would also provide a good maintenance check and keep the bus safely in their garage before we left. What a relief to have the support of a professional outfit. The story of the intended destination and purpose for this bus took these London drivers away from their day-to-day reality, and they offered their support for our work.

There wasn't time to do a complete make-over inside but we pulled out many of the seats upstairs to make sleeping spaces, leaving only the four front seats at the top, with more seating downstairs in the kitchen/dining area.

While trying to work out who would be in the team, we made a journey to Ireland to try and persuade Johnie and Caroline to join us. Much to our disappointment, they were adamant that they would not be joining us on this trip. Johnie gave us all his blessing, reassuring us that we could do it without him, using tricks he had taught us. While we knew that we were not quite in the same league as someone who had been trained in the Blackpool Tower Circus and with Johnie's unique personality and background, we were definitely up for the challenge.

We set about finding a team of 'entertainers'. I remember Allan trying to describe all the qualities that were needed in a clown, even giving me his active version of what a clown needed to do, when it struck me that he was a strong candidate himself! He also had the added experience of operating in a war zone. Both he and Yoyo knew how much humour was needed by the children they had met on convoys; they were both highly motivated to do more.

We also needed musicians, and two volunteers responded to our plea for help on the radio. One was a guitarist, the other a drummer called Paul who played Djambe (African drum), juggled and was generally very entertaining.

A female actress, Mirella, was also up for clowning around and joined our merry band. There were more keen volunteers, but by now we had all the people we needed.

We had all the ingredients for a vibrant show. It was May 1994.

Our priority was now to get down to Split to join Christophe and Sneijana, as they were itching to get the shows happening.

We were also able to provide transport for some other participants, such as our photographer, Max Reeves, and Christopher, so they could get a feel for what happens on a project. Jerry would go with us as far as Bavaria to see his cousin Tessa. Volunteer drivers that needed to get back to Croatia, such as Peter Gulliver from New Zealand or Raphaelle (France) and Paul Kirwan, our original bus-driver, also joined our trip south.

How amazing to see our bus so shiny and red and ready for action. We proudly set off from Cricklewood Bus Garage and made our way to Charlie's Yard, where the trucks had traditionally departed from. There we had a photo shoot and Allan horsed around riding a horse in their stables, before our big departure for the ferry. Charlie and Linda ran horse-riding for the disabled as well as his transport business from the stables.

Our first port of call was Luxembourg and once again the generous people of Luxembourg and my former colleagues in the financial sector, dipped into their pockets. I was also happy to see my sister Ingrid, who was in Europe working as a nanny in France, wanting to catch up with me where possible and to wish us well. Another important stop was the European Parliament, where we made a presentation and received some small financial grant. It was a huge, empty building and we seemed to be the only people around. The flags of many European countries flew on the flagpoles outside while we took the stage, each with our own podium and microphone, but there was no one to hear what we said being the only visitors that day.

Our next stop was in Germany where Tessa and Wolfgang made us extremely welcome as per usual. With access to a workshop and tools, Wolfgang and Yoyo knocked up a much-needed storage area downstairs for props and costumes, with comfy cushions to sit on. Meanwhile, some of us were suffering from the lack of privacy and quickly sewed some curtains out of sheets, to shield us from prying eyes or bright sun in the wee hours of the morning. The communal sleeping upstairs was a mish-mash of mattresses and personal bags with no spot that you could claim as your own. How spoiled we had been on the first bus with its collapsible bunk beds and storage benches. There was no use complaining; it was as it was. We certainly looked highly dishevelled after a night of sleeping in whatever space we could find.

For now we were more numerous than intended and I had to remind myself that our numbers would reduce once we were properly on our own project.

The bus lurched onwards as we made our way slowly but surely towards Croatia. The seating at the very front, up top, was definitely my favourite spot. I could escape into a dream-world as we chugged along, with all sorts of scenarios weaving in and out of my thoughts.

Now we were on the Adriatic coast near Rijeka and the evidence of war was obvious. Unlike last year we were taking the coastal road rather than the safer ferry. There were buildings reduced to rubble and I saw the word 'Cetnici' graffitied on a wall. A bullet-ridden boat lay half-submerged in the beautiful water and I wondered what battle might have happened there. The weather was warming up and we took a quick break to freshen up in the crystal clear waters of the Adriatic.

It was a rough and winding road and we hurtled along to music like Seal's 'Crazy' with Peter Gulliver's wild hair almost taking flight. He reminded me of a woolly sheep which was quite apt as he was from NZ. He and the other drivers were extremely capable and although we shook violently along the coastal road, we made it to our base camp in Podstrana (near Split). We were given a huge welcome by our convoy crew and neighbours. Part of our cargo included a small accordion, which we had appealed for on the radio. One of the refugee children from next door had lost his musical instrument (and of course much more than that) in the war, and it seemed the least we could do to replace it. There was huge excitement as we crowded around to hear him bring this instrument and his people back to life through his music.

What a relief to finally be there, and just in time. Our bus needed some repair work done to one of its wheels. Fortunately there were two tyres per wheel, so we weren't stranded on the side of the road. We drove it to the Premiere Urgence compound where Kiwi Road Tripper, driver and mechanic, Vince Steur, set about repairing it with the help of his French friend from PU. This was a far cry from the bus garage in London; somehow they managed to get the wheel nuts off, using a very long metal pole, to deal with the punctured tyre.

Things were very stressful in the Premiere Urgence camp and 'family' of aid workers. Just weeks earlier, in April, an entire convoy including 11 Frenchmen, their trucks and cargo had been stolen by Serbians. They announced the men would be tried for 'weapons trafficking'. What an outrage for an organisation that did such vital work to be accused of such lunacy; what would become of the aid-workers held captive? I thanked my lucky stars that we were not planning to go into Bosnia and run such risks. I was also grateful that our group comprised of at least six differing nationalities; we could not be targeted politically as belonging to any particular country.

While waiting for the bus to be repaired we busied ourselves rehearsing for the show. The new Banana Split team was finding its new identities.

We played on the well-known UK television Banana Splits song 'One banana, two bananas, three bananas, four…' or something like that, and tried to create a feeling of being on a bus with chairs lined up in a row, and one of us acting as the bus driver.

Within days, our guitarist was missing his girlfriend and decided to abandon the project, returning to London. We were not shaken by this, although I did wonder why our guitarists left the group so spontaneously (this was the third time), and so early on this time. Fortunately for us, Paul Brett was also an accomplished guitarist as well as drummer, so this role fell to him. He didn't have much hair himself, but donned a bright red clowning wig and pantaloons.

As for Yoyo and Christophe, they seemed to buddy up and became like some naughty French twin clowns, who juggled together, spun diabolos and rode the unicycle as part of the act. Christophe was keen to incorporate the celebrated banana split trick into the show and had great fun skidding on the discarded banana skin afterwards.

Sometimes Yoyo wore a spotted outfit and Christophe his multi-coloured jerkin. Usually their faces were painted white and they wore striped felt hats, similar to the Cat in the Hat.

Meanwhile, Allan, with an enormous painted grin and baggy trousers, interacted with Mirella as some Mr and Mrs Clown couple. Allan was a central clown figure, behaving much like Johnie, when he blew up balloons which popped, flinging him backwards. He would also invite children onto the stage to attempt juggling, as this had proved popular on previous tours. Children loved to get in on the action and give things a go, so audience participation was a key part of the show.

As for me, I had been given a bright purple dress decorated with intricate golden threads and sequins. I wore my fantastic blue and orange fabric hat, which resembled some type of crown with the spikes looking almost like the flames of a fire. The wire within each spike allowed me to shape the spikes to point upwards or downwards or a crazy mixture of both. I'd found the hat at the Camden Market on my birthday so I was very proud to be wearing this as part of my costume. It was amazing how a hat could totally put you in a different space and give you the courage to perform despite the sometimes daunting circumstances.

We had been given a wide range of face-paints from the Treasure House of Make-up including some fantastic gold. Since I had taken on the character of some type of 'magic woman', I enjoyed having a golden face with a star and moon on each cheek and a sun on my chin. On my ankle I sported some bells that shook nicely when arriving on 'stage'. I developed two main tricks as part of my repertoire. I arrived twirling some pois that I had brought from New Zealand. These were like two soft balls on strings that I could swing in circles around my body or like propellers in front of me and above my head. Usually I used both hands but sometimes I managed to have the balls going in opposite directions with the strings being held by one hand. This was something I had learnt to do growing up surrounded by traditional Maori culture in Rotorua, New Zealand. I had participated in various Maori Kapa haka cultural groups at primary school. I had learnt to do various poi tricks in preparation for a scholarship trip to Germany that I had won when I was 16. At the time a girl from my class had given me valuable lessons, so that I had something to demonstrate at an international cultural concert evening, arranged for the touring students from over 20 countries. Who would have known that this skill would be of such use some 10 years later? Once on stage, I would embark on a magic trick.

We no longer had Johnie's velvet magic bag, but I had managed to make a larger one out of a lovely colourful backpack. The trick involved placing three small juggling balls into the bag on stage and getting everyone to shout the magic words, such as Abrakadabra and Blah, blah, blah. To everyone's surprise, when I opened the bag, out came three very heavy and enormous splat juggling balls. I would then show the audience the empty bag and many would be left scratching their heads, wondering how such little balls had become so huge. Yoyo and Christophe would take over juggling these heavy monster balls.

They would then move over to juggling clubs, then fire clubs. One of their amazing acts was where they were blindfolded but managed to continue juggling the fire-clubs, even throwing them between each other without dropping them.

All the while, Paul would be animating the whole show with drum rolls or guitar music in the appropriate places. When he was busy with the guitar, one of us would eagerly take over his Djambe drum; and I certainly enjoyed doing this.

Yoyo had been given a colourful hat with Velcro strips criss-crossed over it. Three balls were designed to cling to this hat. One of us, or members of the audience, would throw the balls towards him, and he would have fun stretching or diving towards the flying ball, in order to catch it on his magic sticky hat.

Thus the show took the form of a collection of circus-styled tricks. We only needed a minimum of basic words on stage, and we were lucky to have Sniejana on board for sorting out any logistical requirements in the local Serbo-Croat language.

Our contact at UNICEF had proved invaluable again helping us sort out an itinerary.

It was a relief to see that the show proved a success as we arrived in front of our audience with a clang and bang of percussion noises, to set the scene for this colourful troupe and its varied repertoire of tricks.

We returned to the barracks housing refugees at Sveti Kaja where we had been unable to perform last time, due to a stand-off between the Bosnian Croatian and Bosniak (Muslim) populations. With the warmer weather we were able to perform outside and drove our big red bus up onto a large concrete area. Our bus provided a backdrop to the show and 'behind the scenes' changing rooms. Many children sat on the flat surface in front of us with rows of children seated or standing behind them. Other refugees, adults and children, stood outside the barracks at a slightly higher level, overlooking the scene. I'm not sure how they managed to organise themselves or whether they all sat together on this occasion, but we at least managed to perform the show they had missed the year before. I was unaware that things had progressed politically with a cease-fire between Croats and Bosniaks, so that probably had something to do with it too.

It was a happy occasion and the fire-clubs came out as the sun began to set, providing the appropriate dusky setting for the torches to shine more brightly.

Ironically, one of the children sitting in the front row thought he would play a trick on us and produced a toy gun to mimic shooting Yoyo the clown. Our photographer managed to capture this moment with the bus in the background and the words 'DON'T SHOOT' on a placard held up by our Cat in the Hat who was painted onto our bus.

While some of us had grown up with pop-guns playing cowboys and indians or soldiers shooting each other, in this context of real-life war, the toy gun took on a different significance. It made me question the value of playing such games as children.

Once again we returned to Obonjon Island as part of our tour up the coast. We missed not having the bus for our props and costumes, or for us to change in or hide behind. We made the journey in the little boat that bobbed its way over the waters to the former scout camp. We were told there were roughly 50 families living there; they had fled from behind the Serb front lines in Bosnia. 'It's a beautiful island,' explained the man who ran the boat, 'but you put people from the mainland on an island and they can never be happy.' I guess that was just a small part of the problem. Many had had to flee awful violence and had left their homes abruptly. We could only imagine the traumas and destruction that they had faced and how this impacted on their state of mind and being.

The weather was far warmer at this time of year, compared to the autumn before, and I remember our face-paints dripping enormously in the heat. We had nowhere to shelter from the sun. Our energetic show was packed full of action, and clowns falling over, but the smiling receptive children made performing in the searing heat all worthwhile. Once again I felt privileged to perform in the ancient setting of a stone amphitheatre, with the blue waters of the Adriatic as our backdrop. I wondered what type of theatre had taken place here previously. Coming from the relatively new country of New Zealand, all of these places with such ancient history felt quite awe-inspiring.

We left the contented children with their faces streaked with face-paints. Bags of balloons and a palette of face-paints were left in the hands of someone in charge as a reminder of our visit and to put to good use later.

Further up the coast we headed to a place near Sibenik where the buildings were reinforced with many sand-bags and long thick branches of wood were positioned in front of the windows. We felt much closer to the action, and were informed that there was shelling less than 10km away. I guess we were in a relatively safe zone, but I hoped the front line would not creep closer to us. We were only here to do our show, but how did it feel for the people living here? Could the situation change overnight and they be forced to flee further?

There were shelling noises in the distance and I felt happy to be on our way. Little did I know that my biggest challenge was about to come running towards me.

Once back at the Road Trip base near Split we had a wild night hooking up with a Spanish group called Pallassos Sense Fronteres (Clowns Without Borders). Unlike us, they seemed to be an existing group that performed in Spain under another name 'Desastre Total', but had made the journey to perform in Bosnia under the umbrella of Clowns Without Borders. Their tour was a comparatively brief 10 days out of their existing performance work and they spoke about trapeze and all sorts, which made me realise they were quite a professional group with loads of equipment. They were on their way back from Zenica I think, and on a high of having managed to accomplish their goal. We had a mad night exchanging ideas, stories and T-shirts.

We didn't all speak Spanish, but we somehow communicated as fellow performers do, with similar humanitarian desires thrown into the equation. The drumming went into the wee hours of the morning as we made the most of their brief stopover before they hit the road the next morning. I was now the proud owner of one of their T-shirts. Their success in Bosnia egged some of our group on, as we heard of the possibility of heading into Bosnia, to the heavily destroyed city of Mostar.

A Dash for Mostar

Mostar had been cut off for two years and had been extremely dangerous to enter until recently, when the Croat-Bosniak war ended with the Washington Agreement. Prior to this ceasefire, The Serious Road Trip had heard how bad it was from a French action journalist, Emmanuel Ortiz, who documented the situation there despite the immense dangers. They had also heard how dire it was from EquiLibre and were eventually persuaded that they too needed to provide assistance with our Bedford Trucks.

Our drivers had loaded the food, obtained the various permissions and headed off in the dark of night. Their timing had been impeccable as unbeknown to them a ceasefire, a result of the Washington Agreement, had been negotiated that very day, on the 18th March 1994. It was already dark when they turned up at the checkpoint and the border guards, who were unfamiliar with our colourful trucks, exclaimed that the circus had surely arrived. Maybe they thought that our 'clowns', who were really just a colourful bunch of drivers, had been waiting for this ceasefire to enter the city. The aid was subsequently delivered without the expected dangers, and now here we were some weeks later with a small gap in our itinerary. There had been a freedom of movement agreement established in the region of Mostar in May which made travel far easier, although not for the locals. They remained confined to this area.

Naturally we were asked if we could consider going to Mostar too? My initial reaction was to fear and reject this new suggestion. After all, we were meant to be focusing on the refugees along the Dalmatian Coast, not entering the war-torn Bosnia. But we had not known about this new possibility when planning the trip, and we had two experienced former convoy drivers, plus Christophe who had spent many months in Sarajevo, and Snejana who came from a border town herself. We also had a photographer on board who was keen to get some action shots of Bosnia. I was definitely in the minority on this occasion.

The people of East Mostar had been through a long siege and surely could benefit from our positive show even more than the refugees sheltering along the coast.

There was a clear desire from everyone to go, although I must say the implications of this decision weighed heavily on my shoulders. As some form of leader of the group I somehow felt responsible for everyone should anything go wrong. Of course, we all made our individual decisions to go, but my heart beat wildly as we chugged towards East Mostar. We entered Bosnia at Metkovic and passed several checkpoints on our way. These were marked by armed soldiers guarding the road and criss-crossed metal spikes a metre high or more, to stop vehicles from driving through before being checked. I remember the music from the film 'The Time of the Gypsies' resounding through the bus as we rambled along without talking. The movie had been directed by Yugoslav Emir Kusturica in 1988 with compatriot, Goran Bregovic, composing the chilling Balkan music. I guess I felt rather gypsy-like myself as we journeyed from one country to another in our mobile home bus.

I took a seat upstairs to really take the scenery in and Christophe delighted in telling me in a rather matter-of-fact manner that we could see three front lines as we entered the Mostar region; he added that there were probably snipers from all sides with their sights on us in our large red bus, much like a giant bullseye on a dartboard. He didn't seem to be bothered by this thought and continued to sit there in full sight, which gave me a certain sense of security, although I did wonder if it was false. Maybe he was beyond caring.

The mountains and hills surrounding the city were where Serbs could watch over the entire valley. Still, no one did take a shot at us and I wondered if anyone did have us in their sights, or whether they too were just surprised to see our beautiful bus rolling towards Mostar.

A few kilometers from town we started seeing women scurrying along the country road towards us carrying water and provisions to destinations further afield, all looking up with perplexed looks and surprised smiles on their faces when the bus came into view. Could this be a peace bus, they seemed to ask? Whatever they thought, it seemed to symbolise something different to them. The ceasefire had endured nearly six weeks and now even a London bus had made it here.

Finally we did make it into what was left of the Bosniak side of the city. Mostar had been divided into two parts during the Croat-Bosniak war, with the main division of the city provided by the intense blue waters of the Neretva river. We saw how the famous old bridge named 'Stari Most' had been destroyed. As the city's name was derived from Mostari (bridge keepers) its brokenness symbolised all that had gone on here. Mosques, churches and synagogues had existed side-by-side for over four centuries and this symbol of tolerance and unity had been purposefully destroyed by Croat forces on 9th November 1993. This famous Ottoman bridge had stood the test of time for some 427 years and had been an extraordinary technological achievement of bridge construction.

Two years of war had also destroyed most of the historic Old Town. I had never seen such destruction, with rubble everywhere, and it reminded me of film footage from WWII, but this was here and now in modern-day Europe. I was thankful that I had not lived through this myself, and that I was here under more peaceful conditions. At least a temporary cable bridge had been erected across the river, but I wondered what the Old Bridge had looked like. It was only some time later that I would see old postcards and images of this fantastic rainbow arched bridge.

We made our way slowly to a central area on the main road and stopped the bus. It didn't take long for a number of children to appear from ruined buildings and they were so curious to find out more. Soon they realised that there were clowns on board, juggling balls, a unicycle and much more. Even if they didn't recognise The Cat in the Hat, I am sure that he and the cartoon figures adorning our bus appealed. A young girl handed me a tender little flower as a small gift. Where in all this destruction and rubble had such a delicate flower managed to grow? One by one we savoured the sweet perfume of this flower as we passed it around the group. It seemed to symbolise the hope that now existed, especially with this ceasefire between Croats and Bosniaks. Nonetheless, it was fragile too, and there was a long way to go.

For a few moments I entertained a few with my bright green fluffy snake on a wire, which slithered around arms, hands and necks, provoking shrieks of glee. Christophe sped around on his unicycle like some Serious Road Trip version of the Pied Piper on one wheel, children eagerly following him.

Sneijana explained to the children that we would do a show for them in an hour. We decided that performing in front of Mostar's theatre (which we could see from where we were parked) would be the most appropriate setting on this bright sunny day. The word spread quickly that we would return with our show later that morning.

We continued down the main road to the far end of town, where there seemed to be no one and we proceeded to get into costume, paint our faces and prepare the various props for the show. This was definitely a far more spontaneous show than the previous ones along the coast, where there had been at least some person in authority that was aware of our planned activity.

When we returned to the theatre we could see a few hundred children gathered in anticipation. The word had spread quickly indeed. My eyes glanced at the numerous graves in the park nearby, under the trees. Apparently this was where many children who had died during the war were buried.

The theatre's front entrance was pitted with gun-shots and there was a huge hole near the entrance where a larger mortar had gone off.

This building provided the natural backdrop we needed and there was a pedestrian square in front where the audience could be. We managed to get the children to sit in a fairly straight line before us, with older children and some adults standing behind.

They responded with huge excitement and were obviously over the moon to be able to enjoy being children. As we performed with so many children before us, the graves of many behind them, I gazed upwards now to the row of destroyed buildings beyond. There were no windows left or roofs, just the outline of some stones where the building should have been. Others were just a pile of rubble.

Participation was an enormous part of our show and enthusiastic children would almost beg to be offered the chance to come and join the clowns and attempt to juggle or unicycle. Allan quickly chose a volunteer. His eyes sparkled as he made his way to the stage area. He was a young boy of maybe eight years, who had lost his arm, but that didn't stop him from wanting to try to juggle. I felt quite emotional about this moment of triumph for him and for us.

As usual, once the show was finished we managed to smear face-paint over as many keen faces as possible. We each had different colours on sponges and the result was beautiful and messy at the same time. I tried to give some children whiskers on their cheeks, but that wasn't always possible. There were just so many surrounding us, and we needed to act quickly.

Naturally we had many wanting to converse with us and I wished I spoke more of the local Serbo-Croat language. Thankfully, through Sniejana, we managed to establish that there were many more children than those present. Unbeknown to us, school had re-started that very day after two years of interruption. As there were so many children and not enough space in the school, the teachers had organised the children into two groups. Some had school in the morning and others in the afternoon. They begged us to return in the afternoon so that those at school didn't miss out. Naturally we were happy to be so appreciated and said we would return around 4pm. We definitely didn't want anyone to miss out.

We wondered if raising our performance area might help, rather than being on the same level as the audience, so decided that we should perform in the area leading to where the Old Bridge had been. That way we could perform at the lower level, and the old existing steps would provide seating and height to the afternoon crowd. Or did we make this decision to perform near the bridge to make some kind of point?

We were exhausted from the day's events, and needed to retreat to the outskirts of town. Here there was a warehouse and locked area, where we could take a break from all the attention we naturally attracted. We relaxed over a cup of tea made in the kitchen of our bus and a bite to eat, as we mentally prepared for the next performance, and tried to escape some of the heat. Our bus was like an oven upstairs, but at least the lower deck had some shelter from the heat of the sun.

Nothing could have prepared us for what was about to happen.

Once again we got into costume, made ourselves up with face-paints and checked the props were in order.

Off we set towards town using the same country road of the morning, except this time there seemed to be many more people heading into Mostar.

Some of them were quite well-dressed and there were definitely many, many children.

We had been seriously kidding ourselves, expecting a similar sized audience as in the morning. All these people were heading into town for something and we were it!

As we drove towards the bridge area where we hoped to perform, we could see excited people everywhere. The bus was back with the clowns. There were some adventurous children even sitting on remnants of roofs to get a better view.

As we slowed down children clambered onto the front bonnet of the bus and hovered around the back entrance in numbers I had never imagined.

The crowds were huge; it was very overwhelming and my mind went into overdrive as to what we should do in this situation? There was no way we could perform by the Old Bridge. That would be dangerous with potential crushes, and besides, every inch of space was gone and was crammed with adults and children. What had we been thinking?

The expectant crowd waited patiently, but to their surprise we didn't disembark. The bus idled while we gathered our thoughts, then we decided to head back towards the theatre where we had performed that morning. We were wondering if that would be the better venue after all, but we found another audience waiting for us there. Word had spread fast and we hadn't written anything down to say where we would be. People were waiting in large groups everywhere.

By now we were really unsure how to proceed.

Those near the bus asked where we were performing. I was speechless and gestured with my hands and face that I didn't know where.

A UN tank rolled towards us, dispersing some of the crowd. It slowly crossed our path before moving onwards. The UN soldiers were amused to see such excitement for a change, but in usual fashion, didn't stop to get involved.

By now I thought the safest thing would be to postpone the show, not seeing a clear way forward. We were worried that crowd control would be a serious issue. Wherever we went, if no one could see they would naturally push forward, as we had experienced in the past. There were so many young children in the crowd who might get crushed and we, our props and possessions were also at risk.

We were approached by some policemen in a car, asking about the show. Abruptly I explained that unfortunately there would not be a show. It was impossible under the circumstances.

They looked bewildered and one retorted loudly in English 'But the Show must go on!'

How apt, I thought, smiling... BUT WHERE?

They understood our predicament but quickly came up with the best idea of the year 'Why not the Handball Stadium?' he said to Sniejana.

They said they would show us the way, so the bus followed the police car extremely slowly, with some of the crowd following behind.

We couldn't take the bus into the stadium as there was only a pedestrian entrance, so one of the police offered to stay with it parked nearby, and we carried our bags onto the sandy pitch.

By now hundreds of the crowd had gathered in the area assigned to them: a long series of stone steps. It was such a large and wide space, it would be hard to make ourselves heard without amplification but that didn't matter. Our show was very visual.

The roar of the crowd was enormous as we made our grand entrance. We had never had a crowd this big and they were kept in place by the nature of the stadium. There were well in excess of a thousand people.

I remember having to cover huge distances from one end of the crowd to the other to make sure that all had at least some moments where they could see what was going on.

The cheering of the crowd meant we really had to rely on our animated gestures rather than our voices, but fortunately this was the nature of our performance anyway.

At least our giant splat juggling balls were seen and the high-flying diabolos certainly held the audience spellbound to the sound of an intense drum-roll of the African drum.

With such a large receptive crowd, I could only imagine what it must have felt like being on tour with the Beatles. At the end we were even swamped with youngsters wanting our autographs. This was the nearest I had been to feeling like a pop-star.

By now the light was starting to go as we had been late starting, but the youngsters begged us to do another show. I tried to explain that we only had the one show, but that was not an issue for them.

'We have had no shows or anything like this for two whole years, we have been living underground and dodging snipers, just trying to survive from one day to the next. We have had no running water or electricity and not much to eat. The same show again would be amazing. Please!' a dark-haired girl of fourteen pleaded.

With darkness upon us now, we had to rejoin the others at the bus, but I felt determined to somehow return with the show as soon as possible.

These children and their families had been through so much. Many had fled from other areas. Some had been forced to abandon their

David Rallings with Bruce Dickinson
and a British Army member.

Truck and Graeme back in Podstrana base with
refugee children from next door.

Arriving in Romania
with 2nd bus and Simon the
clown.

At Mama Puiu's in
Virfu Cimpului, with
Simon, Meni, Harry,
Simone, Mihai,
Daniela, Mama Puiu,
Richard and Ionna.

Jutta setting
up the
stimulation
room at
Ionaseni
Orphanage,
Romania.

The show at Ionaseni Orphanage with Simone, Richard and young boy on unicycle.

The Pink Park Monster, our team, local theatre and children in Botosani, Romania.

Tatarai Institute, Romania. Simone with children outside, 1995.

Alba Iulia Institute. Richard and various children having fun with our parachute.

Storytelling with Harry in a kinder-garten, Romania, 1995.

The street children from Parada, Bucharest and Butsi after our show, 1995.

Simon and Richard getting ready for the festival in Sighisoara, Romania.

Simon and Harry in Sighisoara.

Simone, Simon, Jutta, Richard, Meni and Butsi during the last show of the tour, Sighisoara, Romania, 1995.

Send off from London for Dobrakadabra tour, 1996.

Johnie and Simone, Bosnia.

'Tessa' the Land Rover with David at wheel,
alongside a tank outside an American camp in
Olovo, Bosnia.

Olovo kids (school meals) in winter jackets,
with Niall, 1996.

Caroline and
Girl Puppet in
Bosnia.
Dobrakadabra
tour.

Simone and
Boy Puppet in
Bosnia.
Dobrakadabra
tour.

homes on the other side of the river when the Croat-Bosniak war had started. Former allies became enemies overnight. The HVO (Croatians from Bosnia) soldiers had knocked on doors late at night giving some less than half an hour to pack up their possessions and depart for the other side.

What would you pack in such short and desperate moments? The whole story made me think of the Jews being rounded up before and during WWII. How could this be happening in modern day Europe? At least now there was a ceasefire, but they were still under siege and unable to leave the area. There had been the same 'flight' for Croatians living on this side too, but from what we had seen and heard, that side of the city was relatively intact as they had easier access to more arms. In fact, our convoy drivers, who were required to deliver equal amounts to each side, were able to tell us that the aid which was absolutely vital to the east-side, was overflowing in unattended warehouses on the west-side. While on paper delivering equal amounts to each side sounds fair, it was obvious under these circumstances that this was not fair.

We processed all these dramatic experiences back at the warehouse area where we celebrated our day's success, and some of us managed to catch a few hours of sleep in the bus. I was too wired up from the day's events to sleep.

It was a clear, starry night. It was well past midnight and in the distance I heard what sounded like fireworks. Was there some celebration going on thanks to the ceasefire? But who would be setting off fireworks this late at night? Or was that gunfire? This was a war zone after all! All these thoughts swirled round and round in my head before I conked out for a few moments' rest.

Suddenly daylight was upon us and a brand new day was beckoning us to get going.

We were weary but wired all the same and as soon as the sun came up, the bus heated up.

Christophe and Sniejana had organised the next day's activities. They excelled at this; they were a very effective couple.

There was a small area called Mahala, on the other side of the river, yet still part of East Mostar. They would love to see us there. It must have been a school although I can't remember for sure what the set-up was. We had to cross the narrow suspension bridge, with the turquoise waters of the Neretva flowing beneath us. How had they managed when the Stari Most had fallen? They must have been extremely cut off from the rest of East-Mostar.

Once there, we performed outside again, but this time we were on

h

an asphalted sports area, but much, much smaller than yesterday's show. In the distance were many shelled buildings and there was hardly an intact roof in sight. I remember Christophe being a huge hit on his unicycle but what stuck out for me were the fresh graves in the previously grassy courtyard area between the buildings.

The 15 or so graves were mounds of earth, outlined by bricks and marked with wooden planks with names and dates painted in green. The wooden signs couldn't have been more than 30cm wide by 1 metre in height, shaped like mini-coffins and were decorated with the moon, star and the Bosnian symbol of the Fleur-de-Lys beneath that. I had always associated this with France, but in 1992 Bosnia and Herzegovina had adopted a coat of arms used by the Kotromanic dynasty, consisting of six golden Fleurs-de-Lys on a blue background with a white diagonal line. Below that followed the name of the deceased and their year of birth and death. The one closest to me was someone who had been born a year after me (1967) and had died the year before, in 1993. They were only 26 years old, too young to die, and yet there had been many deaths of people much younger, including many children. What a waste of life. Despite this tragedy, we had to keep up our smiles for those that remained. They were alive and with the ceasefire in place, they could finally start to hope for more out of life.

Talk of the bus of clowns spread and many more wanted to see us. One of the policemen wanted us to visit his village on the outskirts of Mostar. His wife and family had prepared a most amazing welcome for us which included coffee and a fresh salad. They were truly grateful for our visit and they wouldn't let a war get in the way of being hospitable. I remember feeling so privileged to share these moments with everyone in the early days of some hope for the future.

Later, in the heat of the afternoon, while resting back at the humanitarian aid depot, two white vehicles emblazoned with UNHCR logos, drove into the guarded area. They were curious about this big red bus.

Most of our group was taking 'time-out', but these newcomers, dressed rather smartly yet casually in white, were keen to speak to someone. I was always willing to connect and communicate, as was our drummer, Paul Brett. All I remember was that one man introduced himself as Martin. He was middle-aged, spoke with an American accent and there was something familiar about him. He was keen to find out more about our 'aid organisation with a difference' and I proudly told him and his companion all about our bus and our fleet of yellow trucks. He praised the work we were doing and asked if he could have his photo taken with us in front of the bus. We willingly obliged and then they wished us well and started to make tracks elsewhere.

Just before leaving, one of their group shook my hand and then muttered that I had just met Martin Sheen, the movie star! I was gob-smacked. What was he doing in this part of the world? Why had I not taken his photograph? I realised too late. No wonder he had seemed familiar, but I just hadn't expected him in this location and had also been thrown by the UNHCR vehicles. It was only many years later that I heard that he had been filming in the area. The film was called 'Gospa'. He was playing a priest who was persecuted by communist officials for encouraging pilgrimages to Medjugorje, where six school children claimed they had seen the Virgin Mary (Gospa) in 1981. It was a shame I never had the opportunity to say that our bus had inadvertently also been to Medjugorje, as part of the peace convoy that also delivered aid to the besieged Sarajevo in June 1992. The bus and the work of The Serious Road Trip had even been blessed by accompanying monks. Our organisation was not linked to any faith, but I personally found this blessing reassuring.

How amazing to think that the Virgin Mary had appeared so close to a place of such destruction, when no doubt her messages had tried to bring peace.

The next morning, after two action-packed days, we set out to rejoin the convoy drivers in Podstrana, Split and to get ready for our onward leg towards Dubrovnik.

There was much merriment in our camp as everyone celebrated the bus's success in Bosnia. There were some squaddies over from the British Battalion, helping to fix one of the trucks and the Land Rover. It was their day off and yet they chose to work and help us in return for some juggling balls and juggling lessons. Some of them had even worked up to earning themselves a Serious Road Trip T-shirt which was worth its weight in gold I heard. Despite all our short-comings, at least we were appreciated by many. No doubt the juggling also helped relieve some of the stress that the British soldiers endured whilst in service. Our lack of finances and resources seemed to attract the necessary people to keep us on the road.

Some other good news greeted us. The Premiere Urgence crew who had been held hostage by the Serbs had finally been released. We didn't get to see them as they had been airlifted out by helicopter. The President of France, Mitterand, had negotiated something and had paid a huge ransom for their release. What a relief for them and their friends and families. We hoped this didn't set a precedent for future kidnappings; I wasn't so sure our governments would pay such money. At least they were now free and we celebrated this too. Their group was one of our biggest supporters on the ground, and we valued their friendship.

Another group, who we relied upon and vice-versa, was the German 'Schueler Helfen Leben'. They were a group of school pupils/students who had set about helping their peers in these war-torn areas in 1992. Their organisation was run by young people and was for young people. There were definitely some shared goals, but they were much younger than us and virtually straight out of school.

Our contact was the freckly, bespeckled Christian, who got around in a beat-up estate (station-wagon) car and looked as though he was still in his teens. He had another hard-working volunteer with him, Dorothea Fleck. She was small, had a simple bob haircut, and seemed quite meek at first... but she was full of great ideas and action. Eager to help us in any way possible she had organised a beautiful multi-coloured parachute to join our various props.

Christian was more focused on the new Mercedes-Benz Unimog truck that had joined our fleet. They had been responsible for this new addition and it would help transport the many boxes of school supplies, educational equipment and other necessary goods from their warehouse in Germany into Bosnia. These convoys made up a fair chunk of the humanitarian aid the trucks were now shifting. This expensive modern truck certainly gave our organisation a different look from the trusty old beaten-up Bedfords, but blended in with a canary yellow paint job and a depiction of 'Road Runner' stretched out on one side. It became known as the 'Menimog' as Meni drove it initially. All the trucks had names; 'Wolfy', the Sarajevan Olympics mascot truck, was driven by Peter Gulliver, 'Rebel' had a distinctive wizard Smurf image and was driven by Roger Field, 'Suzie' was driven by John Pinkerton and 'Jabba' had been Yoyo's truck.

There was not much room at Magda's with a full team of clowns, convoy drivers and our bus and trucks there, not to mention all the visitors we attracted, so we were eager to get on with the rest of our tour.

With our show taking better shape with every performance, we were raring to continue down the coast towards Makarska and beyond.

The sun shone brightly as we made our way from one hotel housing refugees to the next.

Some of these places were familiar to me from our tour the year before, but everything was also very different as we were travelling by bus with a far bigger team. One main difference was getting everyone up and going in the morning. The year before, with our smaller team and Johnie eager to get going, I was often the last one up in the morning. Being a professional and probably hyperactive into the equation as well, Johnie was always aiming to be ready for a show ahead of time. His words echoed in my head like a mantra. 'Don't leave the children waiting, whatever you do, don't make them wait!'

Now it seemed that if I didn't wake up, the rest would just carry on sleeping and we could easily be late for a show.

It was an exhausting task trying to herd hungry and sleepy performers who could have done with a few extra hours sleep. My role as alarm-clock didn't win me any favours, but no one else wanted to be in that position either, or didn't have a watch to know the time.

It didn't help not having a bathroom on the bus where you could go and freshen up. We had to be happy with a splash of water over the face and a cup of coffee and slice of bread. At other times we did manage to rig up a make-shift shower using a hose-pipe connected to the water container, poked out the 'kitchen' window, right next to our painting of Snoopy. This required more time and there was not exactly much privacy for a proper shower either. I sometimes got around this by showering in my bikini.

Of course, we usually got there on time or at least in the nick of time, but I do remember one day when it had been exceptionally hard to get going and we were an hour late. Instead of an excited crowd of children we were greeted by a handful of mums, who explained that the children hadn't been able to wait and had gone for a swim in the sea instead. In such heat, that was only to be expected. Maybe I was expecting a professional commitment, but we were amateurs after all, with a heavy schedule of at least two shows a day, in different locations. On top of this, two of our clowns, Allan and Yoyo, were expected to drive us there too, with Christophe or Sneijana navigating. All in all we did extremely well under the circumstances.

The colourful parachute was greatly appreciated by children if we had extra time available after a show and the numbers weren't too large. We played games of lifting and lowering the parachute, with children holding the outstretched sides whilst trying to stop a juggling ball, placed on top, from falling. It was simple but beautiful for both participants and onlookers. The crowds continued to be held spellbound by Christophe and Yoyo's blind juggling act. They would juggle clubs blindfolded facing the crowd, which was already something, and then would proceed to face each other and throw the clubs juggling between themselves.

The height of the spinning diabolos also created much suspense as they were thrown between this dynamic duo to the sound of the rolling drum.

My spinning pois, with jingling bells on my ankle and magic bag trick also continued to enthrall. I just hoped that the strings wouldn't get tangled up when I tried to do the spinning pois with one hand. When they did, that created its own humour. With a full face of make-up, hat and double layered costume, as well as much running to and fro, I remember feeling very, very hot at times. At least the receptive crowd would make up for the momentary discomfort. It was the least we could do, when you considered the pain these people had experienced and continued to experience.

The shows blurred into one another, although there was one that stuck out. It was Mirella's birthday and someone had come up with an idea to surprise her. The guys made a rudimentary cream pie made out of whipped cream on a plate. During the course of the show, we started singing Happy Birthday to her as she sat on a chair centre-stage. Her surprise turned to horror as one of the clowns promptly pushed her face into the cream pie, then dowsed her with a bucket of water. It may have looked rather funny to the audience, but it definitely wasn't the type of birthday treat I would have appreciated. Understandably she was not amused but put on a brave face over it all.

We needed to take ferries to some of the refugee centres on absolutely stunning islands. I was amazed at how the bus actually fitted on. We only had three or four centimetres to spare on one journey and even had to let some air out of the tyres. How close was that! We found ourselves on the island of Korcula and whilst wandering around one day we stumbled across a sign stating that here was the house where Marco Polo had been born! We had always associated him with Venice and Italy, rather than Croatia, although we guessed that this land had somehow belonged to Italy at the time. In any case, through our travelling to this region, we somehow felt linked to the Great Explorer himself. We hadn't been expecting that on our humanitarian journey.

The hotels were brimming with refugees who were very displaced in this Croatian island setting. As we travelled from one island to the next, I got chatting to a local who was on her way somewhere else. When I explained that we weren't tourists, but volunteers working with the refugees, she was full of awe for our actions.

'You aren't paying for the ferry ticket are you?' she asked.

In fact we were. She felt moved to speak with the captain of the ferry, to explain what we were doing. He in turn felt inspired to give us the passage for free, saving us a good 200 Deutschmarks. It was

174

touching to see how everyone got into the spirit of giving and helping us on our way.

Once back on the mainland we headed further south. Some of the hotels were splashed with giant holes where mortars had attacked and were riddled with bullet holes too. Someone told us how the tanks had arrived in their village. It felt surreal to see the damage and hear all of this as we approached the beautiful city of Dubrovnik. This jewel in the Adriatic had suffered its own siege from October 1991 to May 1992. We had seen the television footage showing the attack of the city from land, sea and air. This historic World Heritage Site had undergone its own damage but we could also see that, thankfully, much had been rebuilt in the intervening two years.

The streets remained rather deserted however, and it was obvious that tourism was hugely impacted by the war. For a start, the many hotels and small holiday dwellings along the coast were obviously full of displaced persons. Aside from this, most tourists didn't want to be caught up in a conflict. From a distance it was hard to really know which were the safer areas.

By now our energies were starting to wane and we also had our moments of suffering from our own bus version of 'cabin-fever'. People were getting on each other's nerves and arguments started surfacing. No doubt alcohol also enflamed situations. I was starting to be acutely aware that Allan really needed a break from everything. He wasn't the only one. Yoyo had also lived through some intense moments during months of dangerous convoys. He may have headed to London with a mission to embark on a Bananas 4 Split 2, but Allan had left convoys in need of a break when we recruited him for the project. Maybe their previous experiences in combat zones had meant they had joined the project running on empty. I had been grateful to have team members who understood the war situation, but their last energies had been consumed during this worthwhile clowning project; they both needed a serious break from communal living and giving. Thankfully, the trip was coming to a natural end.

We travelled further south to Cavtat, near the Montenegran border, for our final show. I remember being able to freshen up in the sea afterwards and then enjoyed the luxury of an outside shower on the beach. What a journey all down the Croatian coast it had been during May and June with that brief interlude into Bosnia. None of us was really certain of what the future held for us, we had been all-consumed with getting through the tour. The bus lurched up the coast as we travelled without speaking, listening to the Time of the Gypsies soundtrack. This had become one of our theme tunes.

175

The project was over, but we still needed to get back to base, and our next destinations were unfolding day by day.

Once back in Podstrana, there was some exciting news from the London office. Christopher and Goblin (Chris Fleury) were leaping up and down at the end of the phone. A film crew from New Zealand wanted to make a documentary about our unconventional organisation. At last some proper documentation of what we were doing and serious acknowledgement that what we were doing was important.

I had been in London when the researcher for this project had interviewed and filmed several of us in the offices. Jane Cooper was a NZ acquaintance of Goblin's with a background in film. She had approached us asking how she could help. They had come up with the idea of the documentary over breakfast in some nearby greasy spoon café and now here was the fantastic result.

The problem was that they did not intend to come for another month or so. Our clowning project was seriously finished and it was too early to speak about a Bananas Part 3. At first this seemed impossible timing.

However, this was an opportunity that we could not afford to miss, so we needed to get our thinking caps on.

At least the convoys were ready for action and drivers seemed to turn up more frequently than clowns.

Once we managed to work out our own answers for ourselves, I was sad to realise that Yoyo really did need to leave and was not about to stay longer to meet the demands of 'journalists'. Many of the convoy drivers had felt let down by journalists in the past, so there was some lack of trust of them in general, to say the least, and I could understand why he was not prepared to accommodate their schedule. But this was a different situation. This film crew was coming all the way from New Zealand to focus on our project. They weren't journalists seeking a way into Bosnia to cover the situation any way possible. However, he needed a break and his mind was made up to leave.

Mirella needed to get back to her partner in England, so we would be two clowns down, but we still had a team and plenty of drivers with clowning abilities. When held up at checkpoints on the way to Sarajevo, they would pass the time juggling or unicycling, much to the interest of local children and soldiers guarding these road-blocks.

There would be a show of some form and in any case a convoy to film. We just had to recover from our intense project and rethink some of the existing tricks.

Another pressing issue was our accommodation. There were too many of us to consider staying on at Magda's for the summer. We would need to relocate and so we found a new possibility, a house in Dugi Rat, right on the water's edge. There was far more space here to park the trucks and the price was lower, due to the extra distance from Split. We weren't right next to that dangerous stretch of coastal road so it was a much more peaceful setting, even if a little remote. We managed to get rides back to London for Yoyo and Mirella and there were tearful farewells. For a start, this threw our romance into the unknown as I was unsure when and where Yoyo and I would meet again. London or Paris maybe? Maybe it was just a fleeting relationship and we had been thrown together through circumstances. I liked to believe that it was deeper than that, but there were no guarantees. We were young and situations could change day by day. Having also conceived this project together, it was more than a lovers' farewell, as I lost my left-handed 'right-hand man'. It was a real wrench for me and I was pretty emotional for a while.

Then Christophe and Sniejana decided to spend some down time with her family on the nearby border of Croatia and Bosnia.

With no pressing commitments elsewhere, Allan had agreed to stay on as bus-driver and clown. He seemed to have moved beyond the heated outbursts on the bus.

So it was just Paul, Allan, myself and all the convoy drivers for a good few weeks. At times it was seriously isolating being a female in such a male-dominated world. I was happy to find the company of various women from Premiere Urgence and Jutta, who continued to work with the special needs refugees in the area.

We needed to prepare for the TVNZ crew and we set the goal of returning to Mostar for another show. After all, I had been determined to return after the pleas of the children on our first visit. We made a trip to Mostar to set something up and set a date for a show.

There we were able to link up with one of the older teenagers who remembered us from last time. It felt odd not to be there with the whole team, but he and the others we met, were happy to hear of our return. We also met with some of the teachers from school. They excitedly told us of the impact our show had made.

Before our first arrival the children had drawn pictures of soldiers, tanks, bombs and destruction. After our trip the children drew flowers, balloons and clowns and the drawings were full of colour and hope. It filled me with immense joy to know that our trip to Mostar had made such an impact. I was lost in thought. The children had seen people from elsewhere, bringing a slice of life to them from outside a war. I liked to think that this awareness of something other than war might create a new possibility of peace, that we might have been a symbol of something other than fighting. Still, there was a lot to it and it had had a positive effect on the children beyond the enjoyment of the show.

It was also good to see that lots of the rubble had been cleared from the streets of the city.

Even our colleagues from War Child, who shared a London office with us, were setting up a bakery in Mostar, providing much-needed bread.

Another driver from Canada who had joined our group, Peter, could also offer his musical talents for a concert, if we could sort out a sound-system.

And so the return to Mostar with the NZ film-crew started to take shape.

In the meantime, a journalist sent from the Big Issue was also hoping to cover The Serious Road Trip's actions in Bosnia. Things were really picking up for us.

She arrived with the TVNZ crew of three, along with Christopher from London, in a great flurry. All of a sudden there were more females than usual so the drivers were on best behaviour. There were all sorts of interviews with team members that needed to be slotted in, as well as loading up the trucks.

The priority was the convoy. Tony Gaffney had sorted out 25 tonnes of aid to transport through Schuler Helfen Leben, and they wanted to take it to Celic, a place that had not received anything for months, according to Moona from SEA (Scottish European Aid). Yes, our paths still crossed in small ways, but our lives had moved on in different directions. With our trucks being Bedfords and 4 x 4, they were able to reach places where other trucks couldn't venture. They could get over mountainous terrain. Celic was on the front line, some 40km from Tuzla. It was a small township that had been cut off from the delivery of humanitarian aid due to the difficult access, or maybe just forgotten. Our trucks arrived like answers to their prayers as their stores were visibly empty when the convoy arrived. The local people had been worrying about how they would survive another winter, when in rolled our bright yellow trucks bringing hope and much needed food. One of the locals tearfully told the drivers how it meant so much to her to know that other people had thought about them in their hour of need. She and others were extremely moved by this lifeline that The Serious Road Trip had thrown them before winter set in and the already difficult roads would be blocked with snow.

The convoy was not without difficulty and the drivers had heard shelling whilst sleeping out on their way back. As was usually the case, they had parked the trucks in a circle formation and then some slept on top of the canvas covers for comfort. One shell had literally whistled past them, metres away and into the trees beyond, but hadn't exploded. Ironically, the film crew had been sleeping more safely in a UN base further away, but captured the drivers' reactions the next morning over a rough breakfast.

A few days later they rolled jubilantly back to base, another convoy under their belts. The TV crew, and Anna from the Big Issue, had plenty of material for their public.

There was no time to rest though, as we planned to enter Mostar with the bus the very next day, while the film crew was still with us.

We had come up with this fun idea of arriving with the bus packed full of balloons. We didn't have a fancy pump, so it required some serious puffing to blow up a few hundred or more balloons to create the effect we desired. It was everyone on deck to help.

It was incredible seeing the reactions as we drove down the main street with the bus leaving a trail of balloons behind us. Naturally the children followed and we headed to the place where others eagerly awaited our show on the outskirts of town. It was not the Handball Stadium like last time but there were hundreds who had turned up to see us. Our convoy team was there for action too and even those who might have looked too cool to wear face-paints got into the spirit of it all. Roger drove the bus, helped by Graeme who was only too eager to show off his juggling skills. Other drivers Pinkerton, Dave, Trevor, Phil, CJ and Gaffney also got in on the action. At the end of the show featuring Christophe, Paul and myself, all the Trippers grabbed one tub of face-paint each, and with a sponge, we covered as many cheeks and noses as possible, not to mention the occasional child's torso decorated with a love heart or flower.

It felt like one big colour frenzy as there were so many eager children scrambling for their slice of the action.

Later, once everything had calmed down we headed down to the Neretva river to see everyone enjoying some time by the water. Children played clapping games and young adults were diving into the river from the makeshift bridge, as had always been the tradition in the summer. They had even rigged up a platform to dive from the same height as the bridge would have been. Meanwhile, near the entrance to the bridge, there was even a shopkeeper sporting a red hat, who had opened up with a small selection of postcards and trinkets. Now I finally got to see how beautiful the bridge had been as it featured on the dusty cards. It really had been something spectacular. No wonder people used to come from afar to visit this city with its arched Stari Most bridge.

179

There was a long way to go, but at least there was renewed life in this bombed shell of a city. Not far away, there were queues of people carrying water canisters to be replenished in the sweltering summer heat. Had I brought my swimwear with me I might have joined them in those tempting cool blue waters. Instead I was wandering the nearby streets sporting my clowning hat; face-paints dripping down my face with the TV crew in tow. It was important to let people know how the war had affected everyone, and of the vital work we were doing. They were keen to find out our motives. 'I'm here for the kids! I love seeing them smile, jumping around for joy, and I get a lot of energy from the kids just having fun. That's why I'm here!' I proudly declared.

We had come armed not only with balloons and face-paints but also ink. Somehow, on one of our previous trips to organise this day's events, we had heard how a lithographer needed some ink to get his business going again. Christophe's parents and long-time supporters of The Serious Road Trip were also here with us; they sourced the ink just over the border in Croatia. When they explained who the ink was for, the shopkeeper had donated half the ink for his fellow man across the border. It was heart-warming to hear this story of the generosity of one man to another, despite being separated by war. We had provided a link of friendship. It was also signalling a new beginning for the artist. He needed to start making a living through his art, and would be able to make prints of the much-loved bridge that had been lost but not forgotten.

Meanwhile, on a flat area near the steps leading to Stari Most a makeshift café had been set up. The rubble had been cleared even more. There may have only been a couple of tables and a few chairs but nonetheless it was there.

Some of the crew were setting up a sound system in preparation for the concert, which needed to be powered by a generator. With our bus parked at the top of the steps, the crowd was already starting to form. A few of us entertained the children at the back of the bus with face-painting and juggling antics, while the sound-check was completed.

Soon the steps and surrounding walls were covered in people, sitting and waiting for the concert to begin. It may have only been Peter and his guitar in front of a microphone, with Paul Brett on his African Djambe drum, but they gave everyone a concert to remember.

I danced wildly with a circle of children on the small clear space in front of the musicians. The words to one of the songs, ' There's a war going on inside me,' echoed around us. Night was falling and we provided lighting with some torches.

To cap the whole show off, Christophe and Graeme climbed onto the elevated edge of one of the ruins and after some juggling of fire clubs, they proudly blew fire into the night. It was quite surreal with the backdrop of the ruined city. The burning light was magical in the darkness of nightfall. What a way to end an important day.

The concert over, I managed to withdraw to the private quarters of the bus and sleep soundly, declining any offers of joining others for what promised to be a party into the night. Our goals had been reached and I was relieved to have done what we set out to do.

The bus rattled triumphantly back to the coast after a few farewells. The TV crew had managed to catch us all in action and had made many interviews.

Once back in Dugi Rat at Vila Diana, crates of beers were brought in and we celebrated with numerous friends in a fancy-dress party. Many people slept where they fell and the next morning Allan awoke unable to speak. He had literally fallen on his jaw and it had broken. He needed emergency care at the hospital in Split and was unable to eat for weeks, except through a straw, poor chap. He was so ready for a break, having given so much, and with this accident his body was telling him to stop everything, including talking.

Before returning to London with the bus there was one last thing Tony Gaffney wanted to do. A young Bosnian woman had approached us in London. She was studying there, but her parents and young teenage brother were blocked in East Mostar. He was fast approaching the age to enter the Bosnian Army and she feared the worst. Was Tony able to help in any way? He kept this plan very quiet but had linked up with the adolescent boy on our recent trip. Feeling despondent after two years' involvement in Bosnia, and knowing that although there was this ceasefire between the Croatians and Bosniaks, there was no real end to the war. Tony felt he just wanted to do something different, as though he wanted to know that he had 'saved' one person. Of course our convoys had provided vital supplies to starving people, but they were still stuck in the middle of the war that dragged on and on, and our earlier efforts to stop the war had been futile. The plan was to return with the bus and just a couple of brave people, to enable the youngster to leave Mostar concealed in our large costume and props box downstairs.

This was extremely dangerous should they be caught and it was a nail-biting day as we waited to see if they managed this risky rescue. Fortunately the plan worked and he escaped, much to all our relief. It had been the perfect hiding place, but it was not something we took lightly or repeated in the bus.

We did not risk transporting him further than Croatia, but eventually he was able to find a way to England to be reunited with his sister and then went on to join a secondary school rather than the army. What a change in direction that had been for him.

The bus trip back to London was fairly quiet, as I pondered the future. My immediate desire was to hook up with Yoyo if possible. With the bus safely sheltered in Cricklewood bus station, I was free to do what I wanted with the last days of summer.

Chapter 17

Paris – Christmas in Cork, Heavy Metal and Fundraising

Yoyo was in Paris and asked me to join him there. Would this be like the time Moona had called me to join him in Scotland? I was nervous but was prepared to take the risk and, at the very worst, Paris was somewhere I would enjoy being, regardless of how my romantic life panned out. I took the first Eurolines coach possible, as this was the cheapest way to get there, and arrived in my favourite city with heart beating ferociously, relieved to be reunited again. After any project of this nature, it was hard to readjust back to life from before. It was a relief to be in the company of someone who understood, who was a clown and had been there too. Even those in the London office didn't always understand us and had different interests or priorities, despite working theoretically towards the same goals.

Yoyo was waiting for me with his black curly locks and wide toothy grin. We sped around Paris on a Vespa, like there was no tomorrow, with me clinging on for dear life. We were staying in his mother's and stepfather's apartment while they were on holiday. In fact, Paris in August is different in that all the locals are on holiday, yet the city is alive with tourists.

We blended in perfectly as we whizzed over to Sacré Coeur in Montmartre or around the Eiffel Tower. I was introduced to many of his friends and we also hooked up with various truck drivers from Premiere Urgence. We drank little espresso coffees at the counters of

183

cafés and feasted on fresh croissants, baguette breadsticks and Camembert cheese. Yoyo was a pretty good cook too and had numerous friends who were writers and artists. How I loved blending in with every situation that each day brought.

I was in heaven basking in French culture, language and food and loved being in the city of lovers with someone special, who knew the city well. I far preferred speeding around the City of Light above ground, rather than the usual Underground Metro experience of before, and Yoyo whizzed in and out of traffic like an expert.

But as with everything, those carefree moments can't last forever, although we try to hang onto them for dear life. The holiday was over, London was calling and the return to reality was inevitable.

Living in the office at Greenland Street was no easy undertaking and trying to find some personal space was nearly impossible. As a good number of us were living there, it was only natural that we sometimes stayed up working until midnight if needed. We would head onto the High Street for a quick meal at the kebab shop, McDonald's or elsewhere, or we might get a few provisions from the supermarket to heat up in the one pot in the makeshift kitchen in the hallway. We were often drawn into our local pub, Liberties, which functioned almost like the homely living room that we missed in the office. There was usually a good atmosphere and the jukebox and music kept things upbeat. I loved putting Seal's song 'Crazy' on, as it really seemed to sum things up. It was a chance to talk with drivers, over a pint, who had just returned from convoys. These conversations became our version of debriefing. I'm sure it was not quite as official as other organisations' procedures, but that was our way of dealing with things and, of course, we didn't know any better. Most had somewhere else to head to, but needed a few nights to readjust as best they could. Their experiences in a war-zone were something that would change their lives forever.

We were drumming up a fair bit of interest now after The Big Issue had run a feature story about us too. Allan was on the front cover, sporting a bright red wig and his tartan clowning trousers, hitch-hiking in Bosnia!

What a moment that was, when we walked along Camden High Street, to see the various sellers on the street waving their magazines with our very own clown on the front. They were pretty excited too to recognise some of our faces in the magazine.

The article attracted more volunteers of varying ages. One who really stuck out was a teenager, Abi, who had just returned from visiting various concentration camps in Poland as part of a school trip.

She drew parallels between the Holocaust of the Jews during WWII and the persecution of the Muslims in Bosnia. This concept of searching for 'scapegoats' was something deep in the human psyche, whether that was the 'black sheep' of the family or a whole ethnic group. It reminded me how, in history, individuals had been singled out and 'sacrificed' in a scapegoat style such as in mob-lynchings. Whether they were guilty or not, they were blamed for something, even if that was just daring to be different. Even Jesus Christ could be seen as the ultimate scapegoat sacrifice in history and he had willingly accepted his fate. I had written about this theme while in high school after reading *To Kill a Mockingbird* and *Anne Frank's Diary*, and later in my studies at university, doing a dissertation on Haitian literature and the beautiful novel by Jacques Roumain, *Les Gouverneurs de la Rosee*. This theme was now cropping up loud and clear in my everyday life, rather than some remote situation. I still felt compelled to do something about it. Abi was equally fired up to help, and for now that work was fundraising in London.

We even did a promotion for The Serious Road Trip on Sir Walter Raleigh's famous ship, the *Golden Hind*, aided by some professional circus performers; they wanted to fund-raise for our cause at their upcoming season.

The trapeze artist hung gracefully from her trapeze attached to the main mast, while we enlivened things up on deck. To think that Raleigh had travelled around the world on this ship with his dedicated crew risking their lives on the journeys. My mind wandered and drew links between their adventures and our own. To me it seemed that we both attempted to cross new frontiers.

Fundraising was reaching new heights and a new volunteer, Tony Rees, had joined our maverick outfit. He had been fondly nicknamed 'Spesh', because his speciality was setting up special events. He had started with War Child, across the hallway, but he found himself swapping sides. He had been involved in co-ordinating various fund-raising concerts, which could be described as dance or club events. His first one, earlier in the year, involved the famous 'Dust Brothers', also known as the Chemical Brothers and had raised a profit of 6,000 GBP. This was a much needed sum of money and went towards office rent and diesel for our trucks. Musical gigs had been our first fundraising events, just three years prior at the Rising Sun. Now another was starting to take shape, which was going to be even bigger!

One of our original drivers, Graeme Bint, also had plenty of contacts in the music world. He'd been wondering about getting his friend, Charlie Hall, a top underground DJ to be part of a rave fundraiser, but Charlie took it a stage further. Charlie and his friend Lol Hammond from Soft Cell started working on releasing a CD and managed to get a track donated from Orbital, which really got the ball rolling. Orbital were massive in the dance scene, and then many other groups followed, including Laurent Garnier, Leftfield, The Drum Club, the Dust brothers again and The Orb, all willing to donate tracks to our cause.

Melody Maker got involved with the promotion and distribution and when the music was finally released it was a comprehensive package with 3 CDs and 20 fantastic tracks. There was a lovely colourful booklet with information and photos about our work in Bosnia to complete the package. It was fantastic to have such a tangible, quality product that raised our profile, and funds for the projects. I know Christopher was extremely pleased as it made his job in the office so much easier. Trying to make ends meet was a constant battle in the charity world, run with volunteers and with so many pressing needs.

Another major coup was the TV New Zealand documentary that was finally aired in NZ during November, as part of a much-watched Tuesday documentary slot on prime-time television. Our profile was going from strength to strength. The coverage showed off all aspects of our work and included interviews with people whose lives we had touched in Bosnia. At a time when coverage of the war-zone was almost limited to impersonal clips of mortar fire taken at a distance on the news, here the public were presented with raw emotion, showing how people's lives had been affected by war.

It showed the child who had stopped talking because she had been so affected by unspeakable horrors and the cramped living conditions of the families who had been forced to flee. It showed the bombed out buildings and treacherous mountain roads, and pointed out that the footage showed conditions in summer, as opposed to the journeys we made in the cold and snow to get the food through in winter. Our viewers saw the kindness extended to our drivers as they stopped en route to Sarajevo to visit a family. Here they were offered a cup of precious coffee made in a Turkish way with lots of coffee grains floating around. They didn't have much, but they were generous with their time and with what little they had to share.

Even I was able to see more closely what happened on a convoy. Although I had spoken with drivers, it was hard explaining certain things with just words. There was the woman interviewed in Mostar who looked moved to tears, saying that we were the first organisation that had come to help the children to laugh or was it love, she had said, I couldn't tell the difference, and both were important. Either way you couldn't help but get caught up in her emotion of what our actions meant to them in their hour of need.

I remember hearing from friends in NZ that this documentary had finally given a face to the Bosnian conflict which had featured on the news for two years. As a nation, those who had watched the programme were extremely proud of the handful of New Zealanders and international friends, who really were making a difference actively helping in such an imaginative way. Somehow it replaced the feeling of helplessness that viewers get when they see suffering so far away, with a sense that at least someone is doing something about it. The generous donations started to roll in as the New Zealanders banded together making a difference and helping us on our way. It was very heart-warming for us to see, after such a long time of feeling that people just didn't understand, and didn't see the point of funding something so far removed from their lives. Here was a lengthy documentary that had somehow captured the heart of who we were and what we were about. It showed the trucks doing their 'Sarajevo shuffle' as they zig-zagged on convoy avoiding sniper fire. It showed that we were all volunteers and doing it for the love of it. It showed the enormous amount of alcohol consumed before and after convoys, blocking out the fears the drivers faced, or celebrating afterwards that they were still alive; or even passing the time between convoys, along with learning to juggle. Tony Gaffney's words echoed humorously in our heads 'we don't deliberately go to places where no one else goes, we're not the Starship Enterprise...' but he was eager to point out that if we managed to get there, how come the bigger government-funded agencies didn't, after sometimes promising they would? The documentary maker, Trisha Stafford summed us up by saying that 'The Serious Road Trip bring a forgotten spirit of hope to a country at war,' and those few words seemed to encapsulate it all.

While the film featured our bus with the words, 'London to New Zealand' on it, it did not elaborate, however, on the initial goals of this project.

I had been wondering if it was now time to take the bus to New Zealand, as we had originally set out to do. I had clung to this idea, but was starting to realise that it was almost impossible to do.

Most of the original crew were gone or were focused on helping in Bosnia. It would be hard to divert their attention back to the initial goal. After all, most of them had joined for different reasons and mostly unaware of this first plan. Even Yoyo, who had seemed united with me on this NZ goal, could see it would be unlikely, now that other things had happened.

That didn't stop his lust to explore the world and although I didn't want to see it, he was looking for other options for travel.

He no longer enjoyed my regular company and was more interested in a 'see you once a week' type of friendship. He was distancing himself in preparation for his ultimate departure.

Now that I had found romantic companionship, I was reluctant to let go of it so soon. I was far from my family in NZ in an environment dominated by mostly men with big hearts, who were addicted to alcohol and adrenalin.

Fortunately my friends in Ireland were beckoning me to travel there for a break. With Christmas on the horizon, Caroline's family in Cork again offered me a family Christmas away from home. Meanwhile Yoyo was asking for some alone time to work out what he wanted. He was five years younger and not ready to settle into a long-term commitment.

As I set off from London, leaving Yoyo behind, I knew that things would be different on my return, even though I didn't want to admit it.

On arrival in Dublin, I found Caroline, Johnie and Caroline's sister all happily living together. Things were fun and upbeat as per usual in their company. Caroline had a way of repeating how 'grand' things were and what 'great craic' it all was. Johnie, being the natural entertainer that he was, kept things buoyant, never allowing our feelings to sink too low. That was his aim, to keep people smiling. He had made a profession out of it, after all. It was reassuring to be around such good friends, and no doubt they sensed my predicament.

Caroline, Linda and I made our way to Cork to prepare for the Christmas festivities with her parents, brother and ageing bachelor cousin Hugh.

It was a lovely time celebrating with a warm Christmas dinner, which contrasted with my usual BBQ-style summer Christmas in New Zealand. While this was a more intimate family occasion, there was also the visit to the hospital to check on the various patients under Dr Moore's care, who were unable to return home for this day. My parents had sent me warm underwear for Christmas; had I been in NZ, I might have been trying out some new swimwear, shorts or beach towel. We had grown up with Christmas cards showing snowy, wintry scenes and while there was no snow on this occasion, it certainly was winter with no chance of splashing in some surf.

I must have been rather run-down from all the events of that year and my knife-edge lifestyle and I was grateful for this moment to relax.

However, as can often be the way, when you do relax, your body allows itself to become ill, almost because you are in a safe place to do so.

I was developing cystitis (urinary infection) but had no idea what it was. As the days went by, the pain of going to the toilet was becoming excruciating. The consumption of alcohol at this festive time of year was only making matters worse. I had been hoping it would just go away, but within a couple of days I was crippled with pain and back-ache.

Caroline and Linda came running to my aid. Being a time when doctor's surgeries were closed, I was fortunate to be staying with an orthopaedic surgeon.

Caroline needed to go and pick a friend up from the train station, so Linda acted as my spokesperson to her father since I was so embarrassed to speak directly. It was decided that I needed antibiotics and so a prescription was written and medication sourced speedily. I had also added that I was allergic to penicillin.

I opened the bottle and quickly took one of the pills, only reading the label afterwards. That didn't sound like my usual antibiotic. Are you sure it is not penicillin? Linda reached for a medical book to reassure me, only to find that somehow in the 'Chinese whispers' consultation, I had indeed taken an incorrect medicine. Of course, I started to panic and her father was out walking the dog at this stage. Last time I had taken penicillin as a toddler, I had gone into anaphylactic shock and been rushed to the hospital. I imagined I needed to get to the hospital urgently but both parents were now out. Linda went to call an ambulance, as Caroline arrived with her guest fresh off the train. Linda raced down to greet them, requesting that we set off for the hospital instantly, and so I was bundled into the car with no time to lose. I wondered whether my throat was about to swell up or what the reaction might be.

Some 15 minutes later, we arrived at Accident and Emergency to be greeted by staff who had been warned of the situation. They explained that I should have had the allergic reaction by now, so not to be alarmed. I was relieved to think that I wasn't about to choke or stop breathing. However, they did want to keep me in overnight to check that I didn't have a kidney infection and to put me on an intravenous drip.

Now it was the thought of a needle that terrorised me and having to keep it in my arm. The nurse had to proceed gently, using her tactics for terrified children. I overreacted and howled that I didn't want a needle, although I knew that there was no escaping it. How odd to think that I had faced crisis situations in war-zones and orphanages with a brave face, and yet here I was whimpering with fear in a normal hospital in safe Ireland! Still, this time I was the patient.

For the next few days my pace of life ground to a halt as I lay in a hospital bed with drips connected to me. In hindsight, it was probably what I needed to force me to slow down.

I was in a women's ward with 20 or so beds and a variety of ages and conditions. Caroline made sure I was stocked up with girly magazines, grapes and chocolate treats. She even arranged for a handsome ex-boyfriend of hers to visit. There was no chance of a romance, of course, but it felt reassuring to have a man with a gorgeous Irish accent and great sense of humour pay me some attention for a few hours. After all, Yoyo's attentions were being diverted elsewhere, which was not a great feeling for me. It was reassuring to know at least this young man cared about how I was doing, as well as Caroline and family.

I was taken down to have a kidney ultrasound, which was quite a process; with cold gels, and me wearing a hospital gown with my drip in tow. To my relief my kidneys were fine. By now the antibiotics were doing their thing and my backache was disappearing too.

In a matter of days I was discharged and free to return to Cork, then onto Dublin for a New Year's Eve party. My mind wasn't quite so focused on the revelry as I was the only one not drinking due to the antibiotics, and there were many happy couples present, including Caroline and Johnie. I pondered what the New Year of 1995 would bring. The very next day I went back onto the ferry and the Slattery's coach bound for London. Sea-sickness kicked in as the ferry rocked over the Irish Sea, but I was better once on solid land and in the bus. I'd had a break from the London office, humanitarian efforts and my romantic woes.

Once back there my life started to take on a new direction. Various members of The Serious Road Trip office had found a flat nearby in St Paul's Mews, which gave us another place to hang out in and party, other than the office or pub.

I heard that The Serious Road Trip had actually managed to facilitate a concert in Sarajevo with Bruce Dickinson and band. This was big, as he was the lead singer of Iron Maiden. The band had been asked to perform in Sarajevo and then it all looked as though it wouldn't happen when the UN were unable to get them in. Someone had approached The Serious Road Trip to help out with the transport. We were maybe the only people who could get them in. The Skidders (as we were delightfully known) discussed this as a team in Podstrana. Everyone acknowledged the dangers, but with a small break in the convoy timetable, they also thought it might break up some of the boredom of waiting for the next convoy and be good to give the trucks a run. Scottish Dave had volunteered and had driven them in the Unimog, along with all their equipment and one other Kiwi Road Tripper, Vance. Bruce Dickinson had even worn our T-shirt for his concert and on the back was printed, 'More Balls than Most' after the juggling company that donated thousands of balls to our cause.

This was some recompense for a concert that one of our group had tried to set up in Sarajevo with Massive Attack, although that concert didn't happen. It was a tricky thing sending musicians into war-zones when they had important gigs lined up afterwards. Understandably it didn't quite add up with insurance companies and people who just didn't want to take the risk. But not so for this courageous singer and group and our team that made it happen. It was a good boost to be able to celebrate this success.

Some 24 years later (April 2018) I would have the pleasure of meeting Bruce Dickinson at the movie premiere of *Scream for me Sarajevo*. The film showed his dangerous trip into Sarajevo and paid tribute to the British soldiers who engineered the project, The Serious Road Trip who stepped in to help transport them against all odds, and the grateful Sarajevan audience who managed to escape their war reality for a highly emotionally charged concert. Afterwards, at the Q and A session, I announced some of us were in the audience and he announced 'You guys are awesome, come and meet up with us now!' What an amazing meeting this was.

The office was relocating to Bayham Place, which was closer to the Camden Tube Station and pub called the Hope and Anchor, which we nick-named 'The Hopeless Wanker'. This meant that War Child and our group could pursue our differing directions, even if to the outside world we appeared to be helping the same people.

Yoyo had also decided to leave The Serious Road Trip; he had joined Encounter Overland Adventure travel. I would be seeing less and less of him: he needed to leave London for the training preparation for this new job, which involved journeys across Africa and other continents, lasting several months at a time. This was a blow, even though it had been fairly obvious that our relationship was no longer going in the same direction. I would still be able to see him a few more times before he would be ready to travel overseas and I clung onto this possibility, or the thought that he might not like it and come back, so as to soften the final blow. Of course, the final goodbye was tearful and a real wrench for me when it did come a couple of months later.

As for my living arrangements, a reasonably priced room in a shared house in Tottenham (N17) presented itself. I was familiar with the name thanks to football and the more famous Tottenham Court Road in central London, but this was a fair distance from that. The landlord, Nick Putz, was a performer who had volunteered for The Serious Road Trip; he was open to my going on projects at times, leaving the room vacant. It was something of a bachelor pad, and the room was smaller than the others, but it was all I needed and the house-mates were welcoming. Nick was slender, tall and dark with long hair, sparkly eyes and a very wide toothy grin.

I remember him teaching me the art of how to make tea using leaves, a teapot and a well-loved tea-cosy over it to keep it warm. Of course, the teapot needed to be heated up before pouring the water in: all things that you don't know when accustomed to using tea-bags in cups, as I had done till that moment. Nick and I would sit at the kitchen table listening to the radio, having tea and putting the world right. I knew to leave him be whenever the much-loved 'Archers' came on, and various other Radio 4 programmes. He was a member of Equity, which I thought was rather impressive and he was always busy getting ready for some juggling workshop or other clowning gigs on stilts, as that was his speciality. I enjoyed hearing how he found that children that weren't performing well in school could somehow be turned around through developing their confidence learning to juggle. Perhaps it was something in the brain that was kick-started through the juggling, or manipulating of spinning diabolos. Whatever it was, I thought it wonderful that a challenging situation could be turned around through circus skills. We certainly believed this was the case in our projects to date. I had even discovered that the importance of play was enshrined in the UN's convention on the Rights of the Child. Obviously there were many other important articles to do with a child's right to shelter, food and medical care, but article 31 states that: *'State parties recognise the right of the child to rest and leisure, to engage in play and recreational activities appropriate to the age of the child and to participate freely in cultural life and the arts.'*

This reinforced the importance of play and egged me on to continue doing the work that certain projects were focusing on. By now I was becoming known as the Children's Projects Co-ordinator in the office and was wondering what our next project would be. It felt good to have the freedom to choose what might be our next focus, but for now there were many other things to help with in the office, including fund-raising.

Often I didn't return home till late at night. The journey from

Camden was somewhat of a trek, involving the Tube with one change, a bus and then a short walk. Tottenham was a multicultural area of London, but I fitted into the sea of faces and the anonymity of living in a terraced house. My life still revolved around the office, but it was lovely to escape from that to my new home. It was my anchor in the turbulence of our existence in volatile situations.

While The Serious Road Trip remained a charity with predominantly males involved, there were a few women volunteers who would help with fundraising and provide moral support. One such woman was Jayne O'Connell. She was a Londoner and worked as a full-time temp doing accounting work. While that type of work may have been a far cry from what we were doing, she still had her wild and creative side, often singing along with whatever song was booming from the jukebox. I was impressed with her impeccable memory of lyrics and ability to blend favourite songs in compilation style onto cassette-tapes for us to enjoy in the office or at home. We hit it off instantly as good friends. Jayne had a wonderful imagination and wicked sense of humour. She was a faithful fan of The Serious Road Trip and could boost our spirits after a day in the Camden office, wondering where the next funding might come from, amongst many other stresses. Rather than heading to the pub, I felt more sophisticated being able to head to the restaurant called Ruby in the Dust on Camden High Street. A lunch meeting there with Jayne could easily turn into several hours, merging into dinner too. The name also made me think of a favourite song by the Rolling Stones, 'Ruby Tuesday', which Caroline and I had sung along to on Tuesdays in France whilst drinking red wine. Funny how things like this ritual continued.

Jayne and younger Abi weren't shy to don face-paints and a fancy hat and hit the streets of Camden Market, where we had permission to fundraise for our work. When asking for donations, dressing-up in costumes somehow gave us that necessary audacity to ask strangers to dip into their pockets. They seemed to respond to our fun-loving approach and were more generous in return. It felt right to explain about our work with children whilst sporting some of the costumes or props used on projects, such as my fluffy snake puppet.

On another occasion I remember fundraising for another children's charity (NSPCC), whereby we were able to split the proceeds. This gave us the possibility of collecting donations in areas such as the Bank area in central London, where we normally didn't venture. Here we really stuck out as we were surrounded by office-workers in suits, off to their financial institutions. What a contrast to our lives and to the

j

life I had led not so long ago as a full-time temp in the financial services, some three years earlier. To think that I too had been one of those workers taking the Tube and heading off to the office, even if it had been a temporary contract and I was a Kiwi on her OE in Europe blending in with the local Londoners.

If it hadn't been for my burning desire to use my foreign languages, maybe I wouldn't have found myself in the financial services in Luxembourg and then meeting someone about to leave for Romania, inviting my two friends to go with them on convoy. Ultimately that had led me from a more conventional path to this quite extraordinary one, although at the time, working in Luxembourg had seemed quite extraordinary for a Kiwi too.

After a hard day rattling the donation boxes, we were well rewarded with heavy canisters, brimming with one pound coins and plenty of silver and copper and the occasional note. Our arms and feet would ache, but we would be well rewarded with a cup of tea before heading over for a pint at the neighbouring Hope and Anchor. On top of this, there was the possibility of enjoying a few drinks with some of the office gang and friends now living in St Paul's Mews.

The office was now reserved for more focused work, although there were always distractions with people coming and going. We tried to steer away from having a dormitory area, although this was inevitable sometimes. Fortunately our Bayham Place office also offered upstairs and downstairs areas. Theoretically, upstairs people focused on fundraising, PR and project co-ordination, whilst downstairs folk would welcome the foot-traffic of volunteers, both new and returning, and a high level of general enquiries. Christopher Watt continued to be the main spokesperson, co-ordinator and general 'blagger' in London and was the anchor person day in and day out. It was amazing how he managed to keep it all going, and always with a sense of humour, despite dealing with such 'serious matters'. He was constantly on the phone dealing with some journalist or television contact drumming up interest or giving regular updates. His free moments would be spent looking forward to a football match or joking about meeting an illusive 'babe' somewhere. While I longed for another project to get my teeth into, and to be involved with children and organisations elsewhere, he seemed to be quite content with his world in London.

I would be asked to answer questions on projects where relevant or be interviewed on Sky News and the like. I even remember having to get up super early for an interview with James Whale on London radio LBC, where he tried to understand my motivation to help others without being paid. He jokingly likened me to some modern-day Joan

194

of Arc with a similar hair-cut. Some may have taken offence to this comparison, but I saw it as a compliment; although I didn't focus on her terrible fate and I continued to be driven to help those in desperate situations, despite the difficulties we faced. Somehow our challenges seemed to pale in comparison with the refugees and orphans we endeavoured to help, thus justifying our hand-to-mouth existence.

Another dedicated office volunteer, Toby Hoyte, had joined our ranks; he was helping with recruitment and fund-raising. He was from London and his girlfriend Libby worked for a clothing company. She showered us with end-of-the-line dresses and outfits; for volunteers, or to be sent to Bosnia. It felt good to be wearing some of these Hippi-Chic mini-dresses, rather than the tom-boyish jeans and sweatshirts most people were accustomed to seeing me in. They might have been more suited to summery weather, but I would make sure I had warm tights or leggings and the colourful fashionable attire lifted my spirits in grey, wintery London.

This also highlighted the fact that I was a woman, and I remember enjoying a few compliments, which were highly appreciated now that the distance with Yoyo was widening. If only he could see me now, I remember thinking. Meanwhile he was busy preparing for his first journey with Adventure Tourists to Africa.

Chapter 18

Return to Romania
(1995)

By now our next children's project was about to be sparked off by the arrival of our Austrian friend, Jutta Feuerstein. She had been working with disabled young adults in Austria, and missed the adventure of working in Croatia, where we had initially met.

She had popped over for a holiday to see friends, but together it was decided that the next project should focus on Romania again. She was trained in the field of working with disabilities and yearned to bring her expertise to those that needed it most.

I told her fondly of the children I had met in Ionaseni orphanage for the so-called 'irrecuperable' children and that more than 18 months had passed since my last visit with project 'Mania 4 Romania'. Jutta was all fired up to build a stimulation room, where children who had been severely deprived could stimulate their senses of touch, sound and sight. She was not shy to perform alongside clowns and musicians, but she wanted to leave a more concrete resource for the children, and to train some of the local staff to work differently with them.

We were both determined to get to Romania and were pleased that we already had the perfect project vehicle almost ready-and-waiting at Cricklewood bus garage.

We drafted a project proposal with our aims and requirements. I was relieved to be heading into more familiar territory, without the stress that a war-zone brings and looked forward to the thought of seeing some of the familiar faces. I couldn't wait to see the reaction of the children on seeing the big red bus again.

'Let me help with presenting your proposal,' offered Angus

196

MacIntyre, one of the office volunteers on Wednesdays. He had read about us in the Big Issue and being what some could describe as a computer geek, he had initially helped by building PCs for us, using old, broken machines that had been donated, and scavenging parts from them to make a few working machines. These had eventually become frustrating to run an office on and Christopher had embarked on investing in some Apple Macintosh's. Angus, with all his expertise in IT, had helped plan and set up the Mac network. Our proposal and others now took on a slicker, more professional look. He busied himself with many other useful things such as developing websites too. He slotted in well to the 'mayhem' of our office and thought that we 'proved that a bunch of lunatics who really care can do amazing things.'

I was pre-occupied with recruitment for the Romanian project, temporarily dubbed 'Mania 4 Romania part II', although this name would change.

People drawn to the project were starting to present themselves, or I found them by wading through scores of volunteer forms.

With Johnie and Caroline busy doing their own tour in Russia, I was grateful when Simon Smoleskis turned up as our new star clown. He had a slower energy than the hyperactive Johnie or Allan, but could carry the show in a calmer manner. This was another way of doing things that I would have to get used to, but would grow to love. Simon was dark-haired with a little goatee and had eyes that seemed to gaze at you, smiling, with some mad idea going on in his head.

He brought with him the ideas of running circus skills workshops from juggling to spinning plates. He was also a skilled craftsman in working with wood and dedicated many weeks preparing our bus for the trip. For this I was very grateful.

Each team-member would have a dedicated wooden storage space upstairs, which was large enough to double up as a base for a bed with a foam mattress for sleeping, or comfy seating. This also meant our possessions could be stored away in an organised and more secure fashion, so we would know where things were!

How luxurious when I compared that with the previous trip where our backpacks were stored in a messy heap upstairs and we had slept on the carpeted floor with not much more than our sleeping bags for cushioning. Still, now we had more time on our hands and the right man for the job. Unlike the year before, when we had to spend this lead time sourcing an appropriate vehicle and having it painted red in a matter of weeks.

Richard joined the team from the North. He'd been walking past the old office, seen the 'Who's Clowning around in Bosnia' poster and felt he could help. He was tall and lanky with long curly hair. He could play the banjo with great expertise and was also an avid juggler, unicyclist and circus performer. His manner was also far gentler, if not somewhat more serious, than previous performers I had worked with.

Another performer to join our team was Harry, who was originally from Australia. He was experienced in many community theatre projects and was a keen storyteller too. He was the eldest, with short grey hair, a strong Ozzie accent and usually dressed casually in dungarees.

Jutta was in her late twenties, blonde, and smiling. She usually wore something colourful and artistic. With Jutta and her specialised skills in working with the disabled, it felt like the team was generally more prepared and experienced to work with disabled children in the Romanian institutions. These weren't truck drivers or volunteers that had been converted into performers to fill a need. The average age was probably a good 10 or more years older than those in the previous project. While that made us theoretically more 'mature' it also meant we were more set in our ways and lacking some of the spontaneity of a more youthful and naive group. Of course, I was completely unaware of this difference initially. Needless to say, every project was different and brought various positive and negative aspects with it.

We busied ourselves preparing for the journey with letters to theatre groups in Romania. Harry also organised for us to construct a huge 'park monster'. This was a giant costume constructed out of one large length of tubular stretchy fabric. It was bright pink and needed to have giant yellow spots screen-printed onto it. We helped with this exciting task. The next part of the project were large hoops which needed to be attached to various holes, where participants would be able to walk along with their upper and lower bodies outside the tube, but joined by the giant fabric costume in a caterpillar shape. I had never experienced anything like it. What an impact this bright monster would make. It was amazing to see the team taking shape; the preparations brought us together before leaving, rather than on-the-road as with previous trips.

Another of the volunteers I had met in the office had also made the most exquisite hand-stitched wall hanging using bright-coloured fabrics. It was a scene of The Serious Road Trip bus and a clown heading through the countryside towards a rainbow and a giant tree, with a miniature teddy bear sitting beneath it. She wanted it to be given to the orphanage at Ionaseni. In fact, she would have loved to come along with us for a couple of weeks but we were going for a couple of months and her role within that period wasn't clear. How times had changed since our own original setting off with very loose roles some three years earlier and not much experience either. But I remained firm, as we had limited space on the bus and I would already be busy with the number of people we had.

We were still missing the necessary bus driver and I put the word out to our own experienced drivers and those with Premiere Urgence to see who could help us. I was stuck on the idea that we needed two drivers, since we would be covering such long distances, and we had had the luxury of two or more bus drivers the previous year. There was a huge part of me that wished Yoyo would abandon his plans for Africa and come along to Romania, but sadly his heart was looking for a different kind of journey.

Meni returned from Bosnia to drive the bus, but he needed to persuade Jutta and me that he was the right one. Someone had jokingly questioned his driving skills and this had worried us. He had returned from several months in Bosnia where he and a couple of other Serious Road Trippers had been helping with a reconstruction programme in Mostar. They had been using the trucks to deliver the necessary building materials, so that some of the thousands of displaced people could finally have homes again. It had been organised through the German Technisches Hilfswerk government agency, who were known for providing rapid and efficient technical relief in emergencies, mainly in Germany.

Here they were helping to rebuild Mostar, but they needed the more robust trucks and drivers that The Serious Road Trip had at its disposal. I was happy to hear that Mostar was entering this phase of reconstruction and that our drivers were again answering a special need. Now Meni had given this up to answer our need. We may have hesitated, but taking him on as driver was the best decision we made; those that know Meni, know that he is more than just a driver. He wasn't a performer, but with his naturally calm disposition, he became a solid rock in our team; he had a great sense of humour.

In the meantime, Premiere Urgence finally found someone who they thought might be up for the trip to Romania. Roy had been one of those French drivers taken hostage by the Serbs; the experience had really shaken him up. Understandably, with some 13 of them confined in 11 square metres for a couple of months, thinking they might be executed at any moment; it can't have done anyone much good. Consequently he was looking for something to do outside a war-zone. I was happy that we both were seemingly needing each other. He made his way over from France within days, in preparation for our imminent departure. He was rather quiet and not quite as confident as I had been hoping. I hadn't realised how nerve-wracking it might be for him driving on the other side of the road, and a red double-decker bus wasn't quite the same as the trucks he was accustomed to.

The bus was still at Cricklewood, being prepared by the 'boys' at Metroline with a general mechanical check and wash at their bus depot. How amazing to have this level of practical assistance the past year. Simon, Jutta and Harry were busy packing the various props, costumes and equipment for the project. Meanwhile I was busy making sure the paperwork was in order and the ferry booked. I also needed to communicate with the various organisations expecting us along the way, and in Romania, as well as a fund-raising team in Luxembourg.

I hoped to see Yoyo before we left but as fate would have it we set off some moments before he arrived. After so many times when I felt that I was waiting and hoping to see him and he didn't appear, I had thought it was unlikely, after all, that he really was coming to see us off. Maybe it was easier not seeing him, but the pain in my heart still ached with a yearning to be with him. Nonetheless, we had a good fan-club waving us off as we finally left from Bayham Place, bound for Calais, late afternoon one Friday in April 1995.

I remember a huge sense of relief finally to be on the road. It had taken some months of preparation and hardship living in London on a shoestring, but now the project was happening and the bus would be our home.

We chugged towards the ferry port where we queued to go through the passport control.

Finally we were waved forwards and then the unthinkable happened. CRASH! Our bus literally wiped out a small prefab the officials used for sheltering. Roy was not used to driving in a cab on the right-hand side and his natural instinct had been to adjust the angle to allow for the vehicle to be on his right, consequently crashing into the shelter. We were all shaken including the men on duty. They could have easily been injured in this accident, but were outside at the time.

The bus was relatively unharmed however. Fortunately we had our insurance and green-card handy and were at least covered for this incident, but who would have thought we would need it before even leaving England. It didn't feel like a good omen so early in the tour.

Meni managed to calm us all down, and not long after we were on the ferry and reflecting on the project to come. It would be fine when we were driving on the other side of the road. Once on the continent Meni drove at first, but as he had not had any sleep that night, it was decided that Roy should take over. More to the point, he needed to get 'back on the horse' so to speak. I would navigate as I had made this journey several times before. In hindsight that wasn't such a great decision for either of us. I wasn't exactly rested myself and hadn't slept a wink on the overnight ferry to Calais. We had opted for the overnight ferry as it was cheaper and there was space at such short notice.

In any case, neither of us was functioning properly. Roy rose to the challenge and all seemed to be going well along the motorway, until all of a sudden there were road-works ahead and there were all sorts of different signs with directions. Of course, I was not used to what the various colourful road signs and symbols meant. Maybe I said we needed to take a turning to the left, but unfortunately for us, I think that was the road for smaller vehicles, with trucks and larger vehicles needing to take another turning. Whatever happened was a blur, but in the heat of the moment Roy took the turning, both of us realising this huge mistake too late.

The road curved and narrowed tremendously and with Roy's instinct to drive with the bulk of the vehicle on his right, we crashed through various orange traffic cones and into a metal barrier. Fortunately we came to a grinding halt and there was no oncoming traffic, but we were blocking the road for any traffic heading in that direction. The police were alerted and came to investigate. Our left-hand front fender was severely damaged and we were naturally shaken once again, but there were no casualties. What a relief! We managed to move the bus to a safer spot, handing out our insurance details once again and recovering from the shock of it all.

Several hours later we limped into Luxembourg rather than roaring into town.

Fortunately we knew where to head. The local bus garage had supported us before and they too had their own red double-decker bus. Both Roy and Simon busied themselves alongside Meni to fix the damage. Our very own clown was most handy in this type of thing and the bus garage had the equipment and tools needed.

We then took Roy aside for a chat. Meni knew what was best and I needed to translate into French for him.

He calmly said: 'I'm sure you are a good driver and with the right training you could drive our bus, but on this trip we have no time to train you. Everyone likes you so you are welcome to stay and help me looking after the bus and navigating, but no driving.' Roy was touched but his response was to the effect that if he couldn't help with the driving then he might as well go back to France. He volunteered to do this now rather than later, as we were not far away. This was an unexpected turn of events but felt right for everyone. A part of me felt

201

guilty that I may have contributed to this second accident, but Meni was right and Roy had made his choice.

After several fundraising events in Luxembourg we let London know about our hair-raising start to the project, then carried on our journey to Romania.

Harry got many hands busy sewing the hoops into the Park Monster costume, Richard plucked away at the strings of his mandolin and Simon started to think about what type of show he would perform.

Jutta and I were happy to have each other's company and we both felt reassured by having our friend Meni at the wheel.

In Wallsee, Austria, we were welcomed by Jutta's mother. She had arranged a fundraising performance at the kindergarten, where she worked. Jutta also had heaps of equipment to collect for the planned stimulation room, including hundreds of those plastic balls to put inside an inflatable swimming pool. I smiled at the thought of the children of Ionaseni enjoying this experience, it was so exciting to imagine, compared with what they were used to.

Once again we bade farewell to our supporters and set forth towards Hungary. On arrival in Budapest we took great pleasure in parking overnight next to another London bus, on a square near the river, which was set up as an eye-catching café. They were closed so we didn't manage to speak with anyone before we headed off the next day for the Romanian border.

The border guards were not as quick as on the previous trip and only some hours later were we finally let through. Once out of the town we parked and made something to eat in our kitchen downstairs. It felt like a dream when I saw a Bedford truck approaching us. It was not one of ours, although it was the same model, but it was branded with the name 'Encounter Overland'. They were so surprised to see us and stopped to say hello. Their new colleague, Yoyo, had told them all about us. In fact, they were on their way back to the UK and were happy to take some juggling balls and a few balloons to him as a message from us. This coincidence was uncanny and I felt that there was some magical link between us, despite the distance. It felt like the hold-up at the border had had some positive purpose, as we could have missed each other otherwise. At least that's how I saw it.

The meeting was momentary and we lurched on towards the Transylvanian mountains.

We arrived in Cluj Napoca in wonderful sunshine. It had been two years since my previous stop here and the place seemed so much more alive and vibrant. The last visit had been during a wet and freezing cold night, so undoubtedly the weather coloured my thinking, but I'm sure the place felt more open to the changes happening in the country now. The usual children in the street gathered around us and were pleased to receive a few fluffy gifts that we had on board for this type of occasion. Simon was happy to get out his juggling clubs. Richard and he were becoming more practised in passing the clubs between themselves, in preparation for the next show. One person who was attracted by the bus was a tall, blond teenager named Butsi. He was involved in a local theatre group and said he'd love to stay in touch. He did actually join us later and became an integral part of the team. Although this was a random meeting at the time, it fitted in with our goal of establishing links with local theatre groups. We needed to empower others to work with the children in the special needs institutions once we had gone, so his appearance and interest in joining us was good timing.

Life was full of surprises and the next roadside stop was completely unplanned. We were moving very slowly up some steep slopes in the mountains, when the bus started to overheat. Meni pulled the bus over with steam rising from the engine. We were not going anywhere for now. Fortunately it was just a matter of waiting until the radiator cooled. We had stopped on the side of the road in a very scenic spot with gorgeous green hillsides all around us.

People on a horse and cart, which we had previously overtaken, now smiled as they passed us by, slowly but surely.

It was a lovely sunny day and we brought out some folding chairs to sit in as though we were stopped at some café drinking a cup of tea. Simon decided to make the most of the moment and brought out his violin to practice. He really was multi-talented. A few local children appeared from the countryside to see what was happening. Then along came a local chap who also played the violin. He returned shortly afterwards to entertain us all with lovely music and a friend accompanied him with a wooden flute. The music seemed to be the language of the moment as we were all entertained by this impromptu concert by the road-side, with Richard getting out his banjo and guitar. We dished out a few juggling balls and balloons to the curious children who gathered around us.

Once the engine cooled and we replenished the radiator, we set off again. At least our starter motor was working, which compared well with the previous bus in Russia that needed to be push-started every time. We carried on up the mountain slowly, taking in the breath-taking views and sunny weather. It was a promising start to summer, and another vehicle hurdle had been overcome. They were becoming a frequent part of any project.

Many hours later we rolled into Ionaseni to the excitement of many including Mama Puiu's family, especially her grandchildren, Daniella and Mihai. She clucked around us in her usual way, preparing something to eat, although I was the only familiar face. There were too many of us to stay with her, and with our bus set up for sleeping fairly comfortably, we were self-sufficient. I was fond of the family and we could park the bus in their entrance with the gate closed behind us, so their home remained a safe-haven and base for us whilst in the area.

Once again we would visit the various orphanages in the area. However, we had established links with a chap called Vali Racila at the local theatre in Botosani. He was a smiling, bearded man, probably in his late thirties, who greeted us with immense warmth and friendship and enormous bear-hugs. He was in touch with various teenagers living in the town and was keen to work with us. We also had contact with an English volunteer working with our Scottish colleagues: Chris Smith from Bradford. He oozed energy and had long wild wispy hair, a background in performing and was not shy to get his guitar out. He was definitely a bit quirky.

He introduced us to a young theatre group known as the 'Trupul GONG'. We went on to perform alongside each other. They were young and enthusiastic and it was great to link up and exchange ideas. I know Simon, Richard and Harry had much to share theatre and circus-skill-wise.

Together as a team, we started planning a series of workshops over a couple of days, where various youngsters would be exposed to different techniques in performing or working with special needs, and then introduced to interacting with special needs children in the orphanage. This was to take place in a couple of weeks. Jutta and Harry would focus on the special needs children and Simon and Richard would focus on circus skills.

In the meantime, Jutta also linked up with Di, who was the physio extraordinaire who had been there several years and had set up various activities for the children and training for the local workers in the orphanage. Di had already managed to earmark one of the prefabs outside the main building, as a space to be set up as the stimulation room. With her guidance and experience, Jutta made plans to paint and decorate the space appropriately. She wanted it to be a calm sanctuary for children with extreme physical handicaps. They could take refuge there in small groups and be worked with in a more focused manner, appropriate to each child's needs. Some of the people working with the children had visited the UK to receive training. Jutta's plans would enhance their training and increase their exposure to new techniques and ways of working with special needs children.

I was still aiming to provide some of our usual clowning performances at various schools, kindergartens and institutions, and so all in all, the project was taking on a multi-faceted dimension that was at times a strain on my brain trying to co-ordinate it all. What did I expect, having projects within projects? There was room for so many possibilities, it was hard to slot it all in and know what was the priority with so many people wanting their skills to be best utilised in the short time-frames.

Despite thinking I was going crazy at times, and with all sorts of personalities and egos flaring up, Meni restored the necessary calm to get all the plans to fall into place. Having such a variety of projects happening all at once was way more stressful than I had anticipated and I appreciated the steadiness that Meni provided during these storms. He had seen a fair few things in Bosnia and even before, and was wise beyond his years. I loved hearing about his background as it was the stuff you could write about. His parents were from Iraq, from a Jewish background, and Meni proudly announced that he was born in Jerusalem. Before he was born, both parents along with other family members, had spent time in prison in Iraq for their Marxist beliefs. I hate to think what the conditions must have been like.

During this time his father befriended an Israeli professor, also imprisoned, and although they had differing political views, they taught each other their respective languages. This led to his work writing a dictionary that translated Arabic into Hebrew. The Kojaman dictionary tried to bridge some of the differences of two worlds and consequently bring better understanding between peoples. How inspiring, I thought.

On their release many years later his mother and some family left for Jerusalem. His father followed later after another spell in prison. There he was reunited with his wife and they were finally able to start a family after more than a decade or two of major obstacles and captivity. Staying on in Israel also came with problems, so they eventually applied successfully for political asylum in London.

Meni was 10 when he arrived in Britain, but he felt more a citizen of the world now. This unique background and his experience in war-torn Bosnia, made me feel that he had a special part to play in creating peace between people in situations of strife. That also included tricky dynamics in a team of people living in close quarters on a double-decker bus and suffering from our own version of cabin fever! For this I was especially grateful as he managed to bring everyone and everything back down to earth. I knew I could count on him.

Operating without our own telephone or fax also posed its challenges. With the help of our Scottish partners, the orphanage office and many face-to-face discussions, we somehow managed to piece together an itinerary that involved using the talents of all on board.

A new and valuable addition to our team also arrived. Through our links with the Romanian Orphanage Trust on our previous trip, we had managed to secure a Romanian translator called Ionna from Bucharest. Meni regularly teased her with his wise-crack 'Give me hope Ionna' and fortunately she was just the right sort of person to take this in good humour. In fact she became more than a translator. She may have come from an intellectual background with an interest in classical drama, but she too wanted to be a fully participating circus performer in the show. How lucky we were to have her fit in so well, and not mind sleeping on the bus as well. She really understood where we were coming from and represented us well to the various authorities along the way. We wanted everyone to know that every child deserved a chance no matter what their background or capabilities.

As part of bridging the link with Romanian culture we had also decided to rename our tour. Instead of 'Mania 4 Romania part 2', we adopted the name 'Pacala isi cauta Pacaliciul' meaning Pacala is looking for his new toy or something like that. Pacala was a folk hero who was a kind trickster; we never really did get to grips fully with his story, or re-enacting it. Still, it felt good to have a Romanian name for our tour emblazoned along the side of the bus and Simon was, in his way, our lead trickster.

We performed in local schools and kindergartens as well as at institutes for special needs children. Simon wore his patchwork dungarees and hat and would produce all sorts of props and tricks from his leather satchel bag, like some absent-minded Clown Professor. The children loved his long balloon trick, where the balloon would just get longer and longer and longer. He then went on to quickly model a balloon poodle or a flower which he then gave to a teacher or nurse as he coyly fluttered his eyelids. They were either flattered or embarrassed by this added attention, but would accept their gift graciously.

There were all sorts of things to juggle and he and Richard made a clever duo passing their clubs. This was followed by riding unicycles, including a giant giraffe one. Children loved being given the opportunity to ride the smaller unicycle, obviously with help. Their faces beamed with delight as they sped around with two 'clowns' on either side. The audience would then applaud them.

Then there were spinning plates, which Simon spun with great

206

gusto and there was endless entertainment as he would try and get various children out of the audience to embark on spinning colourful plastic plates in unison. This inevitably ended up with plates falling and rolling all over the place.

From the depths of his leather bag, there came a rubber chicken that looked like some dead chook on a skewer, which made the noise of a live chicken as it was thrown into the crowd much to everyone's surprise. I'm sure this type of prop was quite alien to the Romanian audience, but they were familiar with chickens, of course, and got into the spirit of it all.

Harry was dressed as a colourful cleaner wearing his trade-mark dungarees. He would wander onto stage with his broom and shovel, to sweep up Simon or some other person in an attempt to get them off stage. Or he would produce an enormous feather duster, to dust around and tickle under Simon's arms. He did not speak, but blew into a kazoo, with animated high pitched sounds to stress the urgency of his essential cleaning work, or low gentle sounds to show enjoyment whilst tickling.

Meanwhile, Richard plucked away on his banjo or blew on his Irish tin-whistle. Jutta and I waited patiently for our role in the story of the old man with his loaf of bread that the animals stole. This was the simple story that involved a huge chase through the crowd, and then the animals performing for their bread. We had used this story on our previous tours with Johnie and Caroline and here it was again. It was a simple story and easy enough to slot different animals into the story, depending on who was available.

We started with Chris Smith taking the part of the pink squeaking mouse. He was anything but dainty, which added to the fun. He would then play guitar as his trick.

I was the miaowing cat, in a one-piece leopard/tabby suit who would juggle, skip or spin my Maori pois on strings.

Jutta was the yapping dog whose trick was to sit on a balloon, bouncing up and down on it for as long as she could. You could see the worried faces of the older children as they awaited the inevitable pop. The younger children were just surprised as they probably had never had the experience of sitting on a balloon, and were not aware of a balloon's limitations.

Ionna played the role of a squawking parrot, but then eventually helped out as the little mouse, when our tour went further south and Chris stayed in Botosani. She became rather good at spinning diabolos as her trick.

The bus took us to places we had been before such as Dorohoi, where the children were far more capable than those at Ionaseni. Once the show was over, Simon would engage the children further, trying to get them to copy him making elephant faces. This would involve bringing one hand up to hold one's nose, while the other arm and hand had been threaded through the remaining gap, forming a trunk. There was endless giggling as they tried to make various elephant 'trumpet' noises to accompany these actions or to swap hands.

Another activity they loved was the parachute, if time or numbers permitted. There was something special about watching it rise or lower in unison, then the intimacy of hiding under it as a team. It felt like some giant rainbow cartwheel, which symbolised the world in our hands. We would experiment with keeping a ball on top as well, although this took quite a lot of self-control as the tendency was to allow the ball to bounce higher and higher, making it fly from the 'safety net' below. Still, we could always start again, sometimes learning from the previous actions, although there was usually one child that couldn't resist the temptation of letting the ball bounce wildly into the air.

Some kindergartens or schools would love to reciprocate after our show by performing some song or poem with clapping and hand actions. It was quite a sharing experience when this happened and we were very touched by this form of impromptu international cultural exchange.

Our first month revolved around the Botosani area and ongoing activities with the children I was more familiar with at Ionaseni.

One day was particularly memorable: an outing in the big Red Bus for about thirty children from Ionaseni Orphanage. What a sight it was as we all piled into the bus and up the stairs to find seats on the foam-cushioned beds. Richard was there playing songs on the guitar and the one that sticks out that we all seemed to know was 'She'll be Coming Round the Mountain' even if some of them could only sing 'yippee, eye, eye, yippee, yippee eye'.

We chugged through the countryside, looking over fields of people working the land below. The children who were usually 'locked up' behind the walls of their orphanage beamed with excitement and looked like they felt on top of the world for a change. After a good hour or so through villages and the countryside, we stopped at a small roadside café in the middle of nowhere, for refreshments and toilet stops. Fortunately there was a new wooden picket fence to keep our enthusiastic lot from wandering too far and we ordered a bottle of fizzy drink for each child. On either side of the café there were giant haystacks and fields. The café owner was intensely surprised. She may not ever have had any contact with children with disabilities, as they were usually kept out of sight in institutions, and we must have been her biggest customers in such a short space of time. We drank through straws, which in itself was something new to some of the children. They tended to lift the bottle up at the same time as trying to drink through the straw. We all stayed on the terrace of the café sitting on the bench seat, or the white plastic chairs, watching and waving to some of the local farmers as they passed by on their horses and carts. We were blessed with sunshine and it was a happy moment outdoors for everyone. After all, this was like a giant family outing for these children who lived together under one roof. We returned to the orphanage, singing and clapping all the way home.

It was only the next day that we noticed something amiss. I think we may have been giving our friend Rodica a ride into Botosani, as she had missed the local bus and could have ended up walking or hitching a ride for the 30km journey. We hadn't noticed it on the day trip with the children, but the roads had so many pot-holes it was no surprise when one of the tyres became punctured. This was no simple job to repair. Fortunately the remaining twin tyre on the same wheel was functioning but we nonetheless made our way very carefully to the only place where we might be able to have this tyre repaired. That was the Botosani Municipal bus garage. At least there they had pits beneath the ground and were used to this type of repair and size of tyre, although they were gobsmacked when such a large bus rolled into their garage. The director of the garage was most welcoming and only too happy to let his men fix our tyre. They didn't have electric tools to get the nuts off, but were better equipped than the local roadside puncture repairer. It was while the bus was on a level platform above the pit that I noticed it seemed to be leaning to one side, perhaps caused by the puncture?

'What d'ya reckon Meni, it seems to be leaning to one side.'

Meni didn't seem to be worried at all.

A few hours later, once the tyre was repaired, I checked to see if there was any difference.

'Still leaning to one side!'

Meni must have thought I was just being paranoid and shook his head in a manner to calm my worries.

Moments later, the director of the garage came out to see us and we thanked him enormously for the assistance he and his men had provided. We asked what we could pay him for this service, but there was no question of payment as he knew that we were doing such good work with the children of his country.

209

As we looked proudly at our bus from a wee distance, I chatted in Romanian as best I could but pointed out the small lean to one side. I hoped he could put my mind at rest with a 'nema problema' type of statement.

Except this wasn't the case. He could see quite obviously what I was talking about and exclaimed quite loudly 'IMA PROBLEMA!' There was indeed a problem. He immediately called some of the workers over and they were asked to look at this in more detail. The minutes seemed to drag forever before one of them came back with a serious look on his face. The problem was huge. The chassis was broken and it was quite a serious issue. The bus had been in danger of collapsing. Wow! We had closely escaped a serious accident, but what did this mean for our project that was only just beginning? He sent his top engineers to have a closer look but they all returned shaking their heads. It was an impossible task to fix this issue. 'Sigur que da?' Are you sure, I begged, as my mind raced onto the consequences of our project being stopped dead in its tracks. Why hadn't this been picked up earlier in London or had our various accidents and the rough roads taken their toll on our dear bus? Or was it the extra weight of the passengers the day before? There was nothing else for it. The garage director himself needed to take a look at the damage and see what they were talking about.

He scratched his head and pondered over the damaged chassis. It seemed like an eternity and even involved various trips into his office to look at various books, before he finally emerged exclaiming 'E possible!' It would be very difficult but there was a solution. Nonetheless most of the men were very perplexed as to how it could be done, but there was one young man willing to accept the challenge under the leadership of the experienced garage director. In fact, it had been his dream to work on a red London bus, so he would be fulfilling a life-long aim right here in Romania.

I think the young man's name was Mihai (Michael). For almost two days solid he remained on task with some serious arc-welding to rejoin the chassis. He might as well have been called St Michael for managing to rescue us from this almost impossible situation along with the director, who had at least focused on the one per cent chance of success.

The local media and television station were attracted to this story. Neither garage nor Mihai wanted payment for this work, although Mihai did look pleased with some juggling balls, balloons and face-paints for his extraordinary efforts. At least the media were able to give some publicity and a good story out of the garage workers' goodwill.

We were thankfully able to get back on the road. Our projects' success really did depend on the helping hands we had along the way. I had seen this on numerous occasions; our vehicles had a tendency to break down.

It was just as well we were in the area where I had more contacts. Most of the team kept themselves busy with the children of Ionaseni in one way or another. I know Jutta was extremely busy preparing the stimulation room and then there were the workshops we were doing and planning to do with the teenagers from Botosani, in conjunction with the local theatre.

Those who were part of a theatre group called 'Gong' were only too excited to take part in the pink Park Monster's debut. There were nine of them and together we managed to get a group of even younger children to join the adventure through a local rural park. Each child was gobbled up by the monster, and popped up through the various bamboo rings, becoming the legs of the giant caterpillar-like monster. We set off with people guiding it along. As we marched along the monster made all sort of noises, 'Sheesh, konk, sheesh, konk, pssssssss, sheesh' resembling a machine. Every now and then, the monster would come to a grinding halt as part of the story. The chief mechanic, wearing his train-driver's cap, and his helpers would come to see what was wrong and then embark on repairing the monster with an extremely large spanner made out of papier-mache. The appropriate noises were made and then the monster would continue on its way, until the next repair.

It was exciting for everyone to be involved in a story that used noises rather than words and which took us outside along the edge of a forest. I'm sure most of these children were more accustomed to traditional theatre performances indoors and sitting on seats, if at all.

The next step in our work was to link the theatre with the orphanage in Ionaseni.

Harry and Jutta were leading different groups willing to work with the disabled younger children at the orphanage. Harry wanted to run an interactive workshop structured around the story of *Snow White*. (I remember him dashing into the market in Botosani beforehand, as he wanted to find a heart to be part of this story.)

The youths that accompanied him to the show were each allocated a young child to interact with, while he told the story of *Snow White* and various hand-actions were done in unison or they were able to touch one of his props, such as the huntsman's hat. While I had imagined a bright red fluffy heart, it was actually the texture of a real-life animal heart that he had found. The children naturally tried to put the heart in their mouths, and had no concept of what they were doing. I'm not sure this was the intended response and only found this out much later.

I wasn't there participating, as there were other things running concurrently, but the teenagers involved seemed to be quite moved by this first-hand experience in an orphanage and with children with disabilities, most of whom could not speak.

Meanwhile, Simon and Richard were focused more on using circus skills with the older and more capable group at the orphanage. This involved learning to spin plates and a little bit of ball throwing. Here everyone was outside in the sunshine and having a fun time trying to co-ordinate their hands and eyes to balance the plates on sticks and then spin them. It was good to see how everyone struggled at first, but how some did manage to balance the plates. Some of the children with disabilities managed this activity before the able-bodied teenagers or the orphanage staff. Maybe Simon had given them more practice prior to the workshop, but I was still very impressed with their skills.

The teenagers from Botosani met with us all afterwards to share their experiences with the group. Those that had faced the indoor environment, complete with its distinctive smell, as well as meeting children less able-bodied than the plate-spinners, seemed to be more moved by the experience. One 16-year-old girl approached me and told me how meaningful this experience had been for her and such an eye-opener as well. She hoped to work with children one day. I'm sure others would process the experience later and how could we tell what impact, if any, it might make. Maybe it helped for some to be grateful for what they had in their own lives, without the limitations of living in an institute.

Of course, we hoped that somehow this day of forming links within the community would bear fruit in the future and open people's minds to working with disabled people. It had certainly strengthened a link between the local theatre in Botosani and the rural orphanage.

Harry's skill as a storyteller emerged further, when we realised that he had the props needed to tell the very famous story of *The Hungry Caterpillar*, by Eric Carle. He had moulded a very cute little caterpillar out of rubber and painted it with stripes. It was flexible and extremely lifelike. He would put his index finger inside and it would inch along in a caterpillar manner up his arm and over tables and chairs or children, in search of food.

This was a story for young children (3–7 years) who could sit on a mat, such as in a kindergarten setting. The children loved hearing his exaggerated munching noises. Harry had made props out of plywood in the shapes and colours of the various fruits and food that the caterpillar ate each day of the week. There was a cute little hole in each food prop that the caterpillar would peek through. Of course, they loved seeing him grow to a much larger size by the end of the week, and burping loudly and feeling sick having overeaten on Saturday. Ionna was excellent at producing the various props at just the right moment and giving any necessary narrative in Romanian, or words for Harry to repeat. They were an effective duo.

At the end the audience was encouraged to imitate the caterpillar who fell asleep, and they prepared a little bed for him in their clasped hands. Harry managed to get the spell-bound children to be ever so quiet sleeping, interspersed with the odd snoring sound he made.

What joy there was when he awoke, and his hands formed into a butterfly shape with the thumbs crossing, flying into the air. All the children imitated this beautiful butterfly being born. I was impressed by the effectiveness of this simple story to cross into another culture with such ease, and the innocent smiling faces and butterfly hands kept me glowing inside for days. Each time he told the story it was as if I had never heard it before and we were all transformed, children and adults alike, in a way that was pure magic. How lucky we were to have such a multi-talented man in the team, but he wasn't the only one, of course.

Jutta had put the finishing touches on the stimulation room and we were invited to see it in action. The room was painted in a very calming pastel pink and the floor was covered with a clean dark carpet. It was definitely a space to leave your shoes at the door.

On the walls were a few A3 posters made out of card and these were attached to the walls at an accessible height for children. Each poster was decorated with various materials of differing textures. There was a rectangle of rough sandpaper, a silky smooth fabric, a bath sponge and a contrasting metal pot-scrubber. There were all sorts of segments of fabrics, papers or plastics with bobbles or patterns to explore with the hands and stimulate the sense of touch. There was a corner with comfy foam sofa cushions (protected with waterproof sheets in case of accidents) and colourful cushions to make the space even more cosy and inviting. Jutta had filled 2-litre plastic bottles with colourful oil or fluids and sparkling glitter and shapes. These were to shake up and watch carefully with the eyes as the glitter slowly moved and fell.

The fairly large inflatable paddling pool had been filled with hundreds of yellow and red plastic balls and a child who was unable to support himself sitting up, could be gently supported by the balls.

There was a full-length mirror for the children to experience looking at themselves, which was a huge novelty. I don't remember there being mirrors in the orphanage.

There was a CD player playing soft and gentle relaxing sounds and even a light projector that spun with all sorts of colourful shapes on the walls and ceiling.

There must have also been some sort of oil burner or the like to engage the sense of smell as well.

It truly was a magical haven for the children to escape to. It was to target the most vulnerable of the children and they would only be allowed to enter in controlled small groups. Here they could stimulate a number of the senses in ways that the normal orphanage environment was unable to do and the carers could work with them ideally one-on-one. However, this luxury would take some co-ordinating from the committed physiotherapist, Di Hiscock, as there were limited resources and workers to facilitate it. At least it was a start and a tool to work with in the future.

Not long before our departure from the area, Di came to me saying that someone we knew and loved was due to arrive unexpectedly. My mind was completely distracted with our busy schedule, current and future, and this seemed to come like a bolt out of the blue.

Moona was making a surprise appearance at Ionaseni. My mind raced back to the past and the happy memories we had shared here almost three years prior. After all, it was through Moona that I had embraced Romanian culture in greater depth and the challenges faced with humanitarian actions.

I was surprised, as I had last heard he was in Bosnia, but then it all made sense. He and Monica had married when she became pregnant in Bosnia.

Now they were back in the country spending time with her family in Bucharest. Maybe they had intended to introduce their son to the many local friends, but the baby had come down with chickenpox, meaning that Moona made the journey to Moldova alone.

How strange that this set of circumstances was to throw us together again, even if there had been many changes in our lives.

Of course, I was happy to see him again, although we had both gone our separate ways and he was now thrown into family life. He was also surprised to hear about Yoyo. For a moment, we were able to enjoy each other's company once again as friends, in the place that had drawn us together. We wandered around the village together catching up with various mutual friends and speaking Romanian. Wherever we arrived we were greeted with a small glass of Tuica, the local fire-water made from sugar beet. I am sure the locals were rather confused seeing us together again as I certainly didn't look like Monica.

He was hoping to visit his dear friend, Mr Soare, the sky-diving instructor in neighbouring Suceava, the next day and invited me to join him. While I was tempted to carry on down memory lane, I wasn't prepared to change whatever schedule we had in place. Although I had enjoyed seeing him again, it served as a reminder that we were no longer together. Enough was enough. This 'rejection' was obviously something that hit me deeply and I was still processing my latest split with Yoyo.

Meanwhile on the bus, romance was blossoming between Jutta and Simon, which was lovely to see. It seemed that this type of thing was inevitable on projects, from which we had seen several relationships begin.

As a finale to our month in the area, we performed for the village of Ionaseni in the local hall. It was a happy occasion with face-painting and balloons afterwards for all our friends and their children. I was always tearful when it came to saying goodbye and I could never be quite sure when we would next meet.

The next stop was Hirlau, where we would revisit the centre with some 500 residents of mixed ages. I remember that the place seemed improved from the years before, but the familiar smells still greeted us indoors.

We managed to find a space outdoors where we could have the children sitting on blankets on grass, under the shade of trees and in a line along the wide pavement. This served as a natural stage and meant that they could all see us, even though our performance area was very long. It had the usual success, with many children following at least some of the visual action humour.

Meanwhile, there were some children with more acute physical disabilities who had needed to remain indoors. Richard and Jutta went around their rooms, playing gentle music on the guitar and interacting with the children; using balloons for visual impact and soft scarves which would caress their skin.

There was another visit to an orphanage but in order to get there we had to cross over some train tracks. The length and weight of the bus was such that it bottomed out on the tracks. The bus stalled and we seemed to be stuck. How funny it all seemed until we could hear a train tooting in the distance.

In a flash, we all exited the bus, except Meni, and pushed as much as we could. Maybe it was a combination of less weight on the bus, plus us pushing and our guardian angels on our side, but we managed to avoid disaster in the nick of time. We clambered all aboard once again, and made it safely to the expectant orphanage, much to everyone's relief. It had been another close shave.

Once our visit here was over we made our way to Bacau, where I looked forward to catching up with our friend from the theatre, Puiu Gheorghiu, his wife Liliana and their young son Adrian (7). During the the trip before we had actually performed on stage at their local puppet theatre for children. It had been a huge buzz and we looked forward to rekindling the friendship and links.

Since our previous trip, Puiu told us of a few visits he had made to the local orphanage. I felt encouraged to hear that our impact last year had prompted him to give his time to the children in a similar way. He would be part of the team for this part of the tour as we would spend roughly a week in the area. I remember parking the bus in the communal garden area beneath his apartment. It was not a huge block, maybe three floors or so, and they were on the first floor.

The local children flocked around the bus. How exciting for everyone. Harry rose to the occasion and before long he and Ionna were performing an impromptu Hungry Caterpillar story for everyone outside.

There were two other volunteers that joined us here. One was Butsi, who we had met in Cluj on our way into the country. He was now available to link up and continue for the remaining weeks. He came open-minded and with a huge heart ready for action with his beautiful, silky, black and white Pierrot clown suit.

The other was a photographer (NZ) Sami, who had been sent out through our London office to take photos on our project. He slotted in well and would be with us for a week or so. We would be grateful for some professional photos of some of our work.

We welcomed them into our home on wheels.

The first thing we did was visit the local orphanage for special needs children, where we had even arranged another bus trip. Once again it was exciting to see smiling children, and a few staff, embark on an adventure outside the boundaries of the world of the institution.

The view from the bus was really quite something and we chugged along through the surrounding countryside, overtaking the familiar horses and carts that punctuate the rural landscapes. It was an extremely hot day and I remember that the heat upstairs was even more intense. We didn't have the luxury of a café this time, but managed to source some cool fizzy drinks. We stopped on the side of the road and relaxed on a grassy verge a short distance from the road and near some trees. We even shared the space with some grazing cattle. The giant

Johnie, Pip and Simone with little boy from the state orphanage in Zenica, Bosnia.

Johnie and Caroline in Bosnia, 1996.

Johnie's balloon trick in Bosnia.

Show for the Cerebral Palsy Institute in Sarajevo.

Unis Towers in Sarajevo and Dodge truck for clowns.

Simone's poi trick with a volunteer at a kindergarten in Fojnica, Bosnia.

Johnie stuck in a chair with Niall, Caroline and Pip – Zenica, Bosnia.

Pip fire juggling in Doboj (Serb held territory).

Dobrakadabra (Good Magic) trick with Johnie and Simone – Bosnia, 1996

After show
in Celic.
Pip and
Johnie
hugging.

After
show in
Gorazde
area,
Bosnia.

Simone in
Gorazde
Stadium
show,
Bosnia.

Face-
painting
in Olovo,
with
Caroline
and
Simone.

Behind the
scenes in
Olovo,
Bosnia.
Meni on
Dodge truck
and Caroline
in Tweety
costume.

Tweety Bird in Bosnia.

Johnie helping offload some aid in Olovo, with Franck.

The truck that crashed into a ravine.
Outside Lion's Den IFOR base in Olovo, Bosnia.

Simone with an American soldier outside
Lion's Den and minefield in Olovo, Bosnia.

Simone with her pois.

Bronzes made in New Zealand.
The Kiss, Jos (Yosh) and The Magic Kiss.

inflatable beach ball brought some fun into the time together, as did the balloons once back on board the bus.

We spent most of the week visiting various institutions and our show was re-enacted in whatever situation we encountered, usually followed by mad face-painting sessions where the children ended up with bright smudges of colour from our sponges.

Puiu slotted in well, wearing a stripey summer beach-suit and a luminous green curly wig. We visited one institute for adults in the middle of a village and the various local adults and children were spell-bound by the arrival of the clowns on a bus. Our performance outside, under the shade of the trees, was enjoyed by at least a hundred or so of varying ages.

I am not sure where he got it from, but even Meni joined in with some of the fun one day, sporting a short bright red 'Michael Jackson' jacket, which we teased him about.

We rounded the week off by taking an overnight trip on our bus with some of the friends made in the area. We must have driven to a park of sorts, on the outskirts of Bacau. Many stayed up chatting and singing into the night and various people slept outside under the stars in sleeping bags and on blankets.

Harry cooked one of his fabulous breakfasts and we juggled, played music and generally fooled around together.

It was a great way to spend time together before the farewells.

I was sad to be saying goodbye to Puiu's family and they gave me a parting gift of a puppet. It was a small hand-puppet with a bright blue opening mouth and red felt tongue. It was made out of stretchy white fabric resembling a sheep's woollen coat. It had long purple hair that reminded me of spaghetti and had a funny green hat. Its eyes were welcoming and smiling with a button at the centre and these were surrounded by hand-made wire glasses. It definitely made me think of Puiu himself, as he wore glasses and made me laugh. I was very moved by the gift which was carefully tucked away in our props area. I went on to name him Eugene, which was a name I loved. We had a German family friend with this name and it also made me think of the famous Romanian playwright Eugene Ionescu, whose work I had studied at University.

This puppet would feature a few years later, when I returned to New Zealand and crafted a story around his adventures to seek treasure in New Zealand. Eugene was an orphan, who had escaped on The Serious Road Trip bus, so it was based on a true story. At that time, I was missing my work with the clowns, so performing with puppets enabled me to have all the different characters of the troupe.

k

Next stop was Tatarai near Bucharest. This was an orphanage with 50 or so children and a UK charity, operating in the institute, had approached us in Britain asking us to visit. They had some special opening or celebration that they wanted us to animate that day. We were happy to oblige as we were in the area at the right time, and had, in fact, structured our itinerary around this. After a show we ran various activities in the garden with our parachute, beach ball and face-painting. Many of these children had severe disabilities and it was fun for them to be on blankets outside and fooling around under the parachute. I remember one little chap just chuckling and giggling and beaming from ear to ear, as he rolled around interacting with the parachute that wrapped around his body. He seemed to love the texture of the material that didn't tangle as much as pure cotton would. What joy in such a simple moment.

We were lucky to have the access into such orphanages through these other charitable organisations. After all, they were the ones who were providing regular commitment to support them on a day-to-day basis, in conjunction with the local authorities and staff. We were there to enhance existing programmes, to boost the morale of all concerned and open minds to other possibilities. We did not have time to build attachments, although I was still managing to form some through my regular contact with the children in Ionaseni. They, and the village folk who lived nearby, were the ones that had captured my heart. There were a number of similarities as we visited these institutes. Many were in rural settings hidden away from the outside world, and the local village folk were the carers; working there as well as carrying out their own domestic tasks and work on the land.

Our next stop was to be the capital city, Bucharest, where our organisation had done its first show some three years earlier. Who could have imagined, when we first arrived in Bucharest in 1992, that we would be called to fulfil a unique need through theatre. After all, at that time we had actually sent our one street performer back, along with the band, following our fund-raising tour of Western Europe. With that leg of the journey complete we had intended to embark on our serious work during our proposed one-year journey to New Zealand. Wondering what we were meant to be doing on our arrival, we had been asked if we had a show, to which one of the team had said 'yes'. Our simple re-enactment of Old MacDonald's Farm back then may have grown into a far more elaborate show, and yet the simplicity of an interactive performance prevailed. Now we were also blessed to have the guidance of Jutta, who was trained and experienced in working with disabilities.

Christopher, from our London office, wanted to link up with us there too, and Bucharest had flights to London at that stage, which facilitated a short stay for him. He brought letters and cards from our families and friends and was a link to what was happening outside Romania. Meni, Jutta and I were interested to hear how our convoy team were doing, although we really were caught up in our own daily activities. No two days were the same as we continued to string together an itinerary within the capital city.

We visited hospitals and in particular the hospital for the AIDS children or those with HIV+. There were hundreds of young children who had been sent here from other institutions, where they could be 'isolated' together and treated by local and international specialists. With the show over, there was time to interact with the children outside while Richard played tunes on his tin whistle. Some of them just wanted a few serious hugs with the clowns, and this was Simon's speciality. He seemed to be always happy and people were drawn to his warmth.

One of our main points of contact in the city was Vali, who had introduced us to the world of street children in Bucharest. Each of these children had a story to tell, whether it was escape from an abusive family or an orphanage. Glue sniffing was still a huge issue and there were various centres trying to rehabilitate those children who had ended up sleeping rough in the city.

Together we embarked on another day out with the bus. It was a scorching day as we clambered on board. Fortunately we were able to head to a local lake in the city, where we could spend the day by the water.

Some of us swam along with the children, but a good part of the day was taken up teaching circus skills such as spinning diabolos and plates, juggling or having a go on the unicycle. Jutta had come fully prepared with some bubble mixture in a plastic bowl and a giant circular rope that made the most enormous bubbles I had seen. There is something quite mesmerising about bubbles and some of the children even explored making giant bubbles through their cupped hands. Some just wanted to hang out together, and practise short English phrases; some wanted to be photographed with the iconic enormous fun bus. It was a sharing of carefree time together, away from the day-to-day challenges they faced.

It was no surprise that we were soon put in touch with another clown who had focused on working with street children in Bucharest.

His name was Miloud Oukili and he was French-Algerian. When he arrived in Bucharest a few years earlier, he had managed to gain the trust of various street children through performing in the street. They were fascinated by him and the language of the clown entranced them, gaining their trust in ways no one else could. He taught them various skills, but for now it was our turn to introduce ourselves.

Many of the children he worked with were being rehabilitated at a centre run by a Swiss organisation. I think he was the one who had managed to arrange for these children he had met on the streets, to come into contact with the centre where they were subsequently housed and schooled. Some of them only stayed because he would visit them daily and school them in acrobatics and circus skills. He provided a link with their past life on the streets that they could not completely walk away from. It was a part of who they were.

Our bus rolled up outside the centre and we set up our stage on the dusty street, with a length of rope marking the stage area. The children were on the footpath. Some sat on the curb and others leaned against the green metal garden wall of the centre. We performed our show with Simon as the central clowning figure.

Various neighbours in the area also gathered to see the show. It was heart-warming to see a grandfather clutching his small granddaughter under the shade of a tree as they were both intrigued to see what was happening in their very own neighbourhood. Other family groups nearby also joined the audience. If they hadn't seen the bus, they were no doubt attracted by the sweet sound of Richard plucking away on his banjo/mandolin.

Once the show had finished, the street children working with Miloud spontaneously leapt into action and formed a very impressive human pyramid. There were at least eight of them in formation, right in front of the bus. It started with three children, each balanced on the shoulders of three others. Then two smaller children managed to perch themselves in between, on the upper thighs of the lower row, but with their arms holding onto the backs of the knees of the upper row. I had never seen this done before, so was very impressed by the acrobatic formation. There was a genuine mutual understanding of each other. Despite our differences, we were all performers. For Miloud there was a relief and excitement that we also had skills and ideas to exchange with the group. I was in my element, speaking French again, although Miloud did manage some English with a very heavy accent.

Our tour was coming to an end, but Miloud had an invitation for us that would extend our stay till the end of July. His troupe was heading to Sighisoara to perform at the International Youth Festival. It was to be part of a medieval festival in the Transylvanian city and would we like to join them there? Apparently this city's beauty was exceptional, and coupled with a chance to show-case some of our performers as well as to support the street-children in any way possible, it was an offer we couldn't refuse.

This was excellent timing as we had also been invited to a Creative Arts Festival in the area (Brasov) around the same time. There we were able to show how the special needs children benefited from our activities, gaining confidence and self-esteem, and were able to share our skills with other teachers and carers working in this field.

Within a week or so we hooked up with the Parada team on the picturesque cobbled streets of Sighisoara. It was as though we were being reunited with family we hadn't seen for some time, such was the excitement to see them again. Over the weekend there was a bit of a programme we needed to slot into, Miloud explained. Did we want to participate in the Opening Ceremony that evening? Naturally we were keen, although I did wonder what form that might take, as this wasn't our usual setting of an orphanage or hospital. A temporary wooden stage had been erected in the central square of the old Citadel and there were a few acts lined up.

We were allocated the last spot of the evening, straight after the street children. While we could leave Simon and Richard to wow the crowds with some of their juggling, it felt necessary for us all to participate. We three women hatched a plan to perform some type of witches' scene around a cauldron, reminiscent of the three witches in *Macbeth*. We had to quickly find some costumes and decided to focus on the elements of Fire, Earth and Water to create three similar yet different characters. The curtains of our bus provided the necessary fabric to drape around ourselves. Jutta had decorated some of the light blue curtains on the lower deck with fishes and seaweed, so that was perfect for Ionna, the Water Witch. The red curtains draped around me with some orange and gold scarves, topped off with my spiky hat resembling the flames of a fire, was perfect for me to be disguised as the Fire Witch. Meanwhile Jutta made a very convincing Earth Witch in black, browns and greens. We made ourselves up with face-paints, which further enhanced our costumes, to prepare for this big occasion.

While I was petrified of performing before the hundreds that gathered that night, I was well hidden beneath my costume and comforted by the thought that almost no one knew us here and I wasn't alone.

We managed to source a massive cooking pot which was placed on stage and we danced around the pot cackling and mumbling words along the lines of *'Double, double, toil and trouble; Fire burn and cauldron bubble.'*

We each threw various items, such as plastic lizards, frogs and stones, into the cauldron and there were some special smoke effects to add to the atmosphere.

There was an Abracadabra chanting and then we withdrew to the sides of the stage to make way for the clowns. Through our magic, the things we had thrown in had been transformed into various circus props that Richard and Simon discovered within the pot. They then proceeded to wow the crowds with them. There was some atmospheric music, amplified over a huge sound system, to accompany their juggling and other tricks and the big finale involved fire clubs. It was such a relief to have performed to certain expectations and the crowd was genuinely happy to have us there, all the way from England and the various countries we represented. In fact, we were eight people representing seven different countries (England, Austria, New Zealand, Australia, Israel, Hungary and Romania).

We returned to our bus parked in the lower town, which hadn't been able to access the medieval part of the city where the Festival was taking place. We were extremely tired but happy and relieved to have achieved such a feat by being in the right place at the right time. The synchronicity of this invitation was incredible.

The sun was shining the next day as we prepared to make our way into the old city. There were medieval flags draped from poles to decorate the town. The children from Parada were wearing medieval costumes as they prepared to re-enact some famous story involving a king on a horse and characters wearing turbans. They also had various court jesters juggling alongside them. They paraded through the town, with many children and adults watching them pass by, before arriving at the central stage where they re-enacted their story.

Another performance troupe also re-enacted a famous story through the streets of the medieval town. This was a travelling story, with each scene taking place in a different part of the city and the audience following along with them. There was the enchanting sound of a beautiful wooden flute as they roamed the streets and 'changed scenes'.

Harry managed to get his pink Park monster with yellow spots out for the occasion, and it was great to see the children from Parada all parading around like some giant caterpillar through town. It wasn't particularly medieval, but nonetheless it certainly animated the streets.

Jutta decided to dress up as a witch again. She loved this role and

222

really did look authentic, as though she had just wandered into town having spent the night under a haystack. Her face was smeared with black paint which looked like dirt and her hair was all knotted and messed up with wooden pegs dangling from it.

She wore her sack dress with a black piece of fabric for a cape and held a wooden staff in one hand. She was hunched over, limping through the streets with a glass jar that had a small frog inside. She would wander over to onlookers asking them if they knew where she could find a princess, and so she wandered from one cobbled street to the next. It was hilarious, as I'm sure from a distance, some people genuinely thought she was the real thing.

Meanwhile I was dressed up in my cat suit and meowing around the streets. I was looking for a witch and the children would point me in the right direction. I was also very hungry and wondered if anyone had any milk or cream for me. There were some young children who genuinely tried to find me something to drink. I was in my element interacting with the crowd through our roving street theatre, which had surfaced quite spontaneously.

Ionna was dressed up as a parrot, with a sea of colourful balloons attached to her as she squawked around the streets.

Simon also produced a giant maroon-coloured costume that resembled a version of Michelin-woman on stilts. I was amazed that he had that hiding in one of the compartments of the bus and we hadn't seen it earlier. He wandered around spectacularly for a few hours, but the cobbled surfaces and steep climb to the Old City, eventually made it very hard to balance on stilts and the costume was quite a heavy thick one in the summer heat. The things one does for an audience! It was all in all a fantastic and enthralling Saturday.

The next day was the last day of the festival and we were to perform our circus-styled show in an almost impromptu fashion, under the shade of a tree in the square. It was hard to think that our beautiful project was coming to an end along with the unexpected festival. I could never have imagined so much fun performing for hours almost non-stop as walkabout, roving characters. This took street theatre to another level, as far as I could see, and I loved the spontaneity of it all.

Now we would perform our show one last time. The story of the old man, his last piece of bread and the ensuing animal chase delighted the audience, especially those we had met during the festival. I spun my Maori pois on strings with extra enthusiasm, despite the heat, and Simon was happy Simon, with all the team doing their bit alongside him as our central clown.

Richard played his tin whistle like some magic piper and he got us all up dancing at the end. There was a happy train of performers and audience holding on to the shoulders of the person in front and we spiralled around the trunk of the tree energetically as if we didn't want the moment to end.

Well, I didn't want it to end, but of course it did. What a high to end on, though, to carry us all the way back to Britain. The farewells with our Romanian team-members and friends were tough, as we didn't know when or if we would see them again. The rest of us had a few more days together as we journeyed back to Britain.

Not before we side-tracked to Paris to catch up with Isabelle, however. How surprised she was to see a red double-decker bus parked outside her apartment there. Together we made the irresistible tiki-tour to the heart of the city to park below the Eiffel Tower which towered majestically over us on one side, and the Champ de Mars on the other. At the far end of this stretch of greenery there was a caravan recruiting for the French Foreign Legion. What a contrast! Another friend from Premiere Urgence, Hughes, joined us there and we reflected on our humanitarian work in both Bosnia-Herzegovina and Romania. We were surprised to see a number of modern double-decker red buses in the area, but they were sight-seeing tours and quite clearly did not have the London look and were worlds apart from our objectives, as were the Foreign Legion. Coming back to the Western world and life going on as it had before we left on a project, brought with it its challenges.

We really didn't want the project to finish, and when we finally did get back to London, we even spent a few extra nights on the bus outside the office over the weekend. But Monday finally arrived with its hurly burly.

It was the height of summer, and with the bus back in Cricklewood bus garage, Jutta and I even slept outside in the garden at my flat in Tottenham, rather than conform to sleeping inside the house. There would be plenty of time for that in life, we thought, as we savoured the very last moments of a special project; even in London.

But as with every other project, there really was a time to return to office-life. Jutta needed to return to her life and work in Austria, Simon went back to Cambridge and the remaining members all needed to return to various situations. Meni had been called back as a driver to Croatia to undertake a fact-finding mission in Albania with Christophe and Sniejana. Nonetheless, the farewells were tough and we all carried some of the treasure of this project, and the people we had met, in our hearts.

Chapter 19

What Next?
Magic Hat and Puppets?

There were other things to occupy some of my time. My sister Ingrid had moved to London with her boyfriend and she and a few friends took me out on the town. They had jobs in the financial services not far from where I had started temping before my transfer to Luxembourg. It was hard to explain this other life I had led to all my friends and family who hadn't been there.

For now, I still had the company of various Road Trippers back from convoys or setting up various other projects in London and elsewhere. We'd all experienced something similar, to varying degrees, and found a close link being with people who 'understood', even if they hadn't all been on the same projects, and were driven to do something to help.

The music world was open to helping us, and one of the projects Spesh and others had worked on, involved shipping out some high tech music equipment from TurboSound for the Kuk Club on the premises of Sarajevo University.

I remember that, on the night Spesh was due to drive the truck loaded with this sound equipment, I went to see and hear the system in action in a London warehouse packed with all sorts of boxes and goods. He put on one of my favourite songs of the time, 'Children' by Robert Miles. I remember dancing with such a passion: lost in the music and thinking about all the people who would enjoy listening to music at the other end. How they so needed this escape to normal life in a war-zone. While most people and organisations focused on the necessity of food, our organisation was not only trying to provide food to eat, but also food for the soul.

Within days, Spesh managed to get the sound equipment to Croatia and from there he drove it into Sarajevo. It seemed an unlikely cargo, but the necessary paperwork had been completed and it was only allowed through on cultural grounds. Another full-time volunteer, Simon Glinn, had been focused on this music equipment as part of the setting up of what was dubbed the Kuk Project and was there to greet them. With extra sound equipment in place, a pilot music therapy outreach project was established that would run for the next few months initially, but with long-term goals for the following two years. Essentially the project wanted to create opportunities for people of all ages and abilities and needs, to participate in music-making and listening. There was support from various professionals in the UK, such as professors at Edinburgh, Glasgow and Kingston Universities, the Drake Music Project and various community music projects. I didn't get involved in this aspect of TSRT's work, but had often seen Simon busy in the London office with his nose glued to his laptop screen as he prepared for this big undertaking and other earlier ventures. He was experienced with computers and had even designed fabulous posters for us in the past, such as the 'Who's Clowning Around in Bosnia' one featuring Johnie the clown, some trucks and our necessary contact and bank details. However, the music project was truly his major achievement.

Another project that was taking off was an artistic one named True Colours. Three creative women (Sarah Butterworth, Sophie Ebrey and Beth) and a Spanish chap had banded together with a mission to improve the bleak environment of refugee camps in Bosnia-Herzegovina. Armed with paintbrushes and many pots of paints they headed off in October aiming to paint various murals in centres they visited, as well as running all sorts of creative art workshops for children. Generously, British Telecom had donated a Dodge Truck which had previously been used as a personnel carrier and mobile café. It was decorated brightly in Road Trip style with the underlying canary yellow base and splashes of other colours on top. It was a fitting vehicle for the True Colours team as they set off jubilantly for a three-month period bringing their ray of sunshine with them as the bleak, cold winter approached.

Meanwhile, I was busy following up with some of our Romanian contacts and there seemed to be a genuine interest to have Simon, our clown, return there to further some of the work we had kick-started. I was grateful for something to work towards and was focused on helping him return, when all of a sudden the rug seemed to be taken from beneath me. He had just returned to London with the aim of

226

returning to Romania, but as was normal in this ever-changing environment, something else came up! One of the music professors from Edinburgh University was leading a group of teenage students out to Mostar and Sarajevo to hook up with the music project out there. It was decided at short notice that a clown could bring a much-valued lightheartedness to the trip and so Simon was invited to join them. He naturally accepted this opportunity staring him in the face without a moment's hesitation in true clowning manner. He was led by his heart and there was no time to think. He had arrived on a Monday and he was gone by the Wednesday in an amazing disappearing act.

At first I took the change in plans personally and felt that I had been investing too much energy on sending someone on a follow-up project which he promptly dropped like a sack of potatoes when something else had come up. Of course, this feeling was understandable, but it seemed to highlight my uncertainty and lack of direction in London. The unpredictable lifestyle was starting to take its toll on me and I was questioning whether I should carry on with The Serious Road Trip. I remember Tony Gaffney saying that I just needed a decent boyfriend. There may have been some truth in that, and I missed Yoyo sorely, but I didn't let him know that. 'No, I just need to get to know myself better,' I retorted, and of course there was truth in that too.

I didn't want my happiness to depend so much on others and was determined to search more within. I was also happy to spend more time with my female friends in London, rather than the male friends who dominated the London office. There were a few Kiwi women who had recently arrived, including Penny who I remembered from my days as a student in Wellington. This helped boost my spirits at what seemed to be a crossroads in my life.

Financially things were rather tricky. My few savings from my work in Luxembourg were coming to an end, and signing on for some governmental assistance and support was proving to be troublesome on this occasion, even under the Training for Work scheme I thought I was a part of. While I was a British citizen, I still held my Kiwi passport and accent. With a string of periods out of the country whilst on projects, to the outsider it looked like I might be someone who the authorities had decided to label a 'benefit tourist'. I had mistakenly signed off each time I left the country, only to return once again several months later. My explanations of our humanitarian work had flown over the heads of the office staff I was dealing with and I would need to appeal their decision. This would require going before a Tribunal and I needed legal aid to represent me. Unfortunately I can't remember the name of the female lawyer who arrived like an angel to take my case on, but I was fortunate enough to find someone. I provided her with my history of voluntary work, backed up with evidence in the form of letters from our head office and newspaper articles reporting on my projects, and then it was a waiting game to get a hearing date.

Meanwhile, Sarajevo seemed to be a major focal point in the office. Alongside the music and art projects, one of our Kiwi drivers, Peter Hobbs, who was also a musician, had based himself in Sarajevo with another chap called Matt for a few months. They went about setting up a community music and arts festival named 'The Dark Side of Disneyland' (Tamna Strana Disneylanda) in the besieged city. This was a community festival organised in conjunction with many of the talented, creative and artistic Sarajevans who were enduring their fourth year and winter under siege. The Festival was to take place in November 1995 and gave many locals a focal point to aim towards. It was to last a couple of weeks with a variety of bands, choirs, amateur dramatic and theatre groups all finding an outlet for their creative work. Local builders and others were focused on repairing some of the many gaping holes in buildings in order to make this possible; all hands on deck to pull it off. It gave everyone, both participants and audience, a positive focus at an otherwise gruelling and hopeless time. Peter and Matt were integral movers and shakers and naturally Simon, the clown, managed to find his space to perform within the framework of the Festival too, along with the True Colours team who came to support the event. Later Simon went on to be the clown chosen as part of a Circus School project in Sarajevo, which was run by EquiLibre, with lots of equipment and support provided by The Serious Road Trip.

The *Daily Telegraph* photographed some of these creative actions as we had been chosen to be part of a Christmas appeal for Bosnia that year, alongside three other major charities. This was a major development and gave us serious credibility. Years earlier, we had been involved in such a venture providing endless information about Bosnia to the *Sunday Times* for a fundraising campaign, but back then we hadn't even been included as a beneficiary. At least the tide had turned and our tenacity and expertise were being rewarded.

On a personal level, however, somehow I felt I was starting to distance myself from the excitement of these new projects and was spending less time in the office. I couldn't quite put my finger on what was happening, but the balance between my working life and personal life was surfacing and trying to take shape. One of my flatmates, Pip, tried to help me through this difficult time with good moral support. He noticed that my bedroom space really wasn't that homely. There were no real curtains up or even posters on the wall. I had been sleeping there as though it would be only for a few nights and living out of my backpack. He set about helping me find a pair of curtains and setting up a curtain rail. We found a chest of drawers for my clothes and I found various posters and postcards to decorate the walls. At least it felt like a space I could escape to now and make it my own, even if the rest of the house was one giant batchelor pad.

My NZ friend Penny, was keen to venture to Paris and this gave me the perfect excuse to set off to my favourite city. I stayed with Eric in his inviting apartment filled with books and views of the Eiffel Tower in the distance. It really was a bohemian flat, with dust gathering on all sorts of curios and artifacts collected on many travels. I was reminded of the previous trips with Yoyo, but was happy to be speaking French again and introducing Penny to Paris and all that it had to offer the tourist. Some of these places were becoming familiar haunts and I especially enjoyed our visit to the Rodin museum. There were many erotic figures of love and adoration between man and woman, such as the '*l'Eternelle idole*', but it was the total beauty of Danaide's back that evoked deep emotions for me. One could feel his love of the female body and all the sensual curves, yet she was curled up, with her long liquid hair falling to the ground almost like a waterfall, and as the poet Rainer Maria Rilke wrote, '*the face loses itself in the stone as though in a great weeping*'. On some sub-conscious level it was as though I identified and felt for her abandonment and yet I felt the intense love she conveyed as well. I was unable to put this into words but was drawn to this figure merging with the marble.

Alongside this there were obvious faces in contortions such as The Great Burghers of Calais as they walked with nooses around their necks towards their destiny. During the Hundred years war, Calais had been under siege and starving for one year. It was said that Edward III offered to spare the starving inhabitants if six of their leaders would surrender themselves, presumably to be executed. They were eventually shown mercy by the English queen, but you could feel their poignant mix of defeat and heroic self-sacrifice as they headed towards what they thought was certain death. It reminded me of the more modern siege of Sarajevo and the plight of the Bosnians, who had overwhelmed our lives for over three years. There the proud inhabitants of Sarajevo refused to let the war divide them up and there was a mix of all ethnic groups, Serbs, Croats and Muslims, all united in their fight to fend off the Serbs that encircled the city. It was strange, as I was questioning more and more my role in something that wasn't my war, and yet I felt strongly about their plight and the injustice of war.

229

The long weekend was quickly over and we returned to London, but I was convinced that my future lay somehow in France.

On another level, the political situation was evolving in Bosnia and it seemed the end of the war was on the horizon. The needs had already changed and finally, it seemed, our humanitarian mission in Bosnia would no longer be needed, at least not in the form that it had thus far been needed. It was hard to judge these things from a distance as the reality on the ground could be quite a different matter.

Christmas was fast approaching and this year my aunt and uncle were over from New Zealand and managing a pub and nightclub venue on the outskirts of London in Burnham Beeches. This provided the perfect safe haven for me at this time of year, when connecting with family felt so important. Most of the other Road Trippers had family to catch up with after returning from projects and now I was excited to be catching up with some of my cousins and having a traditional roast dinner with family. On Boxing Day there was to be a huge party in the nightclub next door and this was extended to anyone from The Serious Road Trip to join us there. A whole vanload turned up eager for somewhere to dance and drink the night away, forgetting about all the recent stresses in our lives. They had come prepared with sleeping bags and all managed to find a soft piece of carpet or sofa to lay their heads for a few hours before climbing back in the van.

The uncertainty of a New Year lay before me and what shape that might take. I seemed determined to find a way back to Paris, which was a city I loved and would allow me to speak French without limits. Having completed my studies in French, I felt destined to use this language to my advantage and the City of Light was beckoning. Maybe there would be an opportunity to reconnect with Yoyo as he was due a holiday, or so I thought, from a recent letter he had sent. Or maybe I would finally earn some money at last. It was tough on one's self-esteem being an unpaid volunteer, despite the other rewards, and I was contemplating returning to an office job in the financial services, just to get some money. A change in base might just help me make the necessary break from The Serious Road Trip, to which I had devoted so much of my heart and soul, time and energy.

Meni had returned from Albania and Jutta arrived for a break from Austria. While I was at this crossroads in my life, it was so good to reconnect with these two friends. We were invited back to Meni's parents where there was an amazing spread of food served to us. His aunt was visiting from Israel and she enjoyed looking into a person's

230

empty coffee cup and reading the patterns of the grains. She said I was on a never-ending journey and I would soon travel with a friend who looked like a duck. What a giggle we had imagining this duck-like friend. Funnily, however, this would actually make sense later.

The New Year arrived like a breath of fresh air heralding new beginnings, new ideas and people to meet.

I couldn't help but remember that it was the one-year anniversary since Yoyo had left for Encounter Overland and the huge wrench that had caused.

Then, almost like a bolt out of the blue, a magic hat was given to me. It was a pointed magician's hat made out of purple velvet with white stars and a moon adorning it. The rim also consisted of eight points, which could be bent up or down due to a wire within. Spesh had picked it up and thought of me on a recent holiday to Prague. Now I was contemplating how I would utilise this new hat in my desired relocation to Paris. It certainly did make me wonder about a new project, but I rejected this thought in favour of Paris. Regardless, this hat had arrived magically in my life and it seemed to be a reassuring sign of good things to come.

Within days there was a knock at my door in Tottenham and who stood before me but two large life-sized puppets (a boy and a girl), with Johnie and Caroline shouting 'Surprise, surprise, Simone! We're off to Sarajevo!'

I was so taken aback by this spontaneous arrival and overjoyed to see these two again. It was almost three years since our first trip to Romania together and our subsequent trip to Croatia. Johnie had always wanted to return for a trip to Sarajevo and here they were, when I had actually given up hope of doing another project together! In fact, I had given up hope of doing another project and was heading off in another direction.

They clambered through the front door carrying puppets, bags and oodles of enthusiasm, and talking a dozen words to the second in true Irish fashion.

The merriment began as I caught up on all their action since we last met. They had been to many orphanages in Russia on their own, but now Johnie was following through on a promise made earlier, which I had almost forgotten. He had always intended to go to Sarajevo. He felt sure it was the right time to act, due to the peace agreement which had finally been reached after three and a half years of war. The Dayton agreement had been signed just a few weeks earlier, in Paris on 14 December 1995 and this was a huge step towards ending the war. Somehow this important development had provided me with my perfect cue for leaving. However, this also meant that we could finally travel in relative safety to areas that had been too dangerous to reach. He had a clear vision of the show he would do. I asked him, 'Was there a magician in there?' as if his answer would clarify things for me.

'Yes, I can see a magician there, but the face is all blurry like.' It certainly made me wonder and question the crossroads I was at. But it was true that doing a project with Johnie and Caroline would be far simpler than starting from scratch and we were a tried and tested team that worked well together.

Caroline was bursting to tell me all she had seen in Dublin whilst working at a creative arts centre for children named The Ark. How appropriate, I thought, imagining the boat bursting with animals, new beginnings and a rainbow overhead. There had been a visiting group from Italy with life-sized puppets and she had been inspired to make the two figures, a boy and a girl, out of recycled clothes. She had hand-stitched them lovingly together like two giant happy dolls. The girl wore a red and white polka dotted dress with a matching blue and white polka dotted apron attached. The legs were stuffed stockings and her hair was a giant yellow mop tamed into two pigtails. The boy wore a shirt with bright red braces, attached to his short trousers, or were they long shorts? His green face was topped with orange hair made from yarn, poking out from beneath his red cap.

Each puppet had thick elastic bands on the rear of the head, the arms and the feet. The puppeteer could therefore hold them up by the head, leaving one arm and the feet to be slotted over the remaining arm and feet of the puppeteer. As the puppeteer walked, the puppet would walk, and so forth, with the person semi-concealed behind the puppet. I had never seen anything like it and they were both charming and enticing. I was obviously taken by this idea for the project, and the compelling political circumstances, but I had many things to consider. 'This could be a grand finale of sorts for all that we have done!' stated Caroline and Johnie in a very persuasive manner.

What a night for it. There was another knock at the door and another unannounced Irishman walked through. Sometimes things seem to come in threes! His name was Niall McCann and he had just been persuaded to head our team in Bosnia with Tony or Graeme no longer heading the team. I had been so preoccupied with thoughts of my life after The Serious Road Trip, that I was completely unaware of this new recruitment, although these types of things would happen very spontaneously with us. Niall knew Bosnia from working with another NGO and was only too happy to join our ranks. He had seen Christopher and was due to fly out to Split the next day. Was there a

232

spare space on the floor somewhere and what was this about a clowning tour of Bosnia? The synchronicity was amazing, as the timing couldn't have been better.

My flatmate, Pip, was also there and being a clown himself, he was also under Johnie's spell and jumped at the idea of becoming part of the Dobrakadabra tour of Bosnia. It was appropriately named due to Dobra meaning good (in Serbo-Croat/Bosnian) and Kadabra coming from the magical word Abrakadabra. This would be a tour to cast some good magic into the heart of Bosnia-Herzegovina! It was in itself a magical evening and we chatted, drank, danced and laughed into the wee hours of the morning, with Johnie up to his usual hi-jinks. I had missed him and Caroline.

The next morning, Niall headed off with a burning desire to let the appropriate organisations know of the proposed clowning tour of Bosnia. He would advertise our tour amongst the relevant people at the next UN briefing in Split. Understandably his announcement was met with numerous groups hoping for a slot in the busy six-week itinerary from April onwards.

To confuse me further, a letter from Yoyo arrived in the wake of all this excitement saying he was definitely due a break, but nothing was certain. He would love to see me again, it seemed, so the feeling was mutual.

Johnie and Caroline were only on a fleeting visit. After meeting with Christopher and others in our London office, who were absolutely thrilled with the new project, they disappeared to get busy with fundraising in Dublin. The project preparation was now underway. I just wasn't certain it included me and needed more time to make sure I was on board.

Romania was also featuring at this time, with arrivals in London of Miloud and Chris Smith, who I'd met the year before. Plus Richard was back in town with plans to return to Romania. My world was in a spin with so many options.

The accounts for Romania needed to be handed in and a volunteer from NZ, Kathrine, had arrived like a dream to help me and others with such practical tasks. She was also very generous in providing moral support, and was probably too generous for her own good when it came to shouting numerous rounds of beer to our thirsty bunch.

My family was beckoning me to join them in Colorado. My brother and his girlfriend were working a skiing season in Aspen and had an apartment to stay in. My parents were keen to catch up midway as we hadn't seen each other in two years. There was also my pen-pal of 14 years living nearby. Ginger and I had corresponded since our families had become friendly in New Zealand before returning to their lives in America. We would have a mini family reunion in Aspen and my brother would sort out cheap skis and passes for us all. Ginger and her husband and three children would join us for a few days. I decided I would use the time to clear my head and see what my next plans would be.

I boarded the Virgin plane bound for Denver with just a few dollars in my pocket having put the flight on my NZ credit card. There would be a short stopover in Denver before the connecting flight. Typically however, there was a snow storm in Aspen and we were snowbound for 24 hours with only the airport to sleep in. I exchanged the few dollars I had into coins and made a few phone calls, including one to Ginger. Her sister lived in Denver and could sort me out for the night. I was thankful for a bed that night and a warm meal before heading on the last leg of the journey.

Aspen was a magical town, with twinkling lights decorating each tree and snow on the pavements and streets. After all that I had done, it was comforting to be surrounded by my family unit once again and my parents were relieved to have their two elder children together after so much time. The skiing was quite different from Mount Ruapehu in New Zealand and it was my first experience of powder. My brother had various Irish friends there and the apartment we stayed in even had a book to read; written by a nurse who had worked with the orphans of Romania! To think, it even mentioned Moona and focused on the children of Ionaseni, who I knew too.

A couple of the Irish friends of my brother were fascinated to hear I had been to Bosnia and was contemplating a return. This wasn't the first time they had met someone who told similar stories. They had met someone they called 'Coops' whilst diving in Thailand. They had thought he was off his rocker, when he had told them tales of driving trucks and clowning in the war-zone. I couldn't believe this coincidence that they had actually met Allan Cooper, who had driven the bus and clowned on the Bananas 4 Split Part II tour. Whilst I couldn't vouch for all that he had told them, I definitely confirmed that he had indeed been there and done that. 'Maybe Coops wasn't as mad as we thought,' they muttered in surprised shock.

After a week, our family friends, Ginger, Chad and Robyn Woods arrived from different locations with their various partners and children. What a beautiful moment to see such old friends reunited and what a surprise for me finally to be in America for the first time. Ginger and I were exactly the same age. She was married with three children, but we still got on like a house on fire, just as we did as

234

naughty youngsters, climbing onto the roof at church instead of attending Sunday School. We laughed about the time Chad had put on some of the clothes in the closed second-hand clothing store where Sunday School was held next door to church, and had pretended to be a female mannequin to unsuspecting passers-by. Our families had shared many picnics, walks through forests and fishing adventures on the plentiful lakes, where I had grown up. Her positive attitude and cheerful nature was infectious and a great tonic for me as I recharged my batteries.

I bade farewell to my family and journeyed back with Ginger and her family. The car wound around the twisty road as we journeyed by moonlight through the Rockies to their mobile home some hours away. The children were excited to have a visitor and I was able to hear more about my friend's life as a mother. I had juggling balls and face-paints to give and Ginger's husband told me of his earlier days as an entertainer. He even went to a cupboard and produced three ventriloquist puppets that his children had never seen. He had been a talented ventriloquist at an early age, even featuring in newspapers. His children were spellbound to discover their father's hidden past. Generously he decided to give me a large blue rabbit puppet to take with me to Bosnia. He also wanted to make sure I had a decent pair of boots for the snow as I had been slipping over for days. They took me to Walmart to find the right ones, generously paying for half. Now it was starting to sink in that I was indeed bound for Bosnia, armed with boots, bunny and balls. If I couldn't make my mind up the universe was producing all sorts of signs to point me in this direction.

Chapter 20

Dobrakadabra Tour of Bosnia
(1996)

On my return to London, I received a much-awaited letter from Yoyo. Something had come up and he wouldn't be back on his break after all. He genuinely sounded disappointed about this, but it gave me another green light to go on tour, rather than waiting around for him or heading straight for Paris.

Funds were starting to roll in from the *Daily Telegraph*'s Christmas Appeal and Johnie and Caroline's various efforts in Ireland. The True Colours team vehicle had returned, meaning we didn't even have to find a new vehicle as the mountainous terrain had already ruled out the use of the Red Bus for this tour. The Metroline garage once again provided us with mechanical support to make sure the truck was serviced and ready to go.

I also had the hearing at the Tribunal, and made my appearance before the three judges with my lawyer at my side. She put forward my very compelling case of all the good work I helped achieve, and what a relief when they gave me a huge applause. They were most certainly happy to reinstate my allowance. Ironically this happened just before I was due to leave again.

There was a last minute drama having to have a final wisdom tooth extracted but that went surprisingly well. There were a few farewells signalling the end of an era. Chris (Goblin) and Adele were returning to NZ after a few years in London and Kathrine also, who had volunteered in our office for the NZ summer.

I couldn't believe how everything just seemed to fall into place.

On a project level, Meni would be our driver, which was reassuring as he knew Bosnia well and had done a marvellous job driving and holding it together in Romania as well. My flatmate in London, Pip Dance, would be our musician and juggler. He had already toured with the Theatre-go-Round project clowning tour of refugee centres in Croatia and Slovenia and before meeting TSRT had spent four years working with the Mid Powys Youth Theatre in Wales, so was well-experienced. And of course there were Johnie Kavanagh, as our main clown, plus Caroline Moore and myself as co-leaders of the tour and performers and puppeteers.

Caroline came over to do the final preparation for the tour, which was a huge boost. There were the usual dramas getting the vehicle in shape for the trip as it failed its MOT the week before leaving and the starter motor went as well... but by departure date it was running like a dream. Caroline and I made a dynamic duo doing some last-minute fundraising at Camden Market dressed up for the occasion. Our catch-phrase became 'Help Send Tweetie Bird to Bosnia' as Caroline had been given a fantastic yellow costume for the trip. It bore a remarkable resemblance to a duck, making Meni's aunt's earlier prediction spookingly true!

By the third week of March, Johnie arrived and we had the usual party to send us off. It was the 23rd March 1996.

Even Nev made it to the occasion and tried to have a heart to heart with me, but my mind was so preoccupied with the forthcoming trip and leaving London that I have no memory of what was said. I just remember feeling how strange it was that he was so distant from the group now, after having been the founder. Now he was the one needing to talk, and I was the one too busy. Our roles had reversed.

Of course, Johnie made sure that the Dodge personnel carrier truck had Clowntown Express emblazoned across the front. The existing colourful decorations of clowns, flowers, happy children and animals meant we didn't have to do much before feeling happy with our new clowning wheels. There was ample room and storage space for all the props and all our bags inside. We even had bags of materials for distribution to each centre after a show, such as face-paints, balloons and juggling balls. We wanted our visit to leave more than memories. We wanted the centres to have some useful tools to put on shows themselves. On top of this, I had even done a deal with a street seller at Piccadilly Circus who sold me 50 or so miniature red double-decker buses at a bargain price. We spent hours decorating them with our Serious Road Trip stickers and Dobrakadabra tour labels, as we also wanted everyone to know who we were and to have a concrete reminder of our visit.

237

Johnie had made some colourful freestanding backdrops, which would provide a focal point behind the stage area and some sort of area where we could change costumes whilst on tour. How practical and professional this all seemed! We were happy with the table and seating, which were part of a mini kitchen space in the back half of the truck and was ideal for sitting over endless cups of tea and meals cooked in one pot on board. Mind you, we soon realised once setting off that the truck did shake an awful lot whilst moving, so this was not as easy to do or smooth as we hoped. The front cab of the truck, where our driver Meni sat, had space for two others, but the only downside was the cab and the rear were separate entities, meaning neither group could speak to the other. Johnie developed some sophisticated communication system that involved banging loudly on one of the two windows that separated the two areas and then attempting to scribble messages in large letters on A4 paper. If Meni was listening to loud music in the front, or was chatting with the navigator or focused on driving, which was a good thing, these attempts sometimes went unnoticed. That wasn't so good if one of us was busting for the loo. However, we did have other receptacles to resort to if we got desperate... having been on various tours, these were familiar situations to us all.

We set off for Austria as our first stop en route, staying with Jutta for the night. She was only too happy to see old friends with similar goals and was working with specials needs children and adolescents at a centre in Altenhof near Linz. Naturally we obliged with an early form of our show, which was starting to take shape, and it was lovely to see Jutta surrounded by loving work colleagues and youngsters who obviously adored her.

This was the first time Pip had performed with Johnie and they both had to work out various routines involving juggling, unicycles and other props.

Meanwhile Caroline and I were using the wonderful puppets with great gusto. While I would double up as a purple magician with my newly acquired hat, spinning my pois on ropes and with bells jangling around my ankles, Caroline also had a new character to make a change from her days as a pink mouse. The giant Tweety Bird costume she had borrowed was a very bright yellow to match our trucks. I couldn't wait to see her in action, and of course the free-standing back-drop provided a private space for changing, so our entrance as new characters could be a complete surprise.

We left Jutta's bound for Zagreb with Deep Forest music blaring out and a colourful fish blowing in the wind outside the truck. There we were hosted by EquiLibre, where we met two French guys. One was a poet and the other the spitting image of Yoyo. It was quite uncanny and served as another reminder that I wished he was there. It was cold and there was snow on the ground, even if it was sunny. We sped past various burnt out buildings heralding more of what was to come. Johnie was busting for the loo and managed to get Meni to stop on this occasion. Meni quickly warned him against wandering off behind a tree for a number two. There might be land-mines around for all we knew. Conveniently, however, there was a bright green skip placed on the side of the road. He climbed into the skip and all we could see was his happy face bobbing up over the edge as he proudly held up a roll of toilet paper for us to see. You could see his relief that he had managed to find somewhere safe to dump. I was glad I didn't feel the urge to join him on this occasion.

The next stop was Split, although this time we were welcomed by our friends from Premiere Urgence. Our own team was no longer based on the coast and had moved inland to Bosnia with various people in Mostar and Zenica.

Premiere Urgence were only too happy to have us to stay, as it was Saturday night and we provided great entertainment and light relief from their work.

Johnie had a cool trick involving two spoons attached by a long piece of string. The drivers had to line up and then thread the spoon through their clothing, linking them altogether. Then it was a race to do this in reverse or something like that. Pip breathed fire into the dark night. There was the usual juggling, my poi twirling and the drivers all thought Caroline as Tweety Bird was hilarious.

We partied and drank into the wee hours, talking about all that we had planned for the heart of Bosnia. It was a big deal for us all as we had gradually built up the necessary courage over the years to embark on this tour. It was reassuring to know we had many friends we could call on if needed before we crossed the border. In the drunken stupor Johnie had his head shaven by one of the French team who had his own electric hair clippers. This would add to one of his tricks as I would soon realise.

We left for Bosnia, very hung over from the night before. Where there had been many checkpoints on Meni's last journey, the Dayton Peace Agreement was starting to take effect and many of these road-blocks had disappeared literally that very day. What amazing timing for us indeed. We crossed with relative ease after a brief checking of passports and paperwork. We were through! Snow was beginning to melt so that was timely as well. Nonetheless, my heart was pounding as we wound our way to eventually arrive in Gornji Vakuf, where we were grateful to be able to stay with Julia from UMCOR (United Methodist Committee on Relief) at very short notice. This placed us well for getting to our show in Prozor the following morning.

It was somehow very apt to realise that we actually started our tour of Bosnia on April Fools' Day! This day had held particular significance, especially when it came to clowns. We quickly found the school that was waiting for us. The sun was shining brightly which was fortunate as we were asked to perform outside on an asphalted sports area of the school. It provided a clear boundary for our stage. Most of the children stood or sat on the grassy verges of the flat space, and there was some elevation on a small hill nearby providing a good view for those gathered at the back.

Caroline and I started the show with the life-size puppets accompanied by appropriate music on a loud ghetto-blaster portable stereo. There was the girl acting all coyly on one side of the stage area and the boy on the other. Dancing to music, he slowly noticed her and approached her beckoning figure. He was obviously attracted to her golden locks and smiling face. He eventually went down on his knees and offered her his heart literally. He handed her the red cardboard heart Velcroed to his shirt and she gladly took this and placed it on her chest. There was a little dance together, then within a few minutes it was time to disappear behind the freestanding back-drop. Our arms felt like they would drop off even after such a short time, but the adrenalin kept us going and the stage was given to Johnie. He wore his usual patched dungarees and a colourful shirt. His face was painted white with a red nose and mouth and a new addition was a black spiky wig on his head.

He had the relevant words needed to say hello (Dobar Dan/Zdravo!) and would quickly produce a large balloon which he started to blow up. The children loved how he would stop and ask them if they wanted it blown bigger. 'Jos?' (pronounced Yosh) and he would mimic bigger with his hands. They would shout back 'Jos'. This would go on until eventually the balloon was so large that it popped and Johnie went flying backwards over a chair and landed on the floor, still trying to blow up the burst balloon.

The crowd would roar with laughter and were sufficiently warmed up for more.

With Pip also colourfully dressed, more equipment would come out, such as the unicycle or juggling balls and clubs. At first the clowns were clumsy and unable to do the tricks. Pip would produce enormous tools to tighten up a bolt and try and fix the unicycle as though that might be the problem. Then they would require assistance from the

240

audience. A volunteer would come onto stage to help steady Johnie as he mounted the unicycle and then just when they must have been thinking that this clown doesn't really know how to do the trick, he would succeed and scoot around proudly on his unicycle and get the necessary applause. He liked to show that in life we are not perfect and one needs to keep trying and trying until you succeed.

Meanwhile I was behind the backdrop preparing for my next act. For this I needed to put on my purple dress with ornate gold thread and sequins decorating it, my purple hat with white stars and a moon, and jingling bells around my ankles. My face was already face-painted with golden paint, a moon on one cheek, stars on the other and a bright and fiery sun on my chin. My heart was racing as it often did before a performance. It was hard to believe that we were actually here beginning a full-on tour of Bosnia-Herzegovina.

I swept onto stage swinging my New Zealand pois with all the energy possible. They criss-crossed from each hand in front of me before I eventually brought the two strings together and managed a more circular formation. This was always at the risk of the balls colliding, but on this occasion it worked and the crowd seemed intrigued. Johnie then arrived holding out a small blue velvet bag with a wooden handle. He produced three scarves which he proceeded to juggle with. This made a change from the previous balls and clubs and was entrancing to watch as the scarves fell gently. He asked for a volunteer and the excited chosen child ventured onto the stage, wondering what task she might be asked to perform. He motioned that she was to put the scarves into the magic bag, which she did. I then proceeded to dance around them with my fingers and hands motioning towards the bag. We needed some magic words before anything would work and Abrakadabra didn't suffice. The audience needed to shout along with me 'Dobrakadabra' before the trick worked and finally the scarves disappeared. The bag was pushed inside out for our volunteer to inspect that the bag was empty and the scarves were indeed gone. I repeated this act with the audience's help shouting and then the scarves magically reappeared. It seemed apt that the tour had been named Dobrakadabra and we had completed this trick successfully.

Next up was Caroline wearing her giant Tweety Bird costume that trotted out from behind the back-drop. This was extremely visual and such a bright yellow.

Some children were encouraged one by one to start forming a huge long train behind her, holding onto each others' waists. She twisted and turned to the music with a huge line of happy children trailing behind her and waving to the rest of the audience.

1

Following that there were all sorts of clowning antics, but the trick that stuck out for me was Johnie and his blue helmet. He had somehow been given a blue helmet that the UN wore during their peacekeeping efforts. He proudly showed off this helmet and how useful it was. He could put it on his head and then whack himself over the head with a juggling club without hurting himself. He looked so pleased with himself and his new helmet. Then Pip snuck up behind him and removed the helmet and the wig along with it. Johnie carried on as though he still had the helmet to protect him and gave himself a huge whack over the head. BANG! He fell to the ground dazed, but that wasn't the only thing we were laughing about. He was completely bald and the crowd started screaming out 'Celo' (pronounced chello) which was the equivalent to 'baldy' or maybe egg-head. It reminded me of my days in New Zealand where the equivalent would have been 'Kina' which was a spiky sea-egg. Their response was so spontaneous and the chanting infectious that everyone joined in, even though it was at the expense of our clown, who thankfully was begging for this type of response.

After some serious bubble-blowing, next up was face-painting. We chose a couple of children to be on stage and have their faces painted. Once that was done, we each took a sponge and a pot of paint and headed into the audience to put streaks of paint on as many faces as possible. Before long every child had rainbow colours splashed over their faces and sadly this was also our moment to finish. The show was over and we were surrounded by so many happy faces.

Meni had been watching our props like a hawk in the chaos and now it was time to scoop everything up to put it back on the truck. We made sure we handed over a tray of paints, some juggling balls, balloons, bubbles and one of the 'souvenir' red buses to the teacher in charge and then we were off to our next stop. A sea of children gathered around the truck to see us off and were all smiling and holding up their fingers in the V shape for victory. It truly did feel like a victory for us too and I proceeded to blow magical kisses into the crowd. What a fantastic start to the tour!

Meni seemed to be lingering a little longer than we needed at the wheel, when we realised that our vehicle wouldn't start. We waited a little longer and it still didn't start. It was like some cruel April Fool's joke gone wrong! All the usual checks were made, but the truck would not go into gear. We were lucky that we had escorts from IFOR (Implementation Force – NATO-led) and UMCOR who could help and we managed to get the truck back to the British base in Gornji Vakuf.

As if to reflect this change in circumstance, the weather changed

242

and in came the rain. 'Rain, Rain, go away, come again another day' I muttered internally. Based on previous experience, we could have guessed that some vehicle trouble was most likely to happen, but it was still a huge bummer that this had happened on the first day! At least we were only a couple of hours away from our team in Zenica, so we were pleased to see our Land Rover, Ragga roll in, with Andy at the wheel. Help was at hand. While our team tried to work out a way to repair the truck, we were quickly offered the use of this first Land Rover from the early convoys. We had a whole week of shows booked and there was no time for waiting for the truck to be repaired. Ragga had undertaken a huge transformation and was now bright pink with painted flames coming from the wheels. Perfect!

The next show was in a school on the Croat side of Gornji Vakuf.

The 200 or so children gathered eagerly in a gymnasium. Some children kneeled at the front, some stood behind them and there were others holding onto the walls at the back to give them the elevation needed to see us. The noise was quite deafening, but we gave it all we had and there were jubilant cries of excitement.

The afternoon show was postponed due to the rain so we made our way to Zenica. It wasn't quite the jubilant arrival from a day's clowning or beginning of our tour that we were hoping for but our experience showed that these types of mishaps were all part and parcel of our projects and that there was always a solution. That night we managed to find space to sleep in a house that The Serious Road Trip was renting and used as its base. Many of the drivers were now working in Mostar with a rebuilding programme and another of our teams was focused on delivering hot food to schools near the front line area of Olovo. This was dubbed the Olovo School Meals Project. Times had certainly changed since the days of driving convoys of aid into the besieged capital and, thankfully, Bosnia now had different needs.

Rather than faxing our head office to tell them of our mechanical challenge, I was now able to actually send an e-mail. There was the familiar screeching noise as with a fax, except this was the dial-up network in action and within seconds a letter, typed on the computer, departed for London or vice-versa. It was such fascinating technology to me and meant we could save lots of the money normally spent on phone or fax bills and still maintain regular contact.

This also had its downside. Within days of arriving I was to learn that Yoyo had taken leave after all and was now in London, much to my dismay. It may have been a tender e-mail, but I remember feeling hugely torn by this thought and wondered if he would somehow magically appear to fix the truck and carry on with us. I tried not to let it dampen my spirits, but he was clear that he would not be heading over to join us and was enjoying his much needed break in London. What a cruel twist of fate. I was deeply disappointed but had to bury this within, put on my outward smile and get on with such an important tour. Hopefully the following six weeks would pass quickly and we could be reunited.

The first week sped by with shows in the Gornji Vakuf and surrounding areas of Zenica, helped by a few groups including IFOR GB, Red Barnett, Pax Christi and a Norwegian agency. Gornji Vakuf was the area our first truck had driven through and been shot at by a sniper. As previously mentioned, our driver had narrowly missed a serious injury with the bullet landing in his pocketknife and this had prompted the painting of the trucks that bright canary yellow. A British soldier had not been so lucky and had lost his life and yet he too was on a humanitarian aid convoy. I had heard the name of the town mentioned so many times and here we now were in that very region some three years later. Buildings everywhere were shot to pieces, roofs had caved in and windows were long gone. There was rubble and building remains lying strewn along the side of the road. No doubt, before the war, that had been someone's house and home. It reminded me of the devastation I had seen in East Mostar. However, we had little time to reflect on this as we were due to perform to our eager audiences.

The venues varied greatly. One moment we were in a secondary school, the next moment in a kindergarten. Our second day was blighted by the rain but that didn't put the children off from attending an outside show the following day. They were there with raincoats, umbrellas and smiles. They somehow managed to squeeze themselves onto four-tiered wooden planks on some metal structure, probably usually brought out for sporting events. The weather certainly hadn't dampened their spirits.

The school in one area had been destroyed during the war, so we toured the various classrooms that had been relocated to the local mosque and shops on the main road. Somehow, people just had to adapt to the situation that they were thrown into. But how would I adapt if that had been my home, village, school and community destroyed? One of the men we met explained that he had never believed that they would take up arms against their neighbours, but that is exactly what had happened. One day neighbours who had lived alongside each other for generations were being told by the political powers to build barricades down the centre of the town, to separate

244

themselves into Muslims and Croats and then, literally the next day, they were expected to shoot at one another. Somehow people had been 'brainwashed' into doing this or going along with it all. It seemed to be an extremely dark version of an experiment I had heard of in the USA to show how people can be manipulated to turn against each other for something as simple as having brown or blue eyes. The American students had been brainwashed into becoming enemies and exhibiting 'racist' behaviour towards one another, where previously they had been friends. It made me wonder if the political powers had done a similar 'experiment' in Bosnia, and the ensuing war had been the fateful consequence. Where the American students were able to end the experiment after a few days and some may have needed some psychological counselling as a result, what would be the consequences of the death and destruction in this community? How would they recover from these atrocities amongst former friends? It certainly didn't look like this could be reversed as quickly as it had overpowered them.

Still, it felt good to be giving positive messages of love and humour after all they had been through. Somehow my blowing of magical kisses into the crowds summed up how I felt towards everyone, without having to use words. Our puppets coming together showed that love conquered the differences between my puppet having a green face and Caroline's one a pinky colour.

Pip also had a 'love-trick' up his sleeve and managed to kiss his juggling balls whilst juggling.

Johnie's famous bucket trick was revived and it never ceased to amaze me how I could watch the same tricks time and time again, and still get the same enjoyment from them. I guess it wasn't exactly the same as not knowing what is coming next, but I loved watching the reactions of the crowd and the smiling faces, when what they thought was a bucket full of water being thrown at them, turned out to be a bucket full of small pieces of torn-up paper.

We finished the week performing in refugee camps near Zenica and, with an average of two shows a day, we earned a well deserved rest that Sunday, after well over 12 shows. I was amazed at how Johnie could keep his energy levels up so high with all the falling backwards over chairs, knocking himself over the head with juggling clubs and unicycling and clowning antics he had to perform to hold our show together. Still, we were all running on adrenalin, and the buzz of managing to get to Bosnia had certainly not worn off. The excitement, energy and love from the children must have transferred over to us in some magical way, too.

245

We almost hadn't had time to think about our truck and had left it in the capable hands of our own crew, Andy and Tank. Unfortunately it was not going to be a simple repair. The clutch cable had gone and we needed to source another part. Had it been a Bedford like our others, we would have been fine as we had loads of spare parts for them, as Vince Steur, former Road Trip mechanic and fellow Kiwi, explained. Had it been a few months earlier, then we might even have had the support of the KiwiBat soldiers that had been stationed there until recently. He told me how admired The Road Trip had been by them. While there, they had helped with their expertise in truck repairs and various spare parts when possible. He told me about some rugby match that had been played and the infamous haka they had performed before leaving. They had certainly made an impression and left their mark in the area. In fact, they had been the culprits who had painted Ragga pink as some practical joke after repairing it. And Pinkerton had added the blue and purple flames afterwards. So that explained the revamped look!

But there was no quick fix for our truck and we needed to order the part from France. Our Premiere Urgence friends would make sure it got to us in another week or so. In the meantime we would have to make do with the well-loved Ragga and the crew that normally used this Land Rover would have to make other arrangements. We clowns attracted attention wherever we were and I remember at one point, whilst checking on our Dodge, an American Army officer felt compelled to meet up as he had something special for us. He proudly announced that he was from the very place where the kazoo came from and handed us all a kazoo to further enliven our show. It was a kind gesture and the perfect addition to put into our bag of tricks. With Johnie's splattering of Bosnian words, he was able to communicate using the kazoo as any normal clown would do.

The following week was dedicated to the areas of Travnik and Zenica, with UMCOR and Pax Christi being our NGO partners. It was amazing to think that here were two Christian organisations working on both sides of the divide. Niall had done a brilliant job of setting up the itinerary and it was a relief to have this aspect of the tour taken care of, as this side of Bosnia was totally new to all of us apart from Meni. He certainly knew his way around in getting us from A to B and we were generally accompanied by a guide from the different organisations.

As with previous tours, Johnie would get us all moving in the morning with a cup of coffee and a persuasive voice. His energy levels contrasted with Pip's more relaxed way of going in some Yin and Yang way, which had its advantages and disadvantages. No tour was complete without a few moans and groans. Johnie was used to performing professionally to high standard and he had similar expectations, within reason, of us. There was no time for sleeping in with our action-packed tour and I was relieved that this role of time-keeping was one he took seriously.

Meni and Pip tended to ride up front navigating, while Caroline, Johnie and myself got things ready in the back of the Land Rover, if it wasn't too bumpy.

Travnik was some 30kms away but that was at least an hour's drive. It was an alpine village surrounded by mountains. Parts of it almost could have been described as a Swiss village with mosques.

Our first day was spent at a youth centre which had been set up for residents and refugees although most were families who were internally displaced. While there hadn't been much damage to the city, the tide of 'refugees' had moved in from surrounding areas, almost tripling its population.

Whilst there, we were invited to visit the local theatre premises by a group of enthusiastic early twenty-year-olds. An office upstairs had all sorts of portrait paintings, photos and posters from theatre productions that had toured there before the war. What stuck out the most, however, was the large wooden desk with a machine gun pointing out from underneath. In its nozzle protruded a large red rose as a visual statement against war. Flower Power! These guys were generally excited to receive various juggling balls, spinning plates and face-paints. Meni was excited to discover a drum-kit on a stage and sat down to give us a few loud bangs.

It was a break from the usual after-show attention and a moment to connect with some like-minded youths and leave them with some tools and ideas to work with.

One of our goals had been to plant the idea of using creative arts as a means of therapy and we got the necessary affirmation that we were on the right track the very next day when visiting a kindergarten in the neighbouring village of Turbe.

A leading Bosnian psychologist had joined us at the kindergarten and was in raptures over the show.

'This is exactly what is needed to put the children on the road to recovery,' she exclaimed. Our parting gifts would be put to good use as the children would be encouraged into drama and physical activities as a result of seeing our show. We were not there long enough to follow these actions through but the NGOs, teachers and staff working with the children were so appreciative of our visit which enhanced existing work, or kick-started something new. I continued to blow magical kisses into the crowds as we sped away in our Land Rover and was happy to see some children reciprocating. They had had far too many experiences of hatred and it felt good to be somehow negating that.

We spent a couple more days in the area, performing one day in a communal space outside surrounded by numerous blocks of flats roughly 20 stories high. There were a few more in kindergartens and one hospital, and then our focus was Zenica.

We rounded the week off with three shows on the Saturday. The first one was at an orphanage for children who had lost their parents during the war. Here we were faced with the brutal reality that they were orphans as a consequence of the war as opposed to the other orphanage in town which was the state orphanage, where we finished that afternoon. Either way, the children no longer had parents.

The week wouldn't have been complete without a show for the general population of Zenica so we squeezed that one in at lunchtime, performing outside the Café Admiral on the pavement. It was drizzly, so not the best conditions, but that didn't stop a good crowd from gathering and enjoying our comedy. I remember enjoying a well-deserved hot cevapcici afterwards. This was the local speciality and could almost be described as sausages without the skin and very flavoursome. This was accompanied by Borek, which was a pastry pie filled with yummy mixtures of potato and onion, spinach and cheese. All very exotic and tasty. It was all washed down with some local firewater, slivovice (plum brandy) to celebrate. Quite strong but it was enjoyed by most trippers at some point.

You can imagine how we remained collapsed for our day of rest that Sunday. It was freezing cold outside and was good to speak with the various Road Trip drivers who were back from their projects.

The main one was the Olovo School Meals Project where the drivers provided one hot meal in a number of schools in that area to encourage the children to school, where no doubt they learnt more with warm food in their bellies. We would visit this project at the end of our tour.

One of the drivers who I knew as Scottish Dave was a young, tall and lanky chap with a twinkle in his eye and Scottish accent. His claim to fame was that he was the driver up for the challenge when Iron Maiden singer, Bruce Dickinson, and band, needed transporting to Sarajevo for that concert in December 1994. He was pretty chuffed, to say the least, that he'd got them in where the UN had failed.

One of the other drivers I remembered from the Croatian coast days, was Kiwi Vince Steur. Vince was now working for IRC, in a paid role for a change, and he would help us, later in the tour, to get to one of the areas that had been extremely cut off during the war. He was still very fond of The Serious Road Trip so would stay in touch as much as possible, even if working for another organisation. With his mechanical background he would still repair trucks if available. Similarly, Paul Kirwan, our original bus driver, was also the type of person to turn up and help out in between contracts with bigger organisations. It was these types of people, various friends from partner organisations, and all the locals who helped as well, that kept us going despite a lack of major funding.

Week three would see us head into a different area of Bosnia and, on a personal level, I would celebrate my 30th birthday mid-week in the most unlikely of places. I guess if I had been leading a more normal life, I would have thrown some large party or gone out on the town, but I would have to save those types of activities for later. The intensity of our project had helped me forget that feeling you have when you are nearing the beginning of another decade or rather the end of the previous one. Either way, people have a way of hyping it all up for the year leading up to your birthday and you almost can't wait to have it over and done with. Despite these mixed feelings, I was fond of birthdays regardless of the significance that reaching 30 brought. I had been reminded by my mother in a letter that at that age she was married with a house and four children. I certainly hadn't achieved any of those milestones, but I was following through on something I was passionate about and my life had taken a different direction on many levels. As far as I was concerned, those things could wait. You couldn't say I had planned to head into a war-zone on the eve of my 30th. On the contrary, but it seemed as though whatever plans I had tried to make to head off to Paris, the decision to go into Bosnia had come up unexpectedly, and I had freely chosen this detour as well. It was quite liberating to be breaking free from convention, although I knew that I would have to face other realities once the tour was over. It definitely felt like this tour marked the end of an era for me.

This week we would be accompanied by the Minister for Cultural Affairs in Tesanj and a humanitarian officer working with DanBat IFOR. This was part of the NATO-led international peacekeeping force that had begun serving the previous December (1995) to implement and monitor the military aspects of the Dayton Peace Agreement. Although our contact worked for the army, he was responsible for being in contact with the various NGOs working on the ground and his duty was to make sure that all sides of the front lines received equal amounts of humanitarian aid, and that included our clowning shows too. We met outside the army base as specified and he led us in his

Land Rover to Tesanj. This was a Bosniak town with a fortress overlooking the entire city. Our show was to take place in the local cinema which had a lovely huge stage area and even changing rooms out the back. We had two slots that day in the same venue, but what was even more amazing, was that it was the anniversary of the Bosnian Army. It was the 15th April and the army had formed exactly four years earlier, meaning there were a few events on the same stage to mark the occasion.

What a change it made to have the children all sitting on the cinema seats with us performing on a giant stage with proper wings and curtains to disappear behind when changing. Instead of our colourful backdrop, there were large Bosnian flags draped from the wings. We almost felt lost with so much space on the stage and the sea of children sitting tidily below. The roars of laughter echoed in the room as each trick unfolded. What a buzz in the air there was.

We retired to the changing room at the rear to catch our breath and wait for the next show a few hours later.

Meanwhile, from our window above, we looked down upon over 50 soldiers in their military fatigues lining up outside along the edge of the river. They had green berets and white belts and were obviously waiting for the next event happening on the stage that we had performed on. What a contrast it seemed to be having the army there on the same day as us, with them representing the presence of war and us the presence of peace, or so I liked to think. Or were they fighting for peace too? I speculated.

The two hours behind the scenes passed quickly and then it was our turn again on the stage. It made a change having two shows in the same location and so it seemed to take away the apprehension of what to expect, that we normally felt before a show. How wrong could we have been, being lulled into some sense of security. It's all a bit of a blur, but roughly half way into the show we were plunged into pitch darkness as the lights went out. We had no idea what had caused this sudden cut in the electricity. After all, we were in a war-zone and we had taken the lighting for granted up until that point. Anyway, there we were fumbling around in the dark and the children also possibly wondering if this was part of our act. The opportunity to explore onto the stage was beckoning and, before we knew it, there were a few naughty youngsters rustling around in our props bag. We certainly felt very vulnerable in the dark and after a few minutes scrabbling around, Pip and Johnie managed to light the fire-torches to see. We tried to continue with our torches lighting the way but this unexpected situation had thrown us. We finished earlier than expected when we realised that various props were missing. Johnie had lost his precious black spiky wig and some juggling balls; but was particulary disappointed about his wig. I had lost my white pois (balls on strings) in the rumble and somehow a necklace I had been wearing, and had possibly left in the changing room, had also disappeared. It was a NZ greenstone in the shape of a giant circle with a hole in the centre, attached to a string made of leather. It had either been a Christmas present or early birthday gift from my family in NZ and so its significance was more meaningful than its value. With both objects symbolising NZ, I couldn't help but feel very far away from home with a part of my identity 'stolen' by some of the very children we were helping. We pondered over whether the power-cut had been an accident or planned, but this experience had left us somewhat perturbed. I tried to see the silver lining. At least this corner of Bosnia, had a little piece of magical greenstone on its shores. Johnie's wig could be put to use in some other way. I could possibly make some more pois for my magical entrance, although it would be difficult to get them to a performance standard.

The next day we were up early as per usual to get back on the road. Johnie seemed to be whistling happily to himself. He wanted me to check on a few props before leaving, including the velvet magic bag. I did so and found my pois had somehow reappeared in the magic bag. I had been sure I had checked that bag the day before, but there they were, sure as eggs. There seemed to be no logical explanation to this except magic itself. Johnie was equally surprised and swore he had nothing to do with it.

This certainly put me in a good frame of mind as we bounced over the potholes headed for the small villages of Miljkovac and Jablanica, where we were welcomed into the local schools. They were so excited to receive us and had even put up a sign in English saying 'WELCOME TO OUR SCHOOL DEAR GUESTS!' Johnie now wore an orange cap instead of his wonderful wig and the show went on as per usual.

I was relieved that we were travelling in Ragga the Land Rover as the roads were so bad, resembling a dirt track in places. I felt sure our Dodge truck wouldn't have even managed this journey.

Feeling happily relieved to have another two shows under our belt, we were travelling back when, all of a sudden, Ragga came to a stop. Oh no! Not another vehicle. We really didn't want to break down on this remote road as night was falling. A quick check showed that we had run out of fuel. It was empty. This might have been an oversight on our part or maybe we had been robbed of our fuel on the journey, but where would we find petrol in these parts? Luckily for us, the minister accompanying us had just the solution. We waited on the side of the road while he returned to his home on foot, to fetch a jerry-can of petrol. This was like liquid gold in these parts so we were extremely grateful to get out of such a tight situation before night fell. It was wet and cold as well. What a relief to get back to Zenica safely after that. Having broken down on the eve of my birthday in Romania, some two years prior, I was wondering if I was jinxing things at times.

The next day, I was awoken to the sound of Caroline and Johnie giggling at my door before launching into singing Happy Birthday, Simone! Caroline had conjured up a few bars of Cadbury's Milk Chocolate and a couple of squashed packets of Irish Tayto Crisps. Cheese and Onion flavour were my favourite and these little luxuries were most appreciated.

We readied ourselves for another busy day and headed off for Maglaj which was roughly 55 kilometres away. This town was on the River Bosna and as we approached the area we saw a bombed out tank on the side of the road next to an equally damaged shell of a building. It stood there like a monument to the battles this area had seen. The bridge that crossed the river to the town was half destroyed and seemed to collapse into the murky brown waters. Mangled iron rods protruded from the previous structure. On the other side we could see the damaged mosque still standing. There were holes in the main dome roof and a blue tarpaulin covered one of the lower three domes. The top of the traditional pointed tower was no longer there, but the building next to it looked like it had taken the brunt of the hit. On the hill, overlooking the whole area, stood a fortified castle. It was obvious to me that this city had a long history but it was only later that I would find out more. There had been some wooden repairs to the bridge so we managed to cross over and headed to the cinema, which was the cultural centre for the area. It too had suffered, with an enormous gaping hole in the roof open to all weather. This didn't stop anyone from attending, such was the thirst for some sort of normality in a war-zone; not that a visiting international clowning show could be classified as normal. We were greeted by a sparkly-eyed middle-aged man, who was the Cultural Minister of the area and was over the moon to be open again for the children of his town.

Before the war there had been a united blend of the three main ethnic groups with over a third of its married couples being mixed. Then, with the city being under siege by the Bosnian Serbs and the later division between Croats and Muslims, it was literally a 'shell' of what it had been four years earlier.

252

The backdrop of the stage area was decorated with a giant painting of the town's mosque, various Bosnian flags and the dates 15 April 92-96 marking the 4th anniversary of the Bosnian Army as we had seen earlier in the week. The event must have been 'celebrated' throughout Bosnia.

The puppets were the best we had done so far that day.

Johnie was totally in his element on another big stage and he discovered a white chair without a seat on it which became an exciting prop. He sat on it and fell through the gaping hole, but then was unable to get out of the chair. He wandered around on all fours with his bottom protruding through the chair, while Pip and Caroline found volunteers to try and pull him free. It was so simple and yet the comic effect was enormous. For other tricks, Johnie marched up and down the isles looking for eager volunteers to participate in the face-painting or unicycling acts. This type of setting was fantastic, with the children able to sit comfortably and the screams of excitement echoed through the building and up through the gaping hole in the roof.

The Cultural Minister was excited to hear it was my birthday. This called for a celebration and I was invited into his office to share a very stiff drink as he wished me a very happy birthday. He was genuinely appreciative of the two shows and the miniature London bus and various other face-paints, juggling balls and balloons we left him with, but I was equally appreciative of that shared drink.

Once safely back in Zenica, we quietly reflected on the day's events and the various truck drivers from The Serious Road Trip scarcely acknowledged my milestone. I guess most of the new ones didn't know me that well and everyone was exhausted from a hard day's work. There had been no surprise arrival of Yoyo either.

The precious drink shared with the sparkly-eyed man from Maglaj shone out as the highlight of my 30th birthday as well as the happy puppets in love.

We awoke early for the next day's journey to Doboj. This was quite a big deal as we would be crossing a front line to venture into Serb-held territory, so we were all rather nervous. A young British man who worked with refugees in Zenica alongside some German women, had asked if he could accompany us on our trip as he had some photo albums and letters to give to people who were in Doboj. We had agreed and felt this special delivery was important for people with little chance of staying in touch.

Once again we met up with an officer from DanBat outside the IFOR Base but there was a huge commotion within. The man appointed to accompany us that day needed to explain something serious. Normally they had agreed to escort us in one of their own vehicles, however that morning they had lost one Land Rover and two men in a land mine accident. They had been out on patrol as per usual and had possibly lost their way and then tried to do a U-turn, triggering off one of the many lethal mines with fatal consequences. He was understandably shaken over losing two men and the impact this had on their families as well as the remaining men, despite keeping professionally calm under the circumstances. He explained that they were a vehicle down, so that meant no escort. However, he was prepared to accompany us and guide Meni through the mine-fields to get there. He knew there were hundreds of children and adults waiting excitedly at the other end and reassured us that he knew the way, if we were still prepared to travel. We didn't deliberate too long over this as we certainly didn't want to let any children down, or let this tragedy or risky situation stop us.

How odd it looked as the armed uniformed man, wearing his helmet and flak jacket climbed aboard our pink Land Rover and into the navigator's seat, his mine-map fully opened.

Ragga crawled along the muddy road, wondering what lay ahead. The trees were all bare at this time of year and there was a misty greyness that day. We finally reached the river Bosna that we needed to cross. There in front of us was some type of army-bridge, spanning the murky brown water. It was close to the water and looked like a temporary floating bridge. It creaked and groaned as we crossed rather slowly and approached the checkpoint on the other side. We had no trouble getting through and seemed to keep edging towards our goal in any direction but a straight line. Hundreds of mines had been set along this road so Meni followed the instructions, carefully zig-zagging on and off the main road at the right moments. Between the river and the city there seemed to be hundreds of empty houses. None of them had windows and only a few had roofs. We stopped at one point as our guide wanted to point something out. I remember seeing a former football pitch completely encircled in wire with red triangles dangling from it. This wasn't festive bunting at all. The red triangles warned of the mines lying nearby. Still, the mines didn't stop everyone and we spied a man walking towards the river with his fishing rod. I commented on how dangerous that was, but someone else remarked that the war might have taken their lives or freedom away for now, but this person wasn't going to let that stop him from going fishing today. Further along the road, there seemed to be one house that looked inhabited as we noticed a young woman hanging out her washing. Life just needed to go on as normal.

Once we reached Doboj we drove straight to a huge hall where we could hear hundreds of excited children screaming in anticipation. Just as well we hadn't kept them waiting any longer as they sounded almost hysterical; almost like football hooligans. We quickly made our way to the dressing rooms and stage area and it didn't take us long to prepare. The Serb flags adorning the stages clearly told us we were in a different part of Bosnia for now, and yet children were children everywhere we went. This hall was far bigger than any of the previous days' venues and it was jam-packed as well. It seemed as though we might even be closer to a thousand, with people standing in the aisles and at the rear as well. They weren't the only ones there either. There were cameramen from Banja Luka Television. Banja Luka was the second largest city in Bosnia and was a Serb stronghold. Our presence certainly had attracted attention on many levels and it was exciting for us to see television cameras present.

We seemed to float through the show in some magical way, almost spellbound by the sheer numbers and loud responses. What we weren't prepared for was the final response. It really was extraordinary. At the end of the show, when we were taking our final bow, so-to-speak, the children threw roses onto the stage. It was as if we were showered in their love and appreciation through the red roses that were strewn all over the stage. Where had they found these roses? We certainly hadn't noticed them earlier. It was such a unique and beautiful moment within the memories of the tour.

Just before leaving I spoke with a teenage boy aged 17 who spoke good English. He'd been helping translate at that event and I was eager to know what the best part of the show was for him. I was expecting he might speak of some humorous trick performed by Johnie. Of course, he had loved the whole show, but the best bit for him was, 'You performed on the same stage as the Serb Army military rallies, but your message is of LOVE and PEACE, not war!'

Our presence was certainly having a positive impact on the people we encountered and was sending a powerful message. While we may have sensed and hoped for this, it was fantastic to have this clear and verbal confirmation. I am not sure this is the angle the TV took however, although it was good to think that maybe our message and humour had reached an even wider audience.

It was only later that I would learn that Doboj had particular significance during both World Wars and during the Bosnian conflict. During World War I it was the site of the largest Austro-Hungarian concentration camp (Wikipedia). World War II saw Doboj play an important role in the partisan resistance movement until their liberation on April 17, 1945. For all I know, maybe they had been celebrating this 51st anniversary the day before. Sadly, during the Bosnian war, the town had seen ethnic cleansing, with mass executions, homes and mosques destroyed and rape camps set up in a nearby school and in a jam and juice factory. I am glad I didn't know of these horrors whilst there, although I had definitely felt that our visit had had special significance and brought another energy.

We returned satisfied to Zenica to hear that our Dodge truck was finally repaired and ready to go. Maybe things had happened in the right order as Ragga had definitely been the right vehicle for covering the terrain of that week and the Dodge was more suited for the next leg to Sarajevo.

My emotions were all over the place as we headed to the capital city the next day. After all, my fellow drivers and friends had risked their lives continually for over three and half years to provide humanitarian aid and other assistance in this former besieged capital. Such was the importance of this that our initial Road Trip to New Zealand had virtually been transformed into a fully fledged NGO in a war-zone instead.

I wanted to see the city with my own eyes now instead of through news reports, or the 'Miss Sarajevo' documentary made by Bill and Graeme, or the video clips that accompanied some U2 and Passengers songs. Yet I knew it would be different. After all, there was no need for the convoys now and our focus had shifted to other areas of development.

I remember giving some teenagers a ride to Sarajevo and asking some naive question such as did they feel that the war had strengthened their souls? Maybe I was trying to see if something positive had come from their survival. They were quick to reply 'Soul-destroying is more like it!' to which I had nothing more to say. How could I understand what they had been through?

I don't remember any checkpoints as we journeyed to the city and Meni was amazed at how quickly we were there without the usual roadblocks. We were all happy to have our café on wheels back and enjoyed the freedom to make cups of tea and reheat baked beans and other dried or tinned food for easy meals en route. Various puppets dangled from the coat hooks, including the one I had been given in Romania and the blue bunny from America. While they weren't part of the show, it was good to have something to grab and use if children crowded around the truck.

Finally, there it lay beneath us basking in the spring sunshine: Sarajevo in all its glory, free from the limitations and imposed horrors of war that had held it in its grip from April 1992 to December 1995. In fact, the siege had been lifted on 29 February, just weeks before we arrived, but things had moved on in those short months and this didn't feel like the Sarajevo I had experienced second hand or Meni had witnessed. Obviously, with the city no longer under siege and never having physically been there before, it felt odd trying to compare it with the present day. The collapsed Media building and many others served as reminders of what had gone on. We were greeted by the two Simons, who I'd last seen in London and didn't associate with Sarajevo in the least. The Simon who had been in Romania with me was now part of a Circus School Project running workshops for children. The other Simon was busy with his music project. I remember we wandered through the empty corridors of the Kuk club where so many others had shared fond memories during the war, but it was a different time now. It was daytime and this sort of place probably came to life after dark. There were various cartoons decorating the walls and the following words adorned one wall as well: 'Those who do not remember the past are condemned to repeat it.' How true this felt. There was obviously a lot more to it than I was aware of, but it felt as if the lessons we should have learnt from WWII and the persecution of the Jews, had not stopped this war from happening and many others. There seemed to be this underlying tendency to find a scapegoat for problems, rather than acknowledge our own guilt or role that led to a problematic situation. Or were these just excuses given by land-hungry greedy people?

Our itinerary was guided by the various institutes that The Serious Road Trip had helped during the siege and continued to help. One of these was the Cerebral Palsy Institute in Sarajevo. Rather than perform inside we gathered in a central square surrounded by various tower blocks at least 20 stories high. A good crowd gathered there. It was a mix of children of all ages, teenagers and adults. The surrounding backdrop was a very bleak and grey environment which contrasted with our bright truck, multi-coloured costumes and props, and of course the sea of smiling happy children and adults. At last they could move forward in some way from the years of the war, but I guess there was a mix of relief that it was over and uncertainty of what came next, after such devastation and loss on so many levels.

The afternoon show took us into the city right next to the largest Serbian Orthodox church in Sarajevo, known as the Cathedral Church of the Nativity of the Theotokos. It had five domes, with the central dome having a cross on top towering over the other domes and the whole neighbourhood. It was testimony to the blend of cultures present in Sarajevo that the locals had fought so hard to maintain during the war. Many Bosnian Serbs had fought alongside their Muslim brothers against the Serbs that encircled the city, as they fought to maintain their united cultures, rather then being divided up like the rest of Bosnia.

I'm not sure how much publicity this show had been given, but our presence soon attracted a vibrant crowd who were delighted to see what we had on offer. We embarked on all the usual tricks. The sun was still shining on us and the scarves danced in the wind as Johnie juggled with them in slow-motion before getting an eager child, roughly six years of age, to stuff them into the velvet magic bag. There was the usual Abrakadabra chanting followed by Dobrakadabra chants to make the scarves disappear and then reappear, much to the little girl's and audience's fascination.

If only the everyday issues that everyone faced could disappear as simply as that. Or maybe they could if one put one's mind to it; although this was an extreme situation.

While I certainly witnessed the scars of the war, I hadn't personally lived through this war in the way these people had. I had certainly empathised with the people and had been worried for my friends' lives, but I wondered how I would cope had it been my family, home or country devastated by war. The children looked ready to face the daily changes, but the parents carried more heartache. Forgiveness for unspeakable acts could take a long time for some and maybe others saw it as impossible.

Meni found it strange to see Sarajevo in peacetime and functioning as a city. It was a totally different place, but then his friend Samir recognised him in the street and rushed over to greet him. Samir had been in charge of the Bosnian Press on the ground floor of the Unis Towers, which had housed The Serious Road Trip during the war. He was delighted to see Meni again. He also tried to set up a meeting with a musician friend, Don Guido, but it did not work out. Our visits to Sarajevo were fleeting and we had no telephone contact whilst there.

The next day we performed in the Institute for the Disabled in Pasaric and it was reminiscent of the institutes in Romania. Survival during the war had been hard and this was one of the places that The Serious Road trip had helped at this time.

We treasured our rest the following day, which was a Sunday, back in Zenica. I was amazed at how we managed to keep up our two or three shows a day schedule, six days a week. It was especially hard on Johnie's back as he fell over that chair backwards onto hard ground. We tried to minimise the damage by placing a couple of gym mats on the ground behind the chair, but it was still a hard landing each time even if he had done special training for this trick.

The next day was the beginning of three days in the Zenica area, where we performed in kindergartens, schools and refugee centres. The centres may have been our focal point, but in Zeljeca and Stari Vitez, the whole village ended up attending. Such was the power of our show in bringing the communities of all ages together.

Wednesday afternoon saw us heading into Fojnica and you could see that Meni was quite sad. During the early convoys, they had regularly stopped off here en route to Sarajevo. The Serious Road Trip had formed a friendship with a local family who ran a small hotel. Sometimes they would leave the fuel needed for the return journey in their cellar rather than risk having it stolen in Sarajevo, or having to carry it up the many flights of stairs at the Unis Tower. They had been particularly fond of the young teenage son, Ahmet, who soaked up every English word possible and even learnt to drive the Land Rover during their visits. The last visit had been some three years prior on the eve of the escalation of the war between Croats and Bosniaks in that region. The Croatian forces had the upper hand at the time, having taken Kiseljak and a couple of villages on their way to Fojnica. Our crew was being sheltered by a Muslim family and, according to their radio sources, the town was surrounded by the HVO (Croatian Army in Bosnia). This meant they were caught in the wrong place at the wrong time. The father had asked our team if they were prepared to take up arms against their 'enemy' if necessary that night, but this was the last thing they wanted to do. I know the team had feared for their lives and lived as though these might be their last moments. They had been offered machine-guns, shotguns and grenades as they lay in wait for the 'ethnic cleansing' that night, but somehow it was not their time and the next day they were able to find a way out of the town on a mountain back-road covered in snow. Amazingly they got through the Croat checkpoint before the impending battle and made their way back to Podstrana on the coast safe and sound.

The information that had reached them later said that Ahmed and family had sadly perished. It was even in the credits of our CD booklet 'Ahmed and family RIP' and I had wondered about the significance of this. After that time, Meni informed me that The Serious Road Trip did not go through Fojnica to get to Sarajevo as it was no longer the safe road into the capital. Instead, after the Croats and Muslims turned on each other, The Serious Road Trip and other organisations had to go through mountain roads which were maintained by the UN. These were called Diamond and Pacman, but they were unpaved roads and could only be tackled with 4 x 4 vehicles such as our Bedford trucks.

Thus, this was the first SRT visit to Fojnica since that harrowing moment and brought back all the memories of that past friendship for Meni.

We were heading to the kindergarten along the main street of town. I was up front with Meni and I noticed he looked very perturbed by something. He was looking in his wing mirror and exclaimed 'I think I've just seen a ghost.' He slowed down to double-check, and running after us was Ahmed, alive and kicking. What a blast! We stopped on the side of the road, Meni got out and the two gave each other a huge hug. They were both completely blown away by the meeting, but especially Meni who was speechless.

'I've been looking for the yellow trucks for years, hoping to see you guys again passing through. Where have you been?' Meni could barely get the words out, he was genuinely moved.

'We thought you were dead... how is your father?' as Meni thought maybe it was his father that had died.

'He's fine too,' confirmed Ahmed.

All of a sudden we realised how communication, at the best of times, let alone a war-zone, can be like a game of Chinese whispers with people getting the wrong end of the stick. No wonder wars start! To think someone had truly got this drastically wrong. There were lots to catch up on but we had a show to get to, so Ahmed climbed into the truck to give us directions to the kindergarten and reconnect with his old buddy Meni, as we drove through the bustling town.

The show was just as good as ever and was over before we knew it. I think we were all particularly taken by this fantastic coincidence of bumping into Ahmed and were keen to talk more. He came back with us to Zenica where we partied into the night and caught up on his news.

While I had heard that Ahmed was just a youngster when they last met, he now seemed to be an 18-year-old going on 28-year-old after all the war had thrown at him. Some three years earlier, the entire fate of the town was hanging in the balance. The United Nations Commander in Bosnia, Gen. Philippe Morillon of France, had even given a farewell speech in Fojnica just a few days prior, calling it 'a model of hope for this land' but that was about to change almost overnight. The town was encircled by Croatian forces and it hadn't looked good for the Muslims. Open warfare began days later, resulting in excess of 70 deaths on their side alone, but within two weeks the Bosnian Army forces had managed to send the Croatian forces retreating and much of their local Croatian population with them. Ahmed explained that with the English language and driving skills he had learnt through The Serious Road Trip visits, he had managed to get himself a job with the UN's Canadian Battalion stationed there. This enabled him to support at least 20 people through that harsh time of war and now he was just extremely happy to be back in touch with us. He had been forced to grow up extremely quickly, like many of the children of this war. His family's survival seemed to depend on it.

Ahmed was pleased with the renewed contact with our group and you could see he was bursting to get away from Fojnica. He would remain in touch with the guys in Zenica as best he could, now he knew where they were, although many of the familiar faces had moved on by now. There were only so many months or years of operating in a war-zone that people could handle. In other organisations, people were restricted to three or six month assignments at times and for good reasons. Some of our drivers had already endured a good two or three years, which was well over the 'normal' limit, so it was only understandable that many had gone on to try and regain some semblance of normality after these experiences, or at least to try and earn some money elsewhere. Mind you, could life go back to 'normal' after working in a war-zone? I had been warned by a colleague in Luxembourg that life was never the same after witnessing the Romanian orphanages, and he was right. It was not easy slotting back into life as it had been and there was a part of us that wouldn't want to either. I was aware that my time to face this next stage was fast approaching with just a couple more weeks in our tour to go, but we were still very much engaged in every moment that had us almost spellbound.

The next morning we were due for a show at the military amputee hospital back in Fojnica, accompanied by Ahmet. This seemed to be apt as in my world it was April 25 and that was ANZAC Day Down Under, when we remembered the soldiers that had fought for our country. A few haggard men on crutches wandered in through the main lobby but it became quickly apparent that no one seemed to know we were coming. Of course, that had never stopped us in the past and we set up in the street outside, attracting almost the whole town in the process. We were just lucky that we could adapt to virtually any situation.

That night we were invited back to Ahmed's family hotel dining on trout for dinner and enjoying a comfortable bed. What amazing hospitality.

The next couple of days were spent back in Sarajevo and

performing in or outside various centres that had benefited from our convoy aid, such as the Deaf and Dumb School, Kosovo Hospital and an orphanage on the hill.

With this under our belt, we were eager to return to Fojnica and enjoy the warm Bosnian hospitality once again. I enjoyed chatting with Ahmed that night.

We connected and both seemed to share the same spark for life. It was flattering to have the attentions of someone much younger and Ahmed gave me a few badges from the Bosnian Army as a token of his thanks to The Serious Road Trip, and a souvenir of the war. I still have these today and they truly evoke memories of that time, when we seemed to celebrate every moment as though you didn't know if there would be a tomorrow.

That Sunday, the family fired up the spit to roast a lamb for us. After a wonderful feast we farewelled everyone and hit the road. It was a long road to the next point on our itinerary, Tuzla, to the NE of Sarajevo.

We seemed to travel through mountain roads to get there, at one point overtaking a whole herd of sheep. Further down the road we crossed paths with Premiere Urgence trucks returning from a convoy. We stopped to say a quick hello and fool around for a few moments, but it was just a brief interlude before heading off to our various commitments.

In Tuzla we were greeted by the amazing, friendly and dynamic, Dada Hazdic, who welcomed us into her apartment she shared with partner, Pero. It was rather small with an extra five people, but extremely huge compared to our small truck. Before the war Dada had been a business woman running a factory, but now she was working for the International Committee of the Red Cross and was in touch with many refugee centres in the area.

It was pizza for dinner and Caroline and I even had a bed for the night.

We had thought that War Child was organising the shows the next day but they were nowhere to be seen. We managed to sort out one in an orphanage for children who had lost their parents during the war. They were pretty wild and out of control. Johnie, Caroline, Meni and myself had so many experiences of orphans in Romania and Russia and I wondered which was worse. The children before us had known a family life with parents and homes and then lost that and much more, as well as experiencing the horrors and threats in a war. By contrast, many of the Romanian orphans had been abandoned as babies by parents who couldn't support them. They had mostly been starved of love, stimulation and food for different reasons and many couldn't remember life before the orphanage. Many hadn't even learnt to speak, let alone learn vital social skills. It was hard to know which was worse and neither was desirable for any child. To know love then lose it, or not know it at all. I wasn't able to dwell too much on this as these types of thoughts could easily overwhelm me and prevent me from functioning. I needed to shut down or push away my emotions as part of my own self-preservation. I too, was becoming numb to the numerous tragic situations I had experienced and this realisation signalled my need for the approaching break after the tour.

As we visited the city we came across the graves of 72 young teenagers, killed by a shelling outside a café, almost one year earlier on the 25 May 1995.

But that wasn't the only tragic news we heard about that day. Dada was working with the refugees in the area. Some 40,000 refugees had fled there from the city of Srebrenica, when it had been overrun by Serb soldiers some nine months beforehand. They were women and children who had been separated from their fathers, husbands and sons.

Dada waved the pages of a neatly typed list with names and dates of birth marked upon it. She explained that she was meant to compile a list of missing persons. Many hoped against the odds, that their separation was only temporary and that, through the International Committee of the Red Cross, they might find news of their men's whereabouts. With an enormous heavy heart she explained that already some mass graves had been uncovered and it did not look good for the fate of some 8,000 missing men. Many had been systematically executed. She pointed at some names on the paper: 'Look, here there are listed twin boys who share the same birthday as my son. It's not just men, there are boys missing too.' You could see that she was choked up with this enormous responsibility and news, although nothing was absolutely clear for now, except that there would be few happy reunions.

Just the mention of mass graves and I had images from the Holocaust spinning in my mind. Hadn't we all learned from that horror? This Srebrenica massacre later became known as the worst genocide on European soil since WWII, but at this time I was getting the first glimpse of what had actually happened there. The media had been so focused on the plight of the besieged Sarajevo, that it was no surprise that these other areas were almost overlooked. But these other areas were also encircled, starving and suffering from a lack of medical supplies, not to mention the shelling, shooting and other methods of killing.

We were due to visit the refugee centres where some of the Srebrenica women and children were two days later, but we noticed that the next day there seemed to be a day off in the middle of the week. Since the airing of the TVNZ documentary which showed our trucks delivering aid to Celic, I had almost expected that our itinerary would include a visit there and yet it didn't. It was just over an hour's drive away and this was our only chance to get there. The others agreed, even if our bodies cried out for a rest day.

Meni was familiar with some of the area and experienced enough with driving in Bosnia to try and find it although he had not been on that particular convoy. We had no point of contact at the other end, but off we set with a map in hand determined to reach the front line town of Celic. Maybe someone would remember the trucks from before, although that was some 18 months earlier.

The roads were muddy and not well signposted. At some point Meni got anxious and stopped quickly. He didn't have a good feeling about the road we were on. His intuition kicked in and we turned around to try and find another way forward. He was worried about land mines and I did start to wonder if this extra detour had been wise. Nevertheless, we followed our noses and eventually found ourselves in Celic. It didn't look anything like the footage we had seen on TV, but that convoy had been during summer and maybe to a different part of the town. He was right, there was an eerie feeling and there were helicopters hovering closely overhead.

Without a definite venue to perform in we decided to set up on the main road as this always attracted attention, but not before driving the length of town announcing our arrival. Somewhere along the line we were told that many of the town had headed over the front line to visit the graves of their dead, but they were due back shortly. It was the 30th April and it had been agreed that there would be a cease-fire to enable the grieving family members to do this. The helicopters were from IFOR and hovered above to protect the civilians as they made their way back from the Serb-held territory, where many had once lived. How odd that we were there on that day of all days. As the long queue of mourners made their way back to town, some of them stopped by our truck to see what was going on. Others continued on past us, understandably lost in their grief. Before long a large enough crowd had formed and there was no stopping us despite the heaviness and poignancy of that day. All things considered, we had come a long way and we would not be able to come back another time.

We positioned the truck on the road with the backdrops in front of the main rear door. Johnie's chair was placed in front of this with enough space for him to fly backwards onto the ground once his large balloon exploded. I captured the moment on camera as he hit the ground after a loud bang of the balloon. It certainly was a 'bang on the front line' in many meanings of the word. There was no doubt that we did help lift the mood of the day for those that were able to stop. The one who we remembered the most was a tall and lanky young man, who looked like the local fool with a permanent grin on his face, smeared with face-paint. He was so happy to see us clowning around and completely understood what we were all about. After the show he and Johnie hugged each other as though they had met their mirror-images. In any case, it was heart-warming to see this shared humanity and genuine love and warmth of one 'clown' for another. In the midst of this madness of war, maybe they were the only sane people able to share love and laughter in such an infectious way and show everyone a way forward.

I had to remind myself of this as we ventured around the various refugee centres or settlements in Mihatovici, Visca and Jezevac the following days as some of the women and children of Srebrenica were coming to terms with the fact that their men and boys had not escaped. In our journey we noticed just one solitary man who had somehow escaped this horror. He looked about our age and I wondered if he had somehow been in a different place, or had he survived this horror, becoming a witness to what had happened? I couldn't ask such questions with so little time, and besides, it wasn't our role. His survival was indeed incredible. Many years later I would see his face on the BBC as he described how he had escaped almost certain death and had miraculously crawled from beneath bodies, escaping into the woods. He would be a key witness in the Hague trials to sentence Mladic, the Bosnian Serb commander, for life imprisonment.

We were helped by the Norwegian People's Aid organisation as we travelled around. Some people were housed in what looked like barracks and others looked like new houses neatly arranged in lines. In any case, they looked isolated from the normal hustle and bustle of nearby Tuzla with little to take their minds off their plight. They were keen to see all the commotion created by our visit, especially the young children, and we gave it our best, despite our aching muscles. The puppets seemed to get heavier by the day but there was no magical replacement for the heavy crumpled up newspaper or rag stuffing at this stage. At least there was nothing like excited children to get the adrenalin pumping, which we certainly needed to push our physical limits. The juggling balls, face-paints and balloons we left behind would hopefully be put to good use. We also liked to think that the

m

magic of our show, and the laughter, could wipe away some of the misery; but the reality was that this would be a long process for most, especially for those old enough to understand. I tried to imagine how I would feel if I had lost members of my family, friends and homes through such tragic war events, but it is hard to really know unless you have experienced such loss. I didn't want to imagine such a harrowing thought, it was too painful seeing the living proof before our eyes.

On our final night in Tuzla, Dada and Pero invited us to a local restaurant. Theirs was a story where the war had brought them together if I remember correctly. They may have known each other when much younger, but only found each other again during this life-changing period. We celebrated love and life, drinking local wine and beer as if there was no tomorrow and we had to live for each day. Johnie was in his element spinning the empty bottles like they were a gun in a Western movie and had us all in raptures. We needed the light relief after a day like that.

They had ordered a local delicacy as a special treat, and a tomato and cheese pizza for Meni, since he was vegetarian.

To our horror, a roasted calf's head was plonked on our table upon a stainless steel platter.

All of a sudden Pip and Caroline also announced that they were vegetarians after all, leaving Johnie and myself to be the reluctant but brave meat-eaters. Well, we couldn't risk offending our generous hosts by rejecting their kindness, and maybe a little part of us was intrigued to see what it tasted like.

Dada and Pero kindly carved and broke it up, placing a piece of the jaw-bone with teeth onto my empty plate. I politely picked this up and nibbled at the roasted gums. Johnie seemed to be excited by the tongue, although it might have been part of an act; he was so believable, and a sliver was also placed on my plate. Tongue had never been a favourite, probably due to the texture, but I found a way to disguise it with slices of gherkins and beetroot pickles. I could see Caroline grinning away as if she was loving the whole thing. Maybe she was, as she had somehow escaped this feast and was smugly chewing on a small tomato and cheese pizza. 'What a shame I'm a vegetarian! Those eyes look so tasty!' she joked.

I hoped that Dada and Pero hadn't picked up on our difficulty eating it as we didn't want to appear ungrateful, especially as all around us were people that may have been envious of such a delicacy.

The next day we left Tuzla after giant hugs and kisses with Dada. She had appreciated our humour and energy enormously and wished us well for the next leg of our tour. She hoped to see us in London one day.

266

We needed to get back to Sarajevo as we were due to travel to the Gorazde area bright and early with the help of Vince. Vince had joined TSRT after reading about us in the free '*NZ News*' paper in London. He'd then moved on to employment with Premiere Urgence in Mostar and then later, to the International Rescue Commission (IRC), who were seeking drivers for convoys to Gorazde. Being a mechanic, he'd helped out with the SRT's Bedford trucks and especially in preparing the trucks for the Olovo School Meals project when possible. Once a Road Tripper, always a Road Tripper. Although we used to put it in another way. 'Once a skidder, always a skidder!' There seemed to be some connection between 'skidders' that didn't stop, even if working or living somewhere else. I was fond of Vince who had helped repair the bus when Banana Split II had toured. Being one of Yoyo's friends, we shared that link as well. It felt reassuring to have him as our guide for the next few days. I sensed there was some pain in his past that he didn't want to talk about. Mind you, we were all experiencing emotional pain working in a war-zone, whether we chose to acknowledge, ignore or numb it. Maybe that is what led some of us there? It's just that whatever we were experiencing seemed to pale in comparison with those that had lost their loved ones, homes and future to war. We were there by choice though, and had the freedom to leave.

Another situation had arisen: Pip was coming down with something. I wouldn't have been surprised if it was connected to all the fire-breathing he did. I was worried he had inhaled some of the paraffin. His teeth certainly looked worse for wear and with a few rotten stubs on display he almost fitted in with the locals, many of whom had rotting teeth too, or teeth missing. I guess the locals' dental hygiene was due to a lack of toothbrushes and poor diet. No doubt regular teeth-brushing and visits to the dentist were hardly a priority or even possible under the circumstances. Whatever the cause in Pip's case, life on tour in a war-zone was far from restful and he was in need of a break. The two Simons were able to offer him an alternative for the following days and we would manage without him. I took advantage of the access to a computer to send a farewell e-mail to London. It was probably no surprise, but it just needed to say that I really was leaving soon. In fact, I debated whether I could handle it till the end.

With Vince leading us in a white Land Rover, we set off towards Gorazde along what was known as the Blue Road, which only aid workers, peacekeepers and journalists could pass through. It was the link between the besieged Gorazde and the rest of Bosnia and had only been set up some eight to nine months prior to this.

Our first stop was the IFOR base with Portuguese soldiers in Rogatica. Unfortunately we needed to postpone the show due to lack of organisation. We improvised with a small walkabout and a few tricks in the street, but decided to reschedule the show for when we would pass back through three days later. We were thankful for Vince leading us through these unknown areas and his link to his colleagues from IRC through the walkie-talkie. This was the sort of equipment that our group had had to manage without.

After some hours we finally arrived in the isolated enclave of Gorazde, crossing the Drina river to get to the main city. The city was on strategic crossroads, linking the Serbian capital Belgrade to Dubrovnik and the Croatian coast and was surrounded by mountains. This idyllic setting initially masked the horrors that this area had endured. Similar to Srebrenica, this area too had been designated a 'Safe Zone' but far from being safe areas, these zones failed to protect the town's residents from constant attack by Bosnian Serb forces, who encircled the areas and attempted to starve the population as well.

At the time I was unaware, that just under one year earlier, the actions of 300 Royal Welch Fusiliers, who had been sent to Gorazde as UN Peacekeepers, had defended a strategic point overlooking the town long enough to stop it from falling into the hands of the ethnic-cleansing brigade and a certain massacre. The Bosnian Army and residents then managed to keep hold of the town during a bloody battle that followed for another few weeks, before the Bosnian Serb soldiers moved on to achieve their gruesome goals in Srebrenica, as we had just been made aware of days before, whilst in Tuzla.

We were quickly introduced to a young and vibrant woman with short, dark hair who would help as our translator for this leg. She spoke about the terrible times they had endured. They had been under attack for years and starving. She spoke about the night treks some of the besieged population had to make to fetch food and other supplies, in which she had taken part. A large group of 200 or so would walk in silence, single-file through the mountains and forests in Serb-held territory to reach Grebak. There they bought essential flour, oil, coffee, salt, sugar, cans and other supplies such as batteries or tobacco on the black market. They would take anything up to 10 hours or more through the cold, mountainous, snowy terrain with a hungry stomach on their way there and would return the following night with a heavy load. She'd managed 20 kilos but others carried far more. They would be in fear of being caught at any moment or of somehow losing the group or just not managing to make it and freezing to death. I tried to imagine carrying the equivalent of 40 half-kilo blocks of butter under

268

such conditions. I just don't know how I would have kept my nerves and stamina through such life-threatening situations, but it was a matter of survival. She looked younger than myself and Caroline. After a year, that life-line no longer existed and Gorazde was completely cut off. There were very few convoys of aid making it through and the people relied on airdrops of aid but no one could be sure where these would land. Another horror of the war mentioned were the hundreds of bodies floating in the river, of people massacred in places such as Visegrad, where women and children, as well as men, had been 'ethnically cleansed'. The Gorazde enclave had so many people arriving from nearby villages in the Drina valley that had been 'conquered' and there were few places to house them, with constant shelling destroying houses and buildings. Far from being bitter or down about these experiences, she was smiling to see us arrive and grateful to be able to share these experiences with the outside world. She radiated a certain happiness that those gruelling times were behind them. I reflected on her situation and could see how having English as a second language had at least opened certain doors for her and vital work as a translator. She looked forward to resuming her studies, which had been cut short by the war. She could finally get on with living her life.

The weekend was jammed full of shows in the Gorazde area as we were making the most of Vince's weekend time to accompany us. We covered places such as a school in Ilovaca, a stadium type venue in Vitkovici, a school in Bare and a village show in Bogucici. In one place the local teacher told us how they had built a stage especially for us so that everyone could see the show. He didn't want any of the few hundred children missing out or being crushed in the attempt to see us, as we were considered very important visitors who had managed to reach them from the outside world. It was very touching to be so appreciated with this extra effort they had made. As we traversed across the beautiful mountains to get to the various venues, I just remember the vast green spaces with breathtaking views. How lucky were we to have vehicles and the Dayton Peace Agreement behind us.

In the evenings we were camped out in premises set aside for Vince and the Premiere Urgence convoy team who were always our faithful fans and supporters. Of course, we provided much needed relief from the work in a war-zone and we sang along to a guitar and drank the nights away with our French friends. Everyone needed to let their hair down and Johnie was always full of tricks in any situation. He was also a great cook in the kitchen with Caroline's help, which everyone appreciated. We laughed about our practical joke played on Premiere

Urgence recruits some three years before, where Johnie had posed as some war-crazed soldier demanding everyone's passports. We laughed about the time they themselves had fooled their own new recruits into believing they had to sleep in cardboard bedrooms within a depot and that they were known on the ground as the very gay and friendly, 'Pede' Urgence. The drivers were some of the ones we had seen on our arrival in Split and I remember Kiki trying to persuade us all that we needed to go to Africa next, as that was where his heart was. It just seemed to be a whole world away from here and quite beyond the realm of possibility.

The following morning we were up bright and early for a new day of action, some of us feeling the effects of the night before.

We were to perform in an outdoor sports stadium in Gorazde, which meant hundreds could gather on the tiered steps and still see what was happening on the cemented sports-ground. Here we seemed to have such a huge space to play within, compared to other more confined settings. It was here that Caroline's Tweety Bird act really came into its own. She danced off around the sports-ground in her giant yellow costume, weaving in circles with a huge string of children following her in a line as they grabbed onto the child in front. It was a new version of the Pied Piper and was extremely pleasing to watch the giggling children trying to keep up.

On our way out of Gorazde we drove through the town where we saw IFOR tanks patrolling through the streets. We could still see the sandbags protecting certain walls and other walls pocked with mortar and bullet holes.

Vince needed to stop at the UNHCR office on the edge of the river and we were introduced to a red-haired Irish chap, Eddie, running the place, and a female doctor, who had been there for two or so years during the siege. We were still in make-up and costume from that morning's show and they were genuinely heartened to meet fellow Irish countrymen, Johnie and Caroline. We had photographs taken in front of the sandbagged offices and the river Drina and chatted for a few moments. In the water below we could see some odd paddle-boat-looking contraptions and wondered what they were. It seems they had been used to generate some electricity during the war. Necessity is the master of invention indeed.

However, there was little time to linger, as we needed to get to Rogatica for the rescheduled show at a local school. This was in Serb-held territory, that we needed to pass through on our way back to Sarajevo. Vince would not be able to accompany us all the way back though after the show, as nightfall was approaching and he needed to

270

get back to Gorazde before dark, along with our lovely translator. There was just an hour's drive through no-man's-land and we should be fine if we got going promptly. After a few photos with the Portuguese soldiers and a rushed farewell, we hit the road still in costume, as we didn't really want to find out what might happen in no-man's-land after dark. There were no other vehicles around to follow either.

We sped off with Meni and Johnie in the front cab listening to some loud music and Caroline and myself chatting away in the back. We were genuinely relieved with how everything had gone and were now very aware that we were entering the last stage of our tour. We must have been on the road for 30 minutes or so when Caroline and I noticed what looked like a policeman on the side of the road waving a large Stop sign. He looked out of place and Meni carried on obliviously. However, Caroline and I could see that he looked rather agitated. We tried to get Meni's attention, but no amount of banging on the windows could be heard, especially with the music cranked up. Meanwhile, this chap jumped into his police car and sped after us with his siren going, even pursuing us through a tunnel and eventually overtaking us. Then he blocked the road with his car.

Finally we came to a sudden halt. The man waved a gun at us, motioning for us to get out. My heart was pounding furiously. He was extremely angry that we had not stopped.

He pointed the gun at us and requested our passports. We fumbled around and gathered the passports up. Reluctantly we handed them over, although this put us in a very vulnerable situation, potentially finding ourselves in a war-zone without identification.

Meni tried to explain that he thought he had motioned us onwards rather than motioning us to stop.

In the spur of the moment, I somehow seemed to naturally put my foot forward to try and explain who we were in the limited Serbo-Croat that I had. We had been far too dependent on translators this tour, but at least I felt confident with a few important words. I'm sure our costumes helped convey what we were all about as well. I mean, there I was with a gold-painted face with a star on one cheek, a moon on the other and the sun on my chin. I mentioned 'Predstava za djeco' (show for children) pointing at our smudged face-painted faces and outfits. I think he said something about entertaining Muslim children, but I was quick to say that we had just been in Rogatica and had recently performed in Doboj. Hadn't he seen us on the Serbian, Banja Luka television? After all we were quite famous, or at least that is what I wanted him to believe and I wanted him to know that children of Serb

271

regions had also seen us. Next I was asking if he needed any balloons, or face-paints... or were a few packs of Marlboro cigarettes more interesting?

Johnie must have muttered a few Blah, blah blahs or some other clowning talk and we could see the harshness on the man's face warming, and he even managed a smile. He realised that we were just a bunch of clowns, quite literally. After offloading a few gifts, which he was genuinely pleased with, we were soon back on the road with our passports safely back in our possession and an exciting tale to tell. It felt like a close shave, to say the least, and we had all left satisfied.

As we rolled towards Sarajevo we could see the cemetery on the outskirts of the city where there seemed to be hundreds and thousands of graves. It was a harsh reminder of those that had not been so lucky. Night was falling and we were relieved to be leaving no-man's-land and heading into the relative safety of the familiar territory of the city itself.

With less than a week to go I was nearing the time when I would hopefully be able to see Yoyo again, although there were no definite plans and there were no telephones to ring with either. It was also the final days of working with The Serious Road Trip and five years' commitment to our cause. That was probably the bigger deal, although I didn't want to think about that too much whilst still on the road.

On our return to Zenica we heard news of Franck Lefebvre, travelling with a Canal+ film crew from France and wanting to hook up with and film the Dobrakadabra clowns in action. Wow, this was big news and good publicity for us. They wanted to film us whilst in the Olovo region as this was where the school meals project was being implemented by our drivers in the yellow Bedford trucks. With Christophe and Yoyo no longer working in Bosnia, Franck was the new 'frog' on the scene, although we had known him for some time now as he had joined our ranks the year before, from Premiere Urgence. Amongst other things he had good contacts with many NGOs and had done an amazing job of managing to actually get this film crew out to Bosnia to cover our story, backed up by Christopher in the London office. There was also some other news. Yoyo had already gone to Paris and would see us all in London. Something didn't feel right, or was I just reading into it all? That night I tossed and turned wondering what to do next?

We would now be heading to another front line area of Olovo (50km north-east of Sarajevo) where our trucks and drivers had been delivering fresh food for soup kitchens operating in 14 schools in the area for the last six months. These provided 2700 school children with a vital daily nutritious meal. This was now in phase II of the project and local staff were being trained and prepared for continuing the project in subsequent years. It had started off with the approaching winter the previous year and had encouraged children to return to their lessons. Many of them had to make long and sometimes dangerous journeys, from outlying rural areas, in the cold winter to get to school in a local village. The region was known for its pine forests and had clear swift rivers running through the mountain gorges. The main danger now was, of course, the numerous mines that had been cruelly planted everywhere. Despite this, the teachers, children and parents were genuinely thrilled that the children could now at least go to school, as there was much to catch up on with their education put on hold the last few years.

The team wanted to head off early to collect a refreshed Pip from Sarajevo en route for Olovo, but I wanted to write a fax to London before leaving.

Ahmet and Belma of PU would make sure the fax was sent and then transport me in Ragga in time for the show in Olovo. It was a hot and dusty day and I just remember clouds of dust as we raced against the clock and hurtled along the road to get there. I even had to drive Ragga back that evening and found it quite a challenge trying to get used to doubling the clutch.

Over the next few days we would visit schools in the outlying regions such as Cunista, Milankovici, Solun, Careva Ciprija and Kladanj. Everywhere there was a warm welcome and delighted children and teachers. It was very clear that the kids loved SRT here and everywhere! The shows also attracted many parents and other local villagers. In the schools we could see various posters outlining the dangers of the mines to the children and how they shouldn't touch them. But that was not the only danger. Driving along the various ravines to get to these villagers, Scottish Dave pointed out where he had had a close shave recently. His Bedford truck had skidded off the narrow and windy road and had landed in the cold and fast-flowing river of the ravine, many metres below. That he wasn't injured in the fall was a miracle. Not only that, he had managed to climb onto the cab of the truck to escape the icy waters and was just lucky that some local folk were coming along the road and saw what had happened. They ran for a rope, which they threw down to him to pull him up and rescue him. It was the talk of the area. He explained how the locals described what had happened. 'The Serious Road Trip looks after the children and God looks after The Serious Road Trip.' Hearing this story I could well believe it on this and many other occasions.

We were even amazed to see the wreck, which the locally based US IFOR soldiers had managed to winch up from the river. The cab was brutally crushed with the impact and goodness knows what else, although it was surprisingly in one piece and now parked or abandoned, outside their base known as the Lion's Den. We were introduced to the American commander who was keen to meet and assist us in any way possible. He explained that he was part American Indian, although I forget which tribe, but he was keen to point out how brave we all were. We left our Dodge truck with the other yellow truck outside the base and were invited, costumes and all, into the camp surrounded by large barbed-wire fences and little red triangle signs marked 'MINES', which I thought was ironic as my surname was Mines.

Once on base we were invited to provide a little light relief in the bar area of the base. Johnie was equipped for all occasions and was thankful to be able to speak more than normal as everyone was English-speaking, although some may have struggled with his Irish accent. I know I had the velvet magic bag and Caroline her bubbles to blow. The only thing I could liken it to was being part of the 'Good Morning Vietnam' film-set except this was the real thing in Bosnia.

The commander and some soldiers had been organising for us to do one last show the next day in a nearby sports ground in Olovo as a finale. They had helped set up a wooden stage there to give us elevation and, of course, we gave it everything we had with a good couple of hundred children attending. The sun was shining and it was hard to believe that this was the very last show, and the long trek home awaited us. We had done a total of 73 performances in six and half weeks, which was quite a task in itself without considering the totally unusual circumstances.

Our American commander friend wanted us to call by the base one last time as he had something to give to us.

He presented us each with a Lion's Den medal of bravery for our courage. It was like a large round golden coin with a Lion's face on it. He said they were not handed out lightly and that each one of us had shown immense courage. Mind you, I couldn't help but think of the many locals we had met during this tour and others, including our own drivers, who could have done with their own medal for the bravery they had to face on a daily basis, just to survive or to try and keep their families and others fed and safe. But there was no denying that we too had been courageous. We had chosen to come to this war-torn country, when we could have turned a blind eye. I, for one, had been petrified at the thought of going into a war-zone when it was first mentioned some four years earlier for the Peace Convoy into Sarajevo. But slowly and surely I had built up to this final tour and had completed it with help from many people.

There wasn't much time to linger on this achievement, as we needed to head back to Sarajevo, accompanied by the Canal+ crew. They had been filming our last couple of shows and had also been interviewing us. All I remember saying, is that we needed more peace and love in the world! There was footage of Johnie carrying boxes of food supplies off the truck for the school meals. Meanwhile Franck explained that The Serious Road Trip had given back the dreams to the children of Bosnia. The TV crew was keen to get the footage back to France as soon as possible and I was aware that our team would now make the lengthy journey back to London. The thought of returning there in a long drawn-out fashion filled me with dread. It was always such an anti-climax going back to the everyday life of London when the team disbanded. It was a world where everything just carried on as normal around us, as though Bosnia didn't really exist for most people. As I had been planning to leave London as soon as possible, before this tour had enticed me elsewhere, I started to wonder why I would return there now. I was tired of trying to second guess or change my plans for men and made a conscious decision to go where I had intended.

Paris had been on my mind and in my heart and I seized the opportunity staring me in the face. Would the Canal+ journalists help me get there? They were up for taking me to Split the following day from Sarajevo. We made the rendezvous at the infamous Sniper Alley part of the city later that evening. It was not the first time I had decided to break with the group, but again, it definitely felt like the right thing for me. I had a new destination and was on a mission. I had to leave some of my luggage on the Dodge to be collected from London at a later date, so I was now down to travelling with my purple Macpack and sleeping bag. There were long and serious embraces with Caroline, Johnie, Meni and Pip. Ironically it was near the spot where it said 'Welcome to Sarajevo' in graffiti, that I actually said goodbye.

I had a fancy meal with the journalists that evening and slept on some cushions on the floor. I don't think I had a wink of sleep that night as I lay awake thinking that I had just gone and done it. I had actually left TSRT!

They needed to leave bright and early to catch a flight from Split. Leaning against my well-loved sleeping bag for comfort, the next few hours were spent silently dozing in the back of the car while the journalists chatted amongst themselves. I had no energy for communicating and couldn't handle any small talk as I dealt with such a huge wrench. They managed to drop me off in Split at the Premiere Urgence base with no big fuss. While in familiar territory I could at least rely on some of our contacts. I needed to find a way to Paris and was on a mission to get there.

I heard Roger was back in town! I got hold of him. He now worked for Médecines Sans Frontières. We had farewelled him in London thinking he was off to Vietnam or Cambodia. However, his Bosnian experience was so valued they had sent him here to be a convoy leader and logistician. He was fondly known to us as 'Cockney Wanker' or 'Tits and Trucks' and it was a relief to hear him at the end of the phone and then see his beaming face. He was one of the first convoy drivers so it was only fitting that he was there. I asked how it was working for one of the big organisations? He explained that he had a small allowance of £100 a month, which didn't sound much, but that they had really good food and living conditions compared to TSRT. We had a little laugh about that, as we really had been operating on a shoestring for all those years.

Premiere Urgence had said I was welcome to stay for a few days, which was a relief too. There were a few surprised faces to see I had left the Road Trip. Did I want a job with them, they asked? They needed someone in Split. Of course, I would have to go through the head office in Paris, so there was even more reason to head there.

Roger informed me about a ferry from Split to Ancona (Italy), so maybe I could get that and then catch a train to Paris. After a little investigation it seemed there was one that evening or one in a couple of days. Which did I want?

I felt like I was on a mission to get to Paris and there was no time like the present. After dropping my luggage just hours before, I was soon collecting it up again to rush down to the ferry.

Chapter 21

On My Way to Paris

It was early evening as I boarded the ferry and waved goodbye to Roger. So that was it!

I made my way to the cabin I had booked and climbed into my sleeping bag. I needed to rest. I had been with everyone in Sarajevo just 24 hours earlier and now here I was bound for Italy and en route for Paris. Fortunately there was no one else in the cabin and I fell into a deep, deep sleep that warded off any sea-sickness and put my brain to rest. I was alone as I headed into a new life away from The Serious Road Trip. It felt hugely liberating. We might not have made it to New Zealand by bus, but we had achieved many of the other goals and more than I had ever dreamed possible.

Who would have thought that what was supposed to be a one year adventure travelling in a red double-decker bus, working with underprivileged children en route for NZ, would turn into an NGO with a fleet of trucks and hundreds of volunteers, including a troupe of clowns, making their mark upon the hundreds and thousands we had come across. One year had turned into five years.

I emerged from the cocoon of my sleeping bag, like some butterfly starting to stretch its wings, as we docked in Ancona the following morning.

I soon found out that there was a train that would take me to Bologna and from there I could travel overnight to Paris.

Wandering through the unfamiliar streets of Bologna, I soaked up the different language, culture and sights, resting in various cafés. What a contrast to where I had just been. From there I could watch

277

people passing by and travel in my thoughts as I waited for the train.

It was unclear where I would head to once I arrived in Paris. Maybe I should let someone know, but I had inconveniently lost my address book or left it on the Dodge. Fortunately I found the number of Zoe, Yoyo's 'spiritual' mother, as he described her, and moments before boarding the evening train I called her. She was older than me and was a writer and would be someone who understood the situation. The phone rang three times and to my surprise a male voice picked up. 'Allo!' I quickly responded semi-wondering if I had dialled the wrong number, 'Allo, je voudrais parler avec Zoe'.

'De la part de qui?' the familiar voice enquired.

'C'est Simone a l'appareil.'

'Simone? C'est Yoyo...'

My heart was pounding, almost cutting my breath off when I realised and I wondered if it could be heard down the phone. So he was still in Paris. Wasn't he due back in London!

'What are you doing there?' I switched into English.

He had just popped around to collect Zoe, as they were going out to catch up while on his fleeting visit back to Paris. He just so happened to be waiting at the door while she grabbed her coat, when the phone had rung.

Now what were the chances of that? I explained that I was on a train for Paris that evening and would arrive at 8am. He was equally blown away as he thought I was in Bosnia or on my way back to London. He would try and change his plans and be there to meet me!

It seemed too good to be true that I would finally have the reunion I had hoped for, and in Paris.

I hardly slept that night as I tossed and turned in the sleeping compartment of the train wondering if he'd be there and if not, why?

Our tired eyes smiled at one another on the station platform. Neither of us had slept well. How wonderful it felt to be reunited. There was so much to explain and the words just gushed out. I was full of news of our tour; Johnie and Caroline; acting on this feeling that I needed to leave, just as he had... and now the present and the future.

However, my impatience to get to Paris was not to pay off after all, even if the timing had seemed perfect. Why hadn't someone tried to warn me? Would I have listened? In any case, I had left before they had time to spell it out. In fact, if I was truly honest, there had been a little old lady in Bosnia who had in fact alluded to this but I did not want to see it. We had stopped somewhere for coffee and the woman had insisted on reading the remnant coffee grains in my cup. She had said

278

that I was to be double-crossed by a friend, and I had not really thought too deeply about it and chose to ignore the warning. After all, what friend was she referring to? It had been rather vague and these were just coffee grains after all.

The happy reunion quickly turned cold when Yoyo decided he had to come clean with me. He had met someone on one of the overland tours; an American woman, who had fallen for him. She mentioned that she was hoping to visit Paris one day, and although he had been unsure if that would ever work out, some weeks later, when she surfaced in London and I was in Bosnia, he had decided to show her Paris.

He went on to explain that he had literally just spent the week with her in Paris. She had only just left.

The betrayal cut like a knife in the heart, even though he tried to reassure me that it was me he wanted to see. He'd even been in trouble saying my name instead of hers. Somehow the magic of the moment had disappeared like a bubble popping. This was not the fairytale ending I so craved. We still enjoyed each other's company, however, and we had some lovely evenings with his vibrant friends as I masked my internal sadness.

I went to see the PU office for the job they had mentioned but it was no longer available. Even that hadn't worked out.

I was invited to see his folks with him again. I bought a small, colourful, bouquet of flowers to give to his mother which she happily received. Within moments, however, I noticed a huge bouquet on the table, with some already wilting flowers. In what seemed like true American style, this new woman had spared no expense the week before, when visiting. As we sat there eating dinner in front of the television, I realised that this was the anticlimax I had hoped to avoid in London. I could only imagine the big celebration there had been the week before when he had arrived back from his travels. Now it was easier for everyone to watch the screen rather than face the emotions of the moment. This just helped to serve as a painful reminder that I was seemingly too late and he had even introduced her to his family. I retreated within and couldn't hide my disappointment the next day. While we hadn't made some pact not to see anyone else, this was all just too close in time and place. It felt like some dog had been peeing on what I had hoped was my territory. At least I didn't have to face this deception back in London amongst all my friends. Or would it have been easier to have their moral support?

Now all the questions of forgiveness arose again. How quickly can a person forgive after a betrayal? How do people get over this type of thing or are they meant to move on and no longer have friendships. People say time heals, but how long is long enough?

While the situations I had encountered in Bosnia-H were far more extreme involving situations where people's families had been murdered or torn apart, sometimes by people they had grown up with, now I was faced with my own story of betrayal again. Admittedly it was on a much smaller scale, but it hurt. I had even broken with the group and gone out on a limb to get to Paris more quickly, almost sleepwalking into this disaster. But maybe I was meant to find out the hard way so I could move on faster.

Yoyo caught up with his 'spiritual' father, Jean-Jacques, while I revisited the Rodin museum and the statue of Danaid. I was alone and yet Yoyo was in Paris.

Within days, Yoyo returned to London to get on with various jobs in his head office. The next few weeks were very hard. There was so much to process.

I was trying to get my feet on the ground in France. Fortunately there was Christophe, Sniejana and the Huette family in Orleans to offer warm hospitality and give some sort of stability. Soon after I even linked up with Isabelle, who lived nearby in the Touraine and had also returned from Bosnia. Our pain was two-fold. We both seemed to have been unlucky in love and were processing the grief of Bosnia and adapting to 'normal' life. Isabelle's ex had given her an old Citroen and we decided to embark on an adventure to the seaside in a 'Thelma and Louise' style. It felt liberating to be on the road again and to see the sea.

We ended up near la Rochelle and made a day trip to the fantastic l'ile d'Aix, where Napoleon had even stayed at one point in exile. There were no cars on the island and this sleepy holiday destination seemed to beckon to us as some sort of sanctuary.

Once back in the Loire Valley, I was introduced to the famous Gerald Bloncourt from Haiti, who had a country home near Isabelle's family and friends. He was a well known person I had read about whilst doing my francophone studies on Haitian literature in NZ. It was amazing to think that I was meeting with such a historical figure in the backwaters of the Touraine region. As a young student he and a small group had started a revolution, starting a coup d'etat. It was short-lived, however, and he was lucky to escape with his life, going into exile in France. He was a celebrated poet, writer, painter, photographer and general action-man. It was lovely to sit there and listen to his stories of leading hunger-strikes for his country, of the dreadful Duvalier regime that I had heard so much about during my studies and also of the many countries he had visited as a photo journalist. He was happy to have someone who had the time and appreciated listening to these colourful stories from his action-packed past. We would frequently toast to 'Liberté, Égalité and Fraternité!' He looked me in the eye and said if there would be another Revolution, a true revolution, he would be ready to fight again for this. He was still very strong and capable at 70, and you could feel his passion for justice and love. The friendship was mutual and I especially enjoyed hearing how he had met his wife Isabelle on the metro in Paris. I was welcomed into the family like some long lost family member and I would visit them regularly when I headed back to Paris to look for work.

Through one of the previous drivers from Premiere Urgence, Hughes, I found accommodation at his parents' apartment. They generously let me house-sit while I got my feet on the ground. One of the gang from Bosnia had even tried to take their life, overdosing on sleeping pills down by a river. Fortunately passers-by had raised the alarm and they ended up in hospital. Hugues and I endeavoured to provide the moral support needed at such a difficult time. On top of this the summer wasn't the best time to find work and there were other things happening. There was the 14th July which I celebrated with Isabelle back on the island. She had managed to get a job there for the summer at the only café.

Yoyo's brother was getting married and I was also invited. The passing of several weeks had not provided any change in our situation and he was due to leave for Africa soon after. It felt like precious time we might have spent together had slipped away and not been savoured as I hoped.

Later, once he had returned to Africa, I headed to London for cousin Grant and Michelle's wedding, where I would find many family members including my parents and even Nev. He had been drinking, was detached from the crowd and danced alone. I also touched base with my friends from London and The Serious Road Trip, who were happy to see me even if briefly. It was reassuring to be surrounded by them, but I was happy I had broken free. The American friend of Yoyo was hovering around London with various Road Trippers and so I was glad I didn't need to stay long. I had other things to get on with back in Paris in the search for a much desired paid job. I wrote numerous applications to some of the French NGOs based in Paris with no success. Mind you, I wasn't really in the right state of mind to head

281

n

anywhere. I tried my hand at translating, which really wasn't my thing, and in the meantime I learnt to touch-type on the French keyboard.

I embarked on trying to find a job with an agency called Kelly Services, once my typing speed improved. Then I managed to pass the various tests and was put forward for a job. I dressed up in a black and white miniskirt and headed over for the interview in La Defense. I would need to be a tri-lingual personal assistant for five scientists working for a pharmaceutical company. Could I start the following week? It was potentially going to lead to a proper permanent job. This was my moment of success.

It was a huge change to my routine, or rather lack of routine, but I was up for the challenge. After all the action of the summer and the visits of various family members to see me in Paris, it was time to start leading a more 9-5 existence with a wage packet coming in. I had been in France almost five months.

I wasn't prepared for the shock of this 'boulot-metro-Dodo' existence but seemed to manage at first. There was, however, something bothering me. I travelled on various metros and trains to get to La Defense where the tall buildings towered over us like ants heading into our various anthills. For security reasons I had to carry an ID badge which I would use to get into the building. This was all very new technology at the time. How odd, I thought, to be heading to La Defense, wearing a badge with the words 'WAR MINES', printed on it. This was the name of the company reduced to an acronym WAR (Wyeth Ayerst Research) and my surname MINES underneath. It was as though someone was trying to send me a message and I was heading into a different type of minefield in La Defense. I was working in the cardio-respiratory department and my boss was the hot-tempered sort who would slam doors and tell everyone to 'F**k Off!' It was not the sort of gentle environment I needed after all my experiences in a war-zone and he looked like he was about to have a heart attack himself at times. On top of that I remembered how friends had willingly sacrificed themselves as human guinea-pigs to be part of drug-trials in London and I hadn't really agreed with it. They had been pleased with a warm roof over their heads, three meals a day and nurses to chat with, not to mention a large sum of money at the end, but nonetheless, I was worried that their health was affected. Some of this money was spent on Serious Road Trip expenses, but working here still didn't feel right, even if everything seemed to be lining up for me at this time. There was the possibility of an apartment in central Paris, which a friend would be vacating. I'd even met a lovely gentleman through the Kiwi Club.

Meanwhile Gerald was even wondering if I would join him on a trip to Haiti as the president wanted to award him with some Golden Medal of Honour. Isabelle felt it was too dangerous for her to go and had their young child to care for.

All of a sudden I heard news that my brother was getting married in January so I would need to apply for time off work to be there. It looked improbable that this would be granted, judging by the busy nature of the role and being new in the job.

Then the lovely gentleman turned out to be married, which he had initially lied about, although going through a period of difficulty with his wife. I would have to be happy with the status of mistress, as well as happy with the thought of being a home-breaker. This didn't sit well either.

The nicely paid job got trickier and trickier to manage. There were so many deadlines from a boss who didn't allow much lead-time, and who would then explode if it wasn't ready. As I tried to get the photocopier to co-operate, entering impossible codes to access it for an impossible deadline, I looked at my watch and then looked out the window at the tall grey jungle outside. I knew my heart just wasn't in it and I knew it was time to give up. I took what transparent slides were ready to the CEO's office for the meeting where my boss had to present his work. The completed ones weren't even at the beginning of his presentation, so I apologised and made a quick exit.

On my return to my desk there was an urgent message from Yoyo's brother, Mickael. He was an incredibly talented, natural comedian and had been going for an audition the day before for what seemed like his lucky break. However, he hadn't got there. He had blacked out, fallen from his bike and then landed up in hospital. No family members were around and could I come and see him?

This seemed to take priority and so I told a few colleagues I needed to leave early. I left knowing I would never return. I was still in the probation period so this was no big deal.

Mickael was recovering for now and we laughed about the events of the last 24 hours, over a bunch of grapes.

I went on to discuss my intentions with various other friends. Even Gerald had decided he wasn't going to Haiti after all. It was far too dangerous. He explained that he must be on someone's hit-list as on a previous visit he had narrowly escaped certain death. He was sleeping on the floor to escape the heat, when someone had started firing a machine-gun through the window towards the bed where he should have been sleeping. He didn't want to risk it at this time and nor did I.

The apartment had even been reclaimed by the owners, when Eric had handed in his notice. My time in Paris, the City of Light, was drawing to a close as I started to look into flights to NZ and packed my bags.

Gerald and Isabelle cooked me a farewell dinner. The candle was lit to remind us of the 'spirit of our ancestors', as was always the ritual in their home, and we drank a 'Petit Ponch' shot of rum from Haiti as we toasted 'Liberté, Égalité et Fraternité!' together.

'But this is the most important thing of all.' He pointed at me, Isabelle and then himself. 'l'Amitié (friendship), l'Amour (love), from one to an-other, pour l'humanité (for humanity), pour tout le monde! (for the whole world).' I totally got it as this had been a driving force in our humanitarian work. The connections we had made amongst ourselves and the people we encountered, had somehow spurred us on to achieve what seemed the impossible. I had several farewells with the various friends I had made. I was sad to be leaving and yet ready to return.

I would leave from London a couple of weeks later with many friends, even Johnie and Caroline, coming to see me there beforehand. It was a send-off full of love as I headed Down Under, in time for the build-up to Christmas.

Chapter 22

The Homecoming

I arrived to a warm welcome from family and quickly found temporary employment as Dad's dental chair-side assistant. I was soon watching the tourist buses pass by from the window as they headed off to either see the local geysers and mud-pools in Rotorua or to some other destination. There were even some with the words 'The Magic Bus' or 'Kiwi Experience' emblazoned across them. How different and yet somehow the same as our own bus experience.

Just before Christmas, I got a message from Johnie and Caroline. They had returned from a Mostar trip with another group called Cradle and were now embarking on a completely new adventure. Did I want to join them to Chechnya and the Republic of Igushetia? It seemed a world away from where I was but they had been invited to go there by French Franck, who was now with Médecins du Monde and would oversee it. I didn't need to think about this for long. My sister was having her own health complications with cystic fibrosis, including time in hospital, and I was the only sibling around. On top of this, almost as if to answer my question, there was a report on the news about a NZ nurse who had been killed by rebels that week. She had been working for the International Red Cross and had been killed in cold blood along with five other nurses as they slept in a field hospital. How cruel this was for people who were helping. This seemed to be a bad omen and the answer was a definite no.

I would later hear how Johnie and Caroline had closely escaped being kidnapped. Two aid-workers in an orphanage they had visited for a day had been kidnapped just minutes after they left, and held for ransom. It certainly sounded more volatile than Bosnia had been, although admittedly our tour had been at a safer time due to the Dayton Peace Agreement and we were known on the ground thanks to the many convoys and other projects.

The summer activities finished with the beautiful wedding of my brother and sister-in-law and then the next chapter started. The lure of returning to Europe wasn't there for now.

My aunt was keen to help me settle back and offered me work as an assistant for her bronze art studio in Auckland. There was much to do and learn. I needed to help prepare her waxes for the foundry and needed to help co-ordinate the various shipments to galleries as well as payments. I also learnt about how to model and sculpt the wax to create figures that would be cast in bronze.

With my clowning projects seemingly on hold I found comfort in recreating some of my friends and children figures in wax. Once cast in bronze the figures and memories would last forever, unlike the brevity of the projects and performances. I started to see that our message of laughter, love, peace and hope could be carried by these little statuettes, even if I was no longer over there performing.

Within weeks of moving to Auckland, I read about a famous visiting clown, who spoke about a planned visit to Sarajevo. I was determined to meet up with him and encourage him. Interestingly he was also a trained doctor who had set up his own hospital. His name was Patch Adams and he was here to do a speaking tour for health professionals. He was promoting joyful caring and an alternative healthcare model not funded by insurance policies. It was wonderful to see how he combined fun and laughter with a serious message. He urged everyone to find their passion and follow it.

There was a movie being made about his story and Robin Williams was chosen to play his role. We would go on to form a friendship by letter and fax and I would promote the film by organising the Premiere as a fundraising exercise for the local Starship Children's Hospital and various charities including The Serious Road Trip. This was a major event with some 500 or so attending and we even managed to get some red London buses (the Party Bus) to transport people to the cinema theatre from the parking at Sky City. We even had wild-haired Peter Gulliver, back from Bosnia, at the wheel driving.

Various people attempted to get me to perform at birthday parties but I couldn't contemplate such a thing. I had done that without payment for the various children in need and the children I met in NZ seemed to have so much more.

I busied myself with the wax figures instead.

286

The statues were cast in bronze. First there was Johnie in his dungarees, sitting on the side of the road, hitch-hiking into Bosnia. This was a one-off.

A small statue of Pip and his kissing trick with juggling balls followed in 'The Kiss'.

Then there was Allan doing the balloon trick with his baseball cap on backwards. I named this one 'Jos' after the children screaming for a bigger balloon.

I sculpted myself wearing my magician's hat and outfit blowing a kiss of love into the world. I named this one The Magic Kiss.

Then I added another smaller Johnie to the collection. It was the anniversary of our show in the front line town of Celic (April 30) and I wanted to recreate him on the ground, having fallen backwards over the chair with a burst balloon in his mouth. 'Bang on the Frontline' seemed to sum it all up.

Each of these smaller ones could be recast in wax and then subsequent bronzes made in the style of a limited edition.

Later I would also sculpt Caroline holding her life-size dancing girl puppet.

Finally I made a larger statue of Yoyo sitting cross-legged in dungarees, sniffing the precious flower that had been given to us in East Mostar.

I started by trying to promote them through The Peace Foundation, eventually selling many through friends and art galleries. I sent one of my bronze clowns to Patch and he sent me a photo of him with Robin Williams, and the message: 'Let all the clowns go into the world to heal.'

It would only be a couple of years later that I would be enticed to perform at a friend's daughter's 3rd birthday party in French. I was missing my performing friends from our projects. I was so used to working in a team with Johnie, or some other clown, the main attraction, that I couldn't imagine playing that role myself, so I always declined. Besides, I had done those shows to meet the needs of the fun-starved children of war-zones, rather than these relatively lucky children of peaceful NZ.

But all of a sudden, my performing needs became greater than I realised they were, and out burst a rather spontaneous show using puppets. I was rather proud of myself, delving deep into my childhood, when I had also performed with glove puppets. Initially I had agreed to do some face-painting but had then felt compelled to recreate a story about an orphan from Romania, who escapes with the magic bus on an adventure seeking some Treasure in NZ. I played all the characters as well as Eugene, the main one. It was very empowering to have found a solution to perform without the troupe and in a fairly normal setting.

It was so liberating to be performing again, and centre stage.

It also felt very real as the puppet had been hand-made for me and gifted by my Romanian friend Puiu.

Eugene would eventually leave the bus to make his own way to NZ, as the bus was caught up in various war-zones and other countries. He was seeking a treasure that the clowns had spoken about, and so a journey by boat was reenacted with the orphan being helped by various new friends along the way such as a dolphin, monkey and eventually a sea monster or Taniwha (Maori). When he and the sea monster finally arrive in NZ, they find various treasures in the waters. The biggest treasure of all is in an old wooden chest. It holds a heart wrapped in a message saying that: 'You are the biggest treasure of all, as you have a heart and the heart can love and love makes the world turn around!' It was the perfect story and would go on to be my favourite puppet show. I performed at many occasions, such as school shows, birthday parties, school holiday programmes, community events, hospitals and nursing homes.

I found a monkey puppet and named her Lucy. She'd escaped on a boat full of bananas from South America, and blew bubbles from a banana whilst draped around me. What a duo we made! Children loved her.

This new performing direction required a return to Europe as I went on to do puppetry training with puppet-masters in Berlin, Bochum (Germany), Paris and Wellington NZ, with two visiting puppeteers from Japan. There I played a frog for the National Children's Theatre, but the Eugene story was still my very own unique story. I was determined to encourage other's creativity and imagination using my puppets.

It was only fitting that after kissing a few frogs along the way, I finally met my husband Mike through friends, whilst setting up for one of these shows. 'What's this about needing to move a pew?' he asked as we struggled to shift the heavy seating in preparation for my show. I'd been around the world but here he was right in front of me in Auckland. It had been a long wait! He valued love, creativity and honesty as much as I did and it didn't take long to recognise this. He even spoke a few languages too. We married the following year.

The curious thing was that he had heard about the initial London cab driving to Australia and had also tried to get a project to drive Down Under off the ground with his mechanic brother and girlfriend. They had bought a cheap Land Rover to repair, but it had proved to be the wrong vehicle and for a number of reasons they didn't get any further down the road in it than Dartmoor, Devon.

He felt certain that he would have joined us on our humanitarian adventure had he realised we existed. It was only fitting that we managed to find each other there in New Zealand, some 11 years after setting off on that journey for love.